WEBER'S
GAS
BBQ
BIBLE

MANUEL WEYER

hamlyn

CONTENTS

This book is all about fun, positive vibes, good company and good food. It's all about barbecuing and cooking outdoors — welcome to the world of the gas barbecue!

THIS BOOK is dedicated to the gas barbecue, its great potential and its many advantages. It's quick to preheat and has a range of different temperature zones, making it ideal for a variety of techniques such as grilling, slow-cooking and other forms of outdoor cooking! And the smoke stays under the lid, making it the perfect smoker.

AS A PROFESSIONAL CHEF, I am passionate about cooking, a skill I learned by working my way through the ranks. I have also been a devoted barbecue enthusiast for years. Building on these foundations, I have acquired extensive knowledge over time, which I am now passing on to you in this book.

PITMASTERS ARE MADE NOT BORN! And it's not that hard to develop those virtuoso skills bit by bit. But you will need the right tools to do it: both the proper equipment and the right know-how. This, of course, includes the barbecue and the key accessories you need to go with it. It also includes the basic principles and techniques, not only for barbecuing but also for cooking in general — a little knowledge of food, appreciation of the importance of quality, as well as a large sprinkling of curiosity and passion, will set you on your way to success.

DO YOU KNOW YOUR WAY AROUND YOUR GAS BARBECUE? If not, it's time to make friends with it and find out what it can do, what accessories it has and how to use them. This book includes the basics such as connecting the gas bottle and knowing how to clean and care for the barbecue and its accessories. It will also teach you the different barbecue techniques available to you — what they are and how you can use and combine them. You will soon find yourself immersed in the world of outdoor cooking, trying out other options besides direct and indirect grilling on your barbecue — cooking foods on a cedar plank, encasing them in a salt crust or smoking them like a professional. I have also included a very

important section on the core temperature and how to measure it to make sure your food is cooked to perfection every time. I'll let you in on my secret right now: measure it once, twice and if in doubt, measure it again! Comprehensive tables provide guidelines on the core temperatures and cooking times of different foods but you have to take into account that the thickness of a piece of meat, not the weight, is of primary importance. Each food has its own characteristics, and depending on the results you want to achieve, you may have to treat it very differently from one recipe to another. This book includes essential information on how to recognize good quality (which is vital), which food is suitable for which preparation method and what you should pay attention to during preparation. And then I have compiled the 11 Commandments of cooking on a bas barbecue!

LEARNING BY DOING — that's what *Weber's Gas Barbecue Bible* is all about. That's why there are so many theory pages with practical examples, using step-by-step photos and instructions. You have to know the rules before you can break them, and know when it makes sense to do so. Over time, you will learn how and why certain things work (or don't), so that as you gain experience, you can experiment with ingredients and cooking methods yourself.

THE RECIPES IN THE BOOK are designed to help you learn more about the different cooking options the gas barbecue has to offer. Why not start with the Top Eleven — the best-known and most popular barbecue dishes? You will also see there's more to barbecueing than meat. This book contains lots of dishes featuring vegetables and fruit, along with sweet treats and pastries — some are well-known classics, others are new and unusual creations. Embark on your own barbecue adventure and discover completely new culinary possibilities. Let your imagination and creativity run riot and have fun with your barbecue!

Manuel Weyer

The principles of
BARBECUING

What's the attraction of barbecuing?

For some, cooking on a barbecue represents pure pleasure and relaxation while others are attracted by the science behind it. Some people even see barbecuing as a sport, in which the best compete to perfect well-known classics or create new dishes of ever-increasing sophistication. But for everyone,

barbecuing is about moving the preparation of food, or at least part of it, outdoors. This is partly because we are drawn to the outdoors when the weather is good and partly because it is more practical and pleasant to sear or smoke food outside rather than indoors. Then, of course, there is the social aspect: there's nothing like a barbecue to bring people together.

It's the perfect opportunity to catch up with family and friends, to chat and have a convivial time. These days, more and more often people are barbecuing in the winter months, too.

It doesn't matter whether you are preparing a quick meal for hungry kids or whether you see barbecue time as your very own 'me time'. When you hear that crackling and hissing, breathe

in the aroma of the sizzling food and get to taste those smoky flavours, you know you made the right choice. And it feels great when beloved classics or even brand-new dishes turn out well on the grill – you get to feel like a hero in your own back garden.

Which gas barbecue is right for you?

This is an important question because a gas barbecue should provide you with service and pleasure for a very long time. The following factors are important when choosing a barbecue:

🔥 Where will you place the appliance – on the patio or a balcony or in the garden? Will it stay in one place, or will it be moved around, perhaps because you have to keep putting it away to store it, for example?

🔥 What and how do you want to cook on the barbecue? Will you only be cooking a couple of steaks and a side dish, or do you also want to experiment with larger joints, hot smoking and slow cooking?

🔥 Do you barbecue occasionally or more frequently?

🔥 Do you usually cook for just two or three people or do you like to invite lots of guests over for a barbecue on a regular basis?

🔥 Do you want to use the extensive range of accessories on offer, keep trying out new things and constantly expand your barbecue repertoire?

By answering these questions, you will quickly work out which gas barbecue is best for you.

Gas barbecue models & sizes

Great taste on the go
Portable barbecue that lights up at the touch of a button, perfect for those who get a sudden hankering for their favourite steak, at home or on the road.

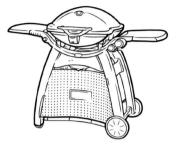

The perfect family barbecue
Mobile gas barbecue with 2 burners for direct and indirect heat, for those who have limited space but want versatility from their barbecue.

The power all-rounder
Mobile gas barbecue with 3 stainless steel burners, with possible additional equipment such as sear zone, side burner or Gourmet BBQ System, for unlimited grilling possibilities.

Built to last
Equipped like the power all-rounder for endless barbecue possibilities, also available as a 4-burner version or in a stainless-steel look.

The ultimate outdoor kitchen
Largest model in the category, with 6 burners and every conceivable feature, such as sear zone, side burner, infrared burner and rotisserie – the dream!

The benefits of a
GAS BARBECUE

- ♦ Ready to cook immediately, thanks to easy ignition

- ♦ Simple temperature regulation with the controls

- ♦ Perfect heat distribution, thanks to the burner layout

- ♦ Consistent heat with easy-to-read temperature, courtesy of the integrated interior thermometer

- ♦ Easy to use different grilling techniques and accessories

- ♦ Fewer flare-ups thanks to the flavorizer bars above the burners

- ♦ Well suited for frequent use, even when catering for many guests

- ♦ Burning off makes the gas barbecue easy to clean

- ♦ Lower CO_2 emissions than when cooking with charcoal

Are there any disadvantages?

Die-hard charcoal fans will miss the smell of charcoal or briquettes when lighting a gas barbecue – and possibly also the 'old-fashioned' way of cooking over an open fire.

Can you taste the difference between food cooked on a gas barbecue and food cooked over charcoal?

Charcoal is nothing more than burnt wood produced by a charcoal burner in a kiln. In a nutshell, charcoal does not impart its own flavour to the grilled food but merely serves as a source of energy for cooking. However, there are two differences: if the charcoal used for cooking is not yet fully glowing and therefore not free of aromatic compounds (which it should be, for health reasons), you get a 'typical' charcoal flavour. In addition, the sugars in the proteins of the food being cooked, such as a steak, caramelize more strongly due to the very high initial heat of charcoal.

A gas barbecue that can reach 800°C (1475°F)? Do I need such high temperatures when cooking with a barbecue?

There are gas-operated 'box barbecues' that cook and caramelize steaks in minutes using directly radiated top heat up to 800°C (1475°F). This is a completely different cooking technique to searing a steak over the sear zone of a gas barbecue at an internal temperature of 250–290°C (480–550°F) then finishing the steak over indirect heat and leaving it to rest. The flames on most gas barbecues also reach around 800°C (1475°F), and the heat on the grate can reach up to 400°C (750°F).

The easiest way to illustrate this difference is by comparing it to taking a bath: anyone who enjoys a hot bath knows that the hotter the water, the shorter your stay in the tub. But spending a short time in very hot water isn't all that relaxing – it's much nicer to stay in the tub for longer at a lower temperature. The same goes for steak. Even if it has a crispy crust on the outside, that doesn't mean that the core is cooked to medium – that is to say, relaxed. That can only be achieved during the final cooking phase over indirect heat and by subsequently being left to rest.

Ultimately, all this is a question of personal taste and one's own (barbecue) philosophy: are you the lone wolf tending the 800°C (1475°F) barbecue or the pitmaster enjoying a barbecue in good company? Whatever method you prefer, it's probably true to say that at a temperature of 800°C (1475°F), the fat burns so quickly, before the steak has a chance to cook perfectly, that a bitter taste develops because the meat is cooked using such intense heat.

Pros & cons of cooking on a barbecue at 800°C (1475°F)

PROS
- Quickly seals and caramelizes the food being cooked.
- The cooked food becomes very crispy.
- Energy-efficient cooking for individual steaks and fish fillets.

CONS
- Requires additional expertise to achieve a perfectly cooked result.
- You can only cook items individually.
- Not suitable for marinated food.
- Increases flare-ups with very high-quality pieces of meat (marbled or with a high fat content).
- Not suitable for cooking for a large number of guests.
- Burn hazard if the cover becomes very hot with the intense heat.
- Difficult to clean.

If you really want an additional tool for your gas barbecue, you should buy a model with a back burner so that you can enjoy the benefits of infrared.

What is a back burner?

Some models of gas barbecue have an infrared back burner. This provides additional top heat and is a game changer for barbecue fans who like to use the rotisserie or enjoy their pizza straight from the pizza stone with particularly crispy toppings.

The infrared burner is fitted horizontally inside the upper lid and provides additional heat. The greater the distance there is between the back burner and the food to be cooked, the less heat the food gets from above.

Do I need a back burner?

You have to answer this question for yourself. A gas barbecue with back burner is nice to have, but not absolutely necessary for getting good results on the barbecue.

How do I prevent flare-ups with a gas barbecue?

- Do not use fatty or oily marinades.
- Dab meat that has been marinated in oil with kitchen paper before cooking.
- Only use a little oil when brushing or rubbing food.
- Always choose indirect heat to cook fatty dishes.
- Clean the grill regularly and empty the drip tray.
- Cook with the lid closed.

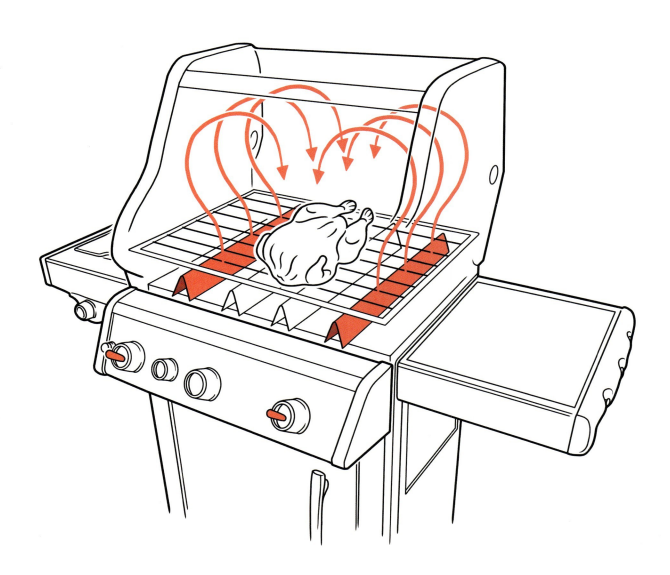

SETTING UP your gas barbecue

Setting up your gas barbecue

- Conduct a visual inspection of the individual components of the gas barbecue.
- Set up the barbecue exactly as specified in the manufacturer's instructions.
- Your gas barbecue must be equipped with a pressure regulator, which is a device to control and maintain uniform gas pressure as gas is released from the LPG cylinder.

Which hose and regulator are suitable for my barbecue?

- Most gas barbecues are supplied complete with a hose and a suitable pressure regulator attached as standard. The data label on your barbecue will tell you which type of regulator you require. The green patio gas bottles commonly used in the UK have a 27mm valve, so you will need a 27mm clip-on regulator.
- Hoses can be made from rubber or plastic. Plastic hoses are cheaper but more difficult to bend when cold. Rubber hoses have the advantage of remaining flexible at low outside temperatures. This is advantageous if you use the barbecue in cold weather and you move it frequently.

- Gas regulators should have a CE mark or a UKCA mark and a recent year of manufacture.
- Regularly check your gas hoses to see if they are still intact and in good condition. Avoid kinking the hose. Older or porous hoses must be replaced. The gas hose assembly on your gas barbecue should be replaced at least every five years.

Do the different coloured gas bottles impart a different flavour to the food?

- The colour of the gas bottle has nothing to do with taste. It merely indicates the type of gas with which the bottle was filled. In the UK, gas for barbecues can be either butane or propane. You'll see butane in blue bottles which are suitable for camping and single-burner appliances, and propane in red bottles which are used for larger appliances and catering vans. Green patio bottles, also filled with propane gas, are commonly sold for gas barbecues. There is a 'cylinder charge' for the bottles that is reimbursed when they are returned, or you can return an empty bottle in exchange for a new filled one.

What do I need to consider when handling a gas cylinder?

- Always transport gas bottles upright, with the valve at the top, in an adequately ventilated vehicle..
- Store gas bottles outdoors or in well-ventilated outdoor areas such as sheds or carports.
- Commercial gas bottles cannot explode, even when stored in direct sunlight.
- Gas bottles that have not been completely emptied must also be stored outdoors or in a well-ventilated place.
- Gas bottles are made from either steel or aluminium, with an inner coating the type of which depends on their use.

CONNECTING THE GAS BOTTLE
and checking the fill level

1. Check that all the burner control knobs are in the 'off' position and open the barbecue lid.
2. Identify your regulator type and follow the appropriate connection instructions in your barbecue's user manual. In the UK, Weber's barbecues are supplied with 27mm clip-on regulators.
3. To connect the clip-on regulator to the gas bottle, first make sure the regulator's gas on/off switch is in the 'off' setting. Never connect or disconnect the regulator with the switch in the 'on' position.
4. Remove any safety cap or cover from the patio gas bottle. Make sure the top of the valve is clean and free from debris.
5. Place the regulator onto the gas bottle valve and press down firmly until you hear a click. This indicates that the collar has locked onto the valve and the regulator is correctly in place.
6. To turn the gas on at the bottle, turn the regulator switch to the 'on' position. You should hear a slight hiss as the gas starts to come through the hose.

HOW TO CHECK FOR LEAKS

Spray the fittings at the bottle and the regulator with a foaming agent – you can either buy leak check solution or make your own soap solution by mixing 20 per cent liquid soap with 80 per cent water. Depending on the type of regulator, either turn on the gas supply by moving the regulator switch to the 'on' position or by turning the cylinder valve anti-clockwise, but do not ignite the barbecue. If no bubbles appear, this indicates that the connections are gas-tight and you can start having fun with your barbecue. If bubbles appear, there is a leak and gas is escaping. Turn off the gas supply and do not use the barbecue. Instead, check the connections and hose and replace if necessary.

WHAT'S IN THE GAS BOTTLE?

The gas bottle or cyclinder is filled with liquefied petroleum gas, or LPG, either in propane or butane form. Propane is better at lower temperatures and it has a higher calorific value than butane. Most barbecues have a 27mm clip-on regulator which is compatible with the green patio gas cylinders filled with propane. If you have a smaller, single-burner barbecue with a 21mm clip you should use the blue butane cyclinders. If your barbecue doesn't have a clip-on regulator to fit on top of the gas bottle, choose a bottle with a screw-in regulator. Some bottles also come equipped with a level indicator.

CHARACTERISTICS OF PROPANE
- Can be used between -30 and +40°C (-22 and 104°F).
- Requires more pressure to remain liquid so comes in heavier and more unwieldy gas bottles.
- Has a slightly higher calorific value than butane gas.
- Cheaper than butane.

CHARACTERISTICS OF BUTANE
- Not suitable for use in winter.
- Cannot be used at 0°C (32°F) or below.
- Liquid butane cannot become a gas at cold temperatures.
- More expensive than propane.

How to check the fill level of your gas bottle

METHOD 1: HOT WATER
- Pour hot water over the outside of the gas bottle. Wait 1 minute, then run your hand over the surface of the bottle. The upper part will still be warm where the bottle is empty. If you move the palm of your hand downwards, it will be quite noticeable where the bottle starts feeling colder. This is because the liquid gas cools the outside of the bottle.

- **Disadvantage:** You can easily burn yourself, and with some gas barbecues, the bottle has to be removed first.

METHOD 2: SCALES
- Place the gas bottle on scales (bathroom scales or luggage scales) and subtract the tare weight indicated on the bottle (its empty weight) from the total weight showing on the scales. The difference in weight is the gas still in the bottle.

- **Disadvantage:** Not everyone has a set of scales to hand that is suitable for weighing a gas bottle.

METHOD 3: ICE DROPLETS
- At temperatures just below 0°C (32°F), both butane and propane settle at the bottom of the bottle. Droplets of water will freeze on the outside of the bottle, but only above the fill line.

- **Disadvantage:** This method only works at temperatures just below 0°C (32°F).

METHOD 4: ESTIMATION
- If you barbecue regularly, you get some idea how full your bottle is likely to be and you should have a spare bottle on stand-by.

- **Disadvantage:** Estimation can be inaccurate, and it's certainly not easy for beginners or those who rarely use their barbecue to know how much gas they are using.

PREPARING
your gas barbecue for use

1. As a rule, the gas barbecue should only be used outdoors.
2. Check the gas bottle is upright, and conduct a visual inspection of the barbecue and bottle.
3. Open the lid and set the controller to zero – follow the manufacturer's instructions before initial start-up.
4. Turn the regulator's gas on/off switch to the 'on' position. If your barbecue has a gas switch valve, make sure it is in the 'on' position.
5. Ignite the barbecue with the lid open, gradually turning all the controlers to their highest settings and igniting them one at a time.
6. Close the lid and preheat the barbecue at 240–260°C (475–500°F) for 8–10 minutes. Then set the barbecue to the desired target temperature and preheat for a further 4–5 minutes before starting to cook.
7. When you have finished cooking and are ready to disconnect the gas, turn the regulator switch back to the 'off' position first, before you turn off the burners, so that any residual gas left in the hose is used up. This makes it safer to store the barbecue until the next time you use it. Then switch off all your barbecue burners before disconnecting the gas bottle.

Why do I have to preheat the barbecue?

If the barbecue is dirty, preheating allows food residue to be burned and brushed off the grate more easily. Make sure that the barbecue has smoked out before you brush or the brush will stick to the residue.

Preheating the barbecue – usually to about 260°C (500°F) for 4–5 minutes, depending on whether you are using an enamel, stainless steel or cast iron grate – results in the food cooking particularly well.

How do I maintain the temperature for a long time?

Barbecuing for a longer period of time requires no major preparation, except that you will need a replacement gas bottle on standby. This is recommended if the gas bottle has already been partly used, if you decide to slow grill (cooking meat at a low temperature for a long period of time) or if you plan to cook lots of food at a barbecue event.

How to regulate the heat

This is quite simple with the lid closed: just turn the dials to regulate the gas supply and consequently the heat. You can easily read the temperature on the interior thermometer and control the heat to the desired temperature using the controls.

TEMPERATURE RANGES FOR COOKING ON A BARBECUE

110–125°C (225–260°F)	very low heat	pulled pork, ribs, brisket
125–140°C (260–275°F)	low heat	sausages, sandwiches, burger buns, fruit
140–150°C (275–300°F)	low to medium heat	salmon flank, fish, whole joints of meat
150–180°C (300–350°F)	medium heat	poultry, dessert/cake, firm vegetables
180–220°C (350–425°F)	medium to high heat	wet fruits, bread, kebabs
220–250°C (425–480°F)	high heat	pizza, tarte flambée, poultry
250–290°C (480–550°F)	very high heat/searing	searing red meat
290°C+ (550°F+)	full heat	cleaning the grate

CLEANING
a gas barbecue

It's fine for your gas barbecue to develop a nice patina – it shows that you are passionate and enthusiastic about using your barbecue. It's a bit like having a new car – of course it has to be maintained properly, but small dents and scratches will happen over time. In the world of barbecuing, you often hear about a grill having character, but it shouldn't start to develop a life of its own.

1. Burn off the residue on the grill after each use with the lid closed and the burners turned up to maximum, then brush off. Wait until the grate has stopped smoking, so the cleaning brush does not become sticky over time. It is advisable to wear barbecue gloves and use a long-handled brush to reduce the risk of burning if the barbecue is still hot.

2. Regularly change or clean the aluminium drip pan.
3. Clean the grease drip tray regularly.
4. If you cannot reach the underside of the grate, simply turn it over, replace it and brush it.

5. Clean the storage rack with the wire brush, too.

6. Clean the inside of the barbecue with the cleaning brush, not forgetting the lid.
7. Never cover the grease trap with kitchen foil. If there is a grease fire, the foil will fuse with the metal of your barbecue, ruining it.

8. Clean the flavorizer bars with the wire brush.

9. Clean the outside of the barbecue with warm water and a little washing-up liquid.

10. If you are using a special stainless steel cleaner, don't use it on the control dials as it could remove the finish in certain circumstances.

11. If you use your barbecue all year round and leave it outside, you should definitely invest in a cover to protect it.

How do I avoid rust on cast iron grates and barbecue utensils?

That's quite simple: after cleaning, simply dab a piece of kitchen paper in a little vegetable oil and rub a thin layer of oil on the grate and any cast iron barbecue utensils you have.

What do I have to consider when storing my gas barbecue over winter?

Clean completely and allow to dry if necessary – this also applies to the cover. Then disconnect the gas bottle.

And what should I do when barbecue season comes round again?

- Simply wipe the barbecue with a damp cloth.
- Check all connections for damage (hose, hose rupture protection, gas pressure regulator).
- Connect the gas bottle, ignite and burn off the barbecue.

USING BARBECUE & OVEN CLEANERS

Indoor grill and oven cleaners should only be used on a cold barbecue, if at all. Otherwise, the metal reacts with the detergent which could cause unsightly stains. Always follow the manufacturer's cleaning recommendations.

BARBECUE TECHNIQUES
with various heat zones

Direct heat & sear zone

Direct heat is when the heat is directly under the food. All the dials are on: preheat the barbecue to the desired temperature and place the food directly over the heat.

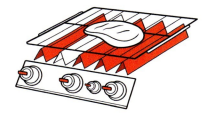

Switch on the additional burner when cooking with the sear zone.

Indirect heat (Method A)

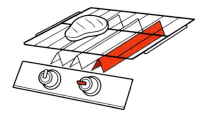

Indirect heat is when the food is on the grate but is not positioned above a lit burner. When cooking with indirect heat, not all the burners are left on after preheating. The burner below the food has been switched off and the control dial set to zero. The options for cooking with indirect heat vary depending on the number of burners your barbecue has.

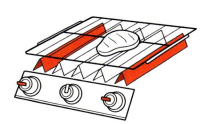

If your barbecue has three or more burners, switch off the burner(s) in the middle after preheating to the desired temperature, then place the food in the middle of the grate and cook, with the lid closed, using indirect heat.

Indirect heat (Method B)

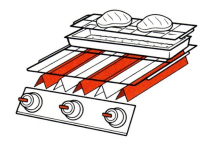

For another method of cooking with indirect heat, set all the burners to the desired cooking temperature and place the food on the storage rack. It is important to use a drip tray under the food if it is fatty, filled to one-third of its depth with water. The advantage of this method is that you can cook other foods over the direct heat on the grate at the same time.

Indirect heat (Method C)

The third method uses a heat shield in the form of an aluminium tray and a small additional stainless steel rack. This technique is particularly suitable if you are cooking a big piece of meat (brisket, ribs, pulled pork) and are using the barbecue exclusively with indirect heat. The aluminium tray provides a shield against the immediate heat under the food and, when the lid is closed, the barbecue is like a convection oven. It is important that the quantity of food to be cooked in this way and the use of the heat shield are always suitable for the barbecue.

Cooking with two heat zones: direct & indirect heat

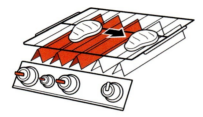

It's common in barbecuing to use a combination of direct and indirect heat. The advantage of this method is that once the desired cooking temperature has been reached, steaks can be cooked over direct heat (in the sear zone) to form the perfect crust then they can be moved to indirect heat to be cooked to the desired degree of doneness without burning.

Cooking with 50/50 heat on a gas barbecue

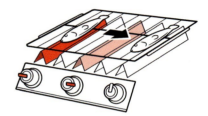

This method is perfect when you want to cook a whole fish or cook on a cedar plank over a low or medium temperature, for example. If your gas barbecue has three burners, turn them all on to preheat the barbecue to the desired temperature. Now turn off the righthand burner and turn the middle burner down low. Grill the fish over direct heat on the left to colour the skin, then finish cooking the fish over indirect heat on the right of the grill to prevent burning.

WHICH GRATE IS BEST FOR COOKING?

Stainless steel grates have the advantage that it is harder for cooked food residue to stick to them, even at high temperatures. They also do not retain heat so well, which helps to regulate the temperature in the barbecue quickly. Stainless steel grates are also particularly suitable for slow grilling in the low temperature range. If, for example, you are cooking ribs at a temperature of 115–120°C (240–250°F) over a longer period of time and you have placed them directly on the grate, you do not have to worry about them drying out or the underside burning.

In contrast, **cast iron grates** retain heat for longer. This is useful when cooking foods with a high water content, such as watermelon or pineapple, because the higher temperature allows the little sugar in the food to caramelize directly. This is definitely something to consider when cooking on your barbecue, no matter what technique you use. In addition, cast iron grates are slightly easier to clean than stainless steel grates.

SMOKE under the lid

Using your gas barbecue to smoke food is child's play. In fact, the most important thing to remember – besides the need for an integrated, mobile or homemade smoker box – is to position the barbecue correctly outside. Because of a gas barbecue's open design, which is necessary to let air circulate, a successful smoke depends, to some extent, on the weather.

Do I need to pre-soak the wood chips?

Pre-soaking the wood chips slows down the creation of smoke. This has the advantage of producing gentle smoke over a longer period of time. The chips should therefore be soaked in water for about 30 minutes before cooking. Avoid adding fruit juices or similar sugary liquids, because the sugar will simply burn and produce a bitter smoke. It is better to pre-soak the chips in plain water or – if you want to be more adventurous – in aromatic liquids such as beer.

If you need to produce smoke more quickly – for example, if you want to serve smoked chicken breasts within 15 minutes to friends who pop over for a spontaneous barbecue – it is better to use a mixture of pre-soaked chips and dry chips. Fill the smoker box with a 50/50 mix of dry and pre-soaked chips and place the box on the flavorizer bars throughout the cooking process.

Which wood chips are best?

Creating smoke under the lid is not only a matter of taste, but is also down to experience and often faith, too. Fruit woods such as apple, pear and peach are recommended for inexperienced barbecue cooks because their smoke is milder. Hardwoods such as hickory, beech and cedar have a slightly more intense taste, which is why you need to be very careful about the quantity you use. You also need to take into account the length of the smoking, the quantity of chips and the type of wood.

How do I position the smoker box correctly in windy conditions?

If the wind is blowing from the right, place your smoker box flush right on the grate after starting the smoke on the flavorizer bars (see right). This keeps the smoke under the lid. If you were to place the box centrally on the grate or flush left, the smoke that forms would be blown away and not stay under the lid to flavour the food. If you have an integrated smoker box, position your barbecue facing into the wind.

DIY SMOKER BOX

To make your own smoker box, simply fill an aluminium drip tray with dry and pre-soaked wood chips, seal the top with kitchen foil and poke holes in the foil so the smoke can escape. Unfortunately, you can't add extra wood chips to such a box during cooking.

You will need a mixture of dry wood chips (left) and some that have been pre-soaked in water for at least 30 minutes (right).

First, place the dry wood chips in the smoker box.

Close the lid of the smoker box.

Remove the grates so that you can place the smoker box on the flavorizer bars.

Place the box on the bars over a high direct heat, close the lid and leave to heat for 6–8 minutes.

As soon as smoke appears, place the smoker box on the grate with the food and begin cooking as normal over the burners.

During cooking, add some of the pre-soaked chips to the box as instructed in your individual recipe.

The smoked food, like these salmon fillets, is ready when it is cooked to your liking.

How it works:
GRILLING WITH A PLANK

Cooking food on a cedar plank is a separate grilling technique in itself. You don't need the plank to produce a lot of smoke under the lid, you just need the smoky flavour to be transferred to the food being cooked. Here are three different ways of cooking food on a cedar plank.

METHOD A (rib-eye steak): charring one side

This method is perfect for grilling fatty or well-marbled pieces of meat. One side of the cedar plank is charred over high direct heat (200–240°C/400–475°F) while the food is being seared on both sides. Then the steak and its flavourings are placed on the charred side of the plank to finish cooking over indirect heat. This allows the excess fat to drain off and reduces the risk of flare-ups and the board catching fire. If you want a smokier flavour or you need to cook the food further at a higher temperature, the cedar plank can be charred on its other side over high direct heat without it being scorched or flames forming due to excess fat. Also, the food does not have any direct contact with the heat source and therefore it cannot burn so easily.

Always pre-soak the cedar plank in water for at least 1 hour before use.

Char the cedar plank on one side over a high direct heat while you sear your steaks on both sides next to it.

Turn the plank over and place the steaks on the charred side of the wood to impart flavour to the meat.

Finish cooking the steaks with any flavouring ingredients over indirect heat on the plank.

METHOD B (salmon): charring both sides

This method is ideal for cooking fish and vegetables, lean meat or chicken breast as these ingredients only need a short cooking time. Charring the cedar plank over a high direct heat (200–240°C/ 400–475°F) allows the smoke to develop more quickly and the essential oils in the wood to be released. The other advantage is that the plank will already be hot when you place the food on it, which shortens the cooking time.

Pre-soak the cedar plank for at least 1 hour, weighing it down so that it stays submerged in the water.

Meanwhile, prepare the seasoning for the salmon or other food you are cooking.

Sprinkle the food with the seasoning mix and marinate it according to the recipe.

Char the cedar plank over a high direct heat on both sides as described in the recipe.

Place the salmon on the plank and cook over indirect heat. It will take on the fine smoky flavour of the plank.

METHOD C (roast beef): double plank cooking

This method is best suited to large joints of meat that are cooked for a longer period of time. In this method, the cedar planks are not charred beforehand. The meat is placed between the planks, then the bundle is charred on both sides over high direct heat (200–240°C/ 400–475°F). Cooking then continues over indirect heat until the meat is cooked to perfection. After being left to rest, the meat can be served on one of the cedar planks, either sliced or whole. For an intense smoky flavour, char one side of each plank before sandwiching the meat between the charred sides.

Place the marinated meat on one of the pre-soaked cedar planks.

Cover the meat with the second pre-soaked cedar plank and tie the bundle tightly with pre-soaked kitchen string.

SMOKING PLANKS & SMOKE AROMA

How many times can you use a plank for smoking?

How many times a cedar plank can be used depends, of course, on how it is used. If you cook for a long time and/or at high temperatures (200–240°C/400–475°F), you can use the plank less often than if you stay within a medium temperature range (120–160°C/250–325°F) and cook for a shorter time. On average, a plank can be used two to four times.

After cooking, remove any residue from the plank and brush the board thoroughly with coarse sea salt and a few drops of lemon juice. Then rinse under running water and leave to dry. That's all you need to do. Soak the plank again before its next use to prevent it charring too quickly or setting alight. Once the plank is really no longer suitable for cooking, chop it into small pieces and use it for smoking in the smoker box.

How do I prevent flare-ups and the plank burning too quickly?

- Always pre-soak the plank for at least 1 hour or up to 1 day before cooking, weighing it down if possible so that it remains fully submerged.
- If you need to transport the plank or keep it moist before cooking, wrap it in clingfilm or vacuum pack it to retain the moisture.
- Avoid using oily marinades when cooking with a plank, as they can drip from the board into the grill, causing flames to form and the plank to catch fire. Thoroughly dab any meat that has been marinated in oil with kitchen paper before cooking.

- If you are cooking heavily marbled meat on a plank, start with an indirect cooking technique after charring the plank. This will allow excess fat to drip off the meat without causing flare-ups. Only then, if necessary, place the plank with the food over a direct heat.
- Do not soak planks in sugary liquids. The sugar will burn and make the board bitter, creating smelly and bitter smoke. It is better to use aromatic liquids which transfer their flavours to the food.

QUICK & DIRTY
short cuts to a smoky flavour

If you don't have the equipment or time for a long smoke, there are other ways you can achieve a good smoke flavour. Quantities are crucial here because nothing is worse than the sensation of biting into an ashtray. Here are a few tips for cooking with smoky flavours.

Smoked salt & smoked paprika

Smoked salt, smoked paprika and other smoky dry spices are popular ingredients in rubs and are particularly suitable for marinades. They can be used in a spice mixture or simply sprinkled on to season food and are great used in sauces to support the smoky flavour or to enhance the food being cooked on the barbecue.

Liquid smoke

This smoke flavouring has been around since the end of the 18th century and was probably discovered by an apothecary. In simple terms, it is filtered and purified liquid smoke. A good rule of thumb is to use 1–4 g (up to ⅛ ounce) liquid smoke for 1 kg (2 lb 4 oz) meat, depending on your taste. Thinly brush the meat with the liquid flavouring as part of the marinating process. You could also mix it with maple syrup, honey or molasses before marinating the food.

Smoked foods

Cooking with ingredients that are already smoked is also a popular way to achieve that smoky flavour in a dish: smoked bacon, ham, sausages, eel, salmon, trout, chicken, tofu, cheese, vegetables and potatoes can give dishes a wonderful smoky flavour. However, make sure that food that has already been cured is not heated too much when cooking.

COOKING WITH SALT
Perfect seasoning three ways

1 **Salt crust:** Cooking food in a sea salt crust not only provides a fabulous treat for the taste buds but when you break open the salt crust to reveal the fish, your guests will be impressed. The food cooks in its own juices inside a salt crust and remains unaffected by external influences, apart from the heat. Moreover, salt is a perfect heat conductor. Even if the lid of the barbecue is opened from time to time, the temperature of the food inside the crust will hardly fluctuate.

Start by beating egg whites in a large mixing bowl to make the crust mixture.

Then mix in the coarse sea salt, some herbs for flavouring and some flour.

Prepare the whole fish as described in the individual recipe.

Line a heatproof ceramic dish with pre-soaked baking parchment then cover with about one-third of the salt mixture.

Place the fish on the salt, cover with baking parchment, then cover with the remaining salt, making sure there are no gaps.

Cook the fish using indirect heat according to the recipe.

To serve, carefully slice around the edge of the salt crust with a knife and remove the top to reveal the fish.

Peel off the fish skin, then remove the perfectly cooked fish fillets and serve.

2 **Quick salt crust:** As well as adding flavour, a quick salt crust is a clever technique for cooking small whole fish or even fillets on the barbecue. First, brush them very thinly with beaten egg white and coat them in coarse sea salt. Then place the fish uncovered in the refrigerator to dry for a short time. The fish can then be cooked whole over direct heat without it sticking to the grate.

For a quick salt crust, you need a small amount of beaten egg white.

Prepare the fish on the flesh side as described in the recipe.

Turn over the fish and brush the skin with a thin layer of beaten egg white.

Coat the skin with coarse sea salt, then place uncovered in the refrigerator for 10–15 minutes. Wipe off the excess salt.

Brush the fillets lightly with oil and place skin side down on the hot barbecue. Once the skin is crisp, turn them to finish cooking.

3 **Steak on salt:** The third method is to cook directly on a bed of salt. The steak is seared on the grill, then placed on the salt mixture to finish cooking. A brown crust forms as a result of the initial grilling, and thus the salt is deprived of its ability to bind moisture or water (hygroscopy) and you obtain a mild accompanying and spicy flavour during grilling.

Mix some coarse sea salt with beaten egg white, water and flour to form a paste.

Put the salt mixture on the plancha, sear the steak on both sides over direct heat, then finish cooking it on the bed of salt.

COOKING WITH KITCHEN FOIL
and why it can be problematic

Cooking with foil is always a bit controversial, but is there any truth behind the concerns?

Any ingredients or foods that contain salt (for example, through seasoning mixtures or rubs) and acidic foods (such as tomato purée and citrus fruits) should not be cooked in kitchen foil on the barbecue or rested in kitchen foil or aluminium trays after cooking. The reason for this is quite simple: salt and acid can cause aluminium to be released from the foil. Small particles pass into the food and are then eaten. You should therefore avoid allowing moist foods containing acid or salt to come into direct contact with kitchen foil or aluminium trays.

Another reason to avoid foil and foil trays is that they cannot be reused and can therefore be considered bad for the environment. Instead, choose barbecue trays and accessories made of stainless steel, ceramic, cast iron or food-safe aluminium.

Cooking safely with foil

You may now be wondering, if you shouldn't use foil, how you are supposed to prepare your ribs with the 3/2/1 method, or your brisket, or what you should use to wrap cooked foods while they rest after cooking.

There are two ways to cook food on the barbecue safely using kitchen foil. If you have to use kitchen foil or aluminium trays, either put off seasoning the food with salt until after cooking it on the barbecue, or avoid using moist or acidic marinades on foods you are planning to cook.

Or simply place a layer of baking parchment between the food and the aluminium tray or foil. This way, the kitchen foil does not come into direct

A pork neck steak has been marinated with salt and lemon, causing the kitchen foil to oxidize.

This meat has been left to rest in foil after cooking. The seasoning has oxidized the foil.

contact with the food, and you can cook as usual or allow the food to rest after slow grilling. When cooking food with little residual moisture over a longer period of time, you should pre-soak the baking parchment for about 15 minutes in cold water before using it to wrap your food. This prevents the baking parchment from burning during cooking.

COOKED IN A PARCEL
Alternatives to kitchen foil

Cooking food wrapped in banana leaves, newspaper, meadow hay or herbs is not only about the taste.

So why do we wrap ingredients like steaks, fish and vegetables in parcels? Partly because it offers a way to lock in the flavour and moisture of the food, but also because it adds theatre and puts your dish centre stage visually! There are many different ways to wrap foods but the best alternatives to kitchen foil are everyday objects which add some value as well as making good parcels. Wood wraps, banana leaves and herbs offer what every barbecue cook dreams of: ease of use, a sophisticated cooking technique and an amazing reaction from their guests. Here, we present our favourite wrappings.

Newspaper

Anything but fake news here. Cooking with newspaper on a barbecue is great fun because the food tastes wonderful. Prepare the food and then wrap it in newspaper, placing heavily marinated food between two sheets of baking parchment first so the marinade does not soak through the newspaper. The newspaper will lock in all the flavours. This technique is suitable for small whole fish, fish fillets, marinated vegetables and small fruits such as apples and pears.

Herbs

Cooking with fresh herbs on the barbecue is now commonplace. But cooking a whole fish, piece of meat or firm vegetables for a longer period of time in this way is still something special for me, and the resulting herby flavour always brings a pleasant surprise. It is advisable to soak the herbs in cold water for at least 20 minutes before cooking so that the essential oils they contain do not burn during the cooking process. The soaking water can be used for cooking if you wish.

Wrap the prepared fish and flavouring ingredients tightly in newspaper.

Place the food in a heatproof dish and covered with pre-soaked herbs.

Cook on the grate over an indirect heat, using a thermometer with a probe to test for doneness, as indicated in the recipe.

Place the dish on the grate over an indirect heat until the food is cooked to your liking. The herbs will flavour the food.

Wood wraps

Wood wraps are wafer-thin sheets of wood which must be pre-soaked for at least 30 minutes so that they do not burn during cooking or tear during wrapping. They are ideal for imparting a smoky flavour during a short cooking time, they tolerate a range of cooking temperatures from low to high and can be used with direct or indirect heat. Small cuts of meat, fish fillets, vegetables or fruit can be cooked successfully using this type of wrap. After pre-soaking, place the food on the wooden sheet, roll with the grain and tie in a neat parcel with kitchen string.

Wood wraps can only be used once, but once cleaned, they can be chopped, pre-soaked and recycled to be used for smoking.

Banana leaves

The banana leaf is one of the oldest, most natural and, ultimately, most sustainable ways to prepare perfectly grilled food. Wrapping food in a banana leaf is easy, and it protects the food from drying out. It is important to grill the leaf briefly first; it will change from matt green to shiny and become more pliable. Use to wrap fruit, rice, skinless fish fillets, chicken breast, small steaks or vegetables such as asparagus.

Cooking food in a banana leaf always makes me think of Malaysia. While I was there I met a cook who didn't at first inspire much confidence but conjured up a fantastic marinated chicken leg for me. It was cooked in banana leaf beneath a mountain of salt over glowing charcoal. The taste sensation was completely new to me.

Meadow hay

Cooking with hay is fantastic! For some the flavour is a leap of faith, for others it is a taste revelation. Meadow hay is simply dried grass with herbs and flowers, so when you moisten this fragrant mixture, wrap it around food and grill it, the wonderful aroma is not only transferred to the food, it also works on your sense of smell .

Wondering where you can get such fragrant meadow hay? I get mine directly from an organic farmer I know personally, because knowing where my food comes from is important to me. There may be organic farmers in your area who would give you some of their hay – just ask. Otherwise, you can buy organic hay in some health food shops or online.

Pre-soak the wood wrap and kitchen string in water for 30 minutes, pat dry, then use to wrap the food.

Briefly grill the banana leaf to make it more pliable, then fill it with the marinated food and tie to make a neat parcel.

Moisten the hay with a little water and wrap it around the food in a heatproof dish, aiming for an even covering.

Cook the wrapped food over direct or indirect heat according to the recipe.

Cook the wrapped food over direct or indirect heat according to the recipe.

Cook using indirect heat according to the recipe, enjoying the tantalizing fragrance.

TOOLS & ACCESSORIES
Must-haves for your gas barbecue

BARBECUE TONGS You will need two or three pairs of robust, long-handled tongs with a locking mechanism. These protect your hands and forearms from heat. You need one pair of tongs for putting raw foods on the grill and moving them around, and a second pair to lift the cooked food off the grill (or you can clean the tongs in between).

BARBECUE SLICE This is an absolute must for turning burgers, fish fillets and chops. It should have a long handle with a slight bend in it, so that the lifting surface is lower than the hand holding the handle. Use it to lift food off the grill easily and safely.

BRUSH Anyone who wants to coat their food with marinades and sauces cannot do without a brush. Preferably, it should have silicone bristles and a long handle.

BARBECUE GLOVE If you want to move a wok or pizza stone on the grate or remove a hot grate, you need thick, long, well-insulated barbecue gloves to protect your hands and forearms from the heat.

CLEANING BRUSH A clean grate is important for barbecue cooking success. To clean the bars thoroughly, you need a sturdy, long-handled brush with stainless steel bristles that won't shed. Smaller brushes are available for cleaning smaller, heavily soiled areas.

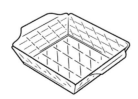

BARBECUE & VEGETABLE BASKET Small or delicate foods such as fish fillets, prawns or pieces of vegetable or fruit can be safely cooked in a perforated barbecue and vegetable basket.

SMOKER BOX Smoking adds a wonderful smoky flavour to your barbecue dishes. Fill the smoker box with wood chips of your choice and follow the instructions for smoking food (see page 22). It is easy to add more chips while the food is cooking. (You can also make your own smoker box, see our tip on page 22).

WEBER CONNECT SMART GRILLING HUB The Weber Connect Smart Grilling Hub is a step-by-step grilling assistant which can send notifications straight to your smartphone, everything from a cooking countdown to letting you know it's time to flip or serve. With a glance at your smartphone, you'll know that the barbecue is working properly and that you'll be serving your guests with perfectly cooked food.

CEDAR PLANK An untreated cedar grilling plank gives barbecued food a special flavour. Soak the plank for at least 1 hour before placing it on the barbecue to prevent it catching fire.

RIB RACK Thanks to this clever tool, whole racks of ribs can stand on the grate instead of being laid flat. This way you can grill three or four racks at the same time, where usually there would only be room for two. Depending on the model, the rack (when turned upside down), may also serve as a cradle for large joints of meat.

SKEWERS Skewers are perfect for meat or veg kebabs, satay or fruit kebabs. They hold all the ingredients together while cooking. Unlike metal skewers, wooden or bamboo skewers must be soaked in water for at least 30 minutes before use. Weber ETGS skewers are fitted in a rack, raising the food above the grate while cooking.

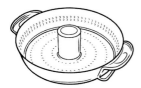

POULTRY ROASTER This is used for cooking a whole chicken or other type of poultry upright on the grate, allowing heat to circulate evenly around it. Some models have an integrated container to hold beer or other liquids. This allows you to steam and flavour the meat from the inside during cooking.

PIZZA PADDLE A sturdy stainless steel pizza paddle makes it safer and easier to place larger items such as pizza or bread on a hot grate or pizza stone. It is also used for lifting the finished food safely off the hot stone.

SEAR GRATE A porcelain-enamelled cast iron grate ensures even heat distribution, adds a professional-looking diamond grill pattern to food and seals meat juices and flavour into your food.

ROTISSERIE (ROTATING SPIT) Chicken, ribs or leg of lamb become deliciously tender and juicy when slow cooked on the rotisserie, with the lid of the barbecue closed to retain the heat.

LIGHT A light that can be easily attached and removed from the barbecue handle is really useful when it gets dark, allowing you a good view of your cooking food.

PLANCHA Made of porcelain-enamelled cast iron, the plancha grill plate is perfect for cooking small items or food that easily falls apart, such as pancakes, prawns or chopped pieces of vegetable.

WOK The age-old art of stir-frying can be achieved perfectly using a wok over a gas barbecue. Ideally, the wok should be made of enamelled cast iron, which absorbs heat well and is not affected by acidic foods. The wok can be placed on the grate or – even better – set into an opening in the middle of the grate, as this provides more direct contact with the heat.

GRILLING BASKET Roast potatoes, chips and even popcorn can be cooked in a fine-meshed grilling basket, which is attached to the rotisserie and turns during cooking. Before adding the food, brush the inside of the basket with a little oil.

DUTCH OVEN You can prepare wonderful soups, stews and braised dishes in a cast iron casserole pot, also known as a Dutch oven, in your barbecue. You can even bake bread in it.

PIZZA & GRILLING STONE A pizza stone is indispensable for cooking pizza, tarte flambée, bread and other pastries. It absorbs a lot of heat from the barbecue and then releases it slowly and evenly, ensuring perfect baking results!

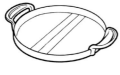

GBS PAN This cast iron pan is designed to be used with the Gourmet BBQ System. In this all-rounder, you can prepare anything from fried eggs and bacon for breakfast to a tasty casserole. This pan is also ideal for gently cooking small vegetables or thinly sliced fish. The range of uses is huge.

ROASTING RACK WITH HEAT SHIELD You can use this to cook over indirect heat by putting the meat on the roasting rack and then placing the rack on the heat shield. Place the whole thing directly on the grate of your barbecue.

CORE TEMPERATURE & COOKING TIMES

Every food has its own unique requirements

Heat is nothing more than energy, which causes the muscle fibres in meat to contract during cooking. The meat juices transport the heat from the outside of the piece of meat to its core. When barbecuing, the aim is to give the food the time that it needs for this to happen, and to only expose it to the cooking temperature this requires.

Every type of food – whether it's meat, fish, vegetables or fruit – needs a different combination of cooking temperature and time to achieve perfect results, and there are enormous differences between them. A beef brisket, for example, is best cooked at a low temperature over a number of hours, while a skirt steak needs just 6–8 minutes at a high temperature. Similarly, the proteins in fatty fish such as salmon and trout start to contract at a core temperature of 37°C (99°F), whereas those in bony fish such as monkfish require a higher temperature, meaning they need a different cooking regime altogether.

Before cooking

Food should never go straight from the refrigerator to the barbecue! Bring the meat up to room temperature first. This will put you on the right path to eventually achieving the perfect core temperature. The reduced grilling time needed when starting with room-temperature food also means that your food can cook more gently and receive the perfect amount of smoke.

However, very marbled or fat-streaked meat such as Wagyu beef requires very careful attention when put on the barbecue at room temperature. Even with an indirect heat, it is difficult to keep the flames in check, as the meat does not contain enough protein to prevent the fat leaking out as a result of the intense heat during cooking.

Caution: Only take out of the refrigerator the food that you are actually going to cook. This is because fresh foods such as poultry and fish do not tolerate temperature fluctuations well and can soon spoil.

During cooking

Adjust the temperature of the barbecue to suit the food being cooked. Smaller pieces of food, such as prawns, thinner cut steaks, sliced vegetables and fruits, are best cooked with intense heat over a shorter cooking time. Large pieces of food, such as brisket, ribs and roasts, generally need lower temperatures and a longer cooking time.

After cooking

Few other techniques are as important as leaving the food to rest after cooking. The intense heat of a barbecue creates tension in the meat fibres, which helps move the meat juices from the outside to the inside, transporting heat with them. Leaving the meat to rest after cooking allows the juices to flow back again and make the meat moister. It's a good idea to turn the food from time to time while it is resting to distribute the juices more evenly and help you achieve an even better result!

When leaving the food to rest, avoid wrapping it in kitchen foil, unless you first wrap it in baking parchment (see page 29). In the warm summer months, you can simply place the meat next to the barbecue to rest. And when it's colder outside, you can rest food in a cool box, because anything that keeps things cold also keeps them warm.

The resting times for meat, poultry and fish depend on the following factors:
- Outdoor temperature, wind and weather conditions
- The temperature of the food (the larger the piece, the more critical)
- The cooking temperature

A USEFUL RULE OF THUMB:
The higher the cooking temperature, the shorter the cooking time and the longer the resting phase until the required core temperature is reached.

The lower the cooking temperature, the longer the cooking time and the shorter the resting phase until the required core temperature is reached.

How to measure the core temperature of meat correctly:

Measure the core temperature of a pork chop close to the bone without touching it.

Push the probe into the side of a rump steak when measuring the core temperature.

Push the probe into the middle of the top side when measuring the core temperature of a roast pork joint.

How to measure the core temperature of poultry

With a whole chicken, measure the core temperature in the thickest part of the leg.

With chicken breasts, insert the probe into the centre of the flesh.

Measure the temperature of chicken thighs at their thickest part close to the bone without actually touching it.

How to measure the core temperature of fish

Poke the probe into the thickest part of a whole fish from the top.

Measure the core temperature of a fish fillet by inserting the probe into the side.

Measure the temperature of chunky fish steaks by poking the probe in the top.

BEEF & VEAL

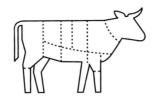

What to look for when buying beef

Maturity and fat content are two important qualities when it comes to buying beef. In particular, the marbling – the intramuscular fat that runs through the meat between the fibres – is an essential clue as to whether a steak, for example, will be juicy and have a great taste once barbecued. Maturation or ageing also plays an important part. During the ageing process, enzymes break down the muscle tissue and make it tender. When buying beef, make sure it has a light red to bright red colour when cut. If it is dark reddish-brown, the meat has probably been on display for too long, or comes from older animals and is therefore possibly tougher.

A distinction can be made between dry ageing and wet ageing. With **dry ageing**, the cuts of meat are hung on the bone in cold rooms or refrigerators. This type of ageing creates a dry surface on the meat which protects the muscles. The cool hanging also removes water and at the same time enhances the flavour.

With **wet ageing**, the meat is cut and packed, preferably vacuum-packed, soon after slaughter. This causes a decomposition process to take place in the meat, which tenderizes it. However, even if the cut is vacuum-packed and airtight during wet ageing, small bubbles can form in the meat juices – a sign that the meat is past its prime. Such meat no longer has any bite, it is tasteless and the structure is not good.

I prefer meat that has undergone a combination of both types of ageing. Cuts are matured on the bone for three to five weeks and are then vacuum-packed.

The cut

The more tender the cut – that's the meat from muscles used less often – the milder the flavour. If you buy expensive fillet steak, you are paying for the rarity and tenderness of the meat. That's why fillet steak costs more than flank steak, even though the latter has a much better flavour. Expensive, tender steaks such as porterhouse and T-bone also come from muscle meat that has been used little, whereas flank and skirt steaks are cut from more heavily used muscle.

The feed

In some countries where there is intensive farming, cattle are not always fed on grass. The animals are fed on grain or concentrated feed and are often kept indoors. They grow quickly, making their flesh watery, soft-textured and not very marbled. The meat is on the tough side, even when perfectly cooked. In the UK, where grass is abundant, cattle are mostly fed on grass. Grass-fed animals are provided with fresh grass on or from the pasture all year round. Cattle may be brought indoors for the final few months for 'finishing', where they may be fed a mixture of grains and silage from other crops to help fatten them before slaughter. Some small farms graze their cattle exclusively in pastures throughout their lives. Their meat has a firm structure, little marbling and an intense flavour. The lower fat content means you have to be careful when cooking this meat on the barbecue, so that it doesn't overcook. It is advisable to let the meat reach room temperature before barbecuing. If you want to ensure you are purchasing grass-fed beef that hasn't been 'finished' on grain but fed only on grass, look for a Pasture for Life label awarded by the Pasture-Fed Lifestock Association or a trusted supplier that advertises 100 per cent pasture-raised beef.

The all-important sear

Regardless of which cut of meat you are cooking on the barbecue, you will get the most flavour when you start by searing the meat over an intense heat. Hot direct grilling causes the sugars in the proteins to caramelize, creating fantastic flavours you can smell and taste. This initial sear does not dry out the meat. On the contrary, searing meat gives it a wonderful crust to protect the moist flesh inside.

Before searing, pat the meat dry with kitchen paper to remove any moisture which might make the meat steam rather than grill. Then rub it with a thin layer of oil and season it with salt. If you are marinating meat with a dry rub, wrap it in baking parchment to prevent a film of water forming on the surface. Always season the meat with salt before cooking, because once the caramelized crust forms, salt cannot easily penetrate the meat. However, you can of course season the cut surfaces after cooking if you slice the meat.

When is it done?

I believe that to achieve perfectly grilled beef, you should cook it medium. However, I only do this when I have a fantastic piece of meat. I rarely go above a core temperature of 56°C (133°F) for quick-cooked beef. But everyone's definition of the perfect steak varies, and the cut of the meat and the cooking technique play as much a part as personal taste.

Doneness	Core temperature	Colour at the core
Rare/blue	37–43°C (99–109°F)	blue/red
Medium-rare	43–49°C (109–120°F)	red/pink
Medium	49–56°C (120–133°F)	pink
Medium-well done	56–68°C (133–154°F)	pink/grey
Well done	at least 68°C (154°F)	grey/brown

The following table is for guidance only. The cooking times and temperatures below are approximate as they will be affected by a number of factors, including the quality, cut and thickness of the meat. External factors such as wind, air pressure and outside temperature also play an important role when cooking with a gas barbecue.

The core temperature of perfectly grilled meat should be measured, not estimated. Cook **smaller cuts such as steaks and chops** over a direct heat for the time indicated in the table or until the desired degree of doneness, turning once during that time, and if necessary finishing over an indirect heat. During the resting phase, the core temperature will increase a little, depending on the heat. The resting phase is usually 3–5 minutes. Cook **roasts or thicker cuts** over indirect heat for the duration indicated in the table or until the desired core temperature is reached. During the resting phase, the temperature increases more than it does with smaller cuts of meat, depending on the size, weight and heat. The resting phase is usually 12–15 minutes but can be up to 2 hours. During the resting phase, the fibres relax and the meat juices are evenly distributed. You can leave the meat to rest in a cool box, for example, to keep it warm.

BEEF	SIZE/WEIGHT	METHOD	COOKING TEMP	COOKING TIME	MEDIUM	DONE
Porterhouse/club steak/ T-bone	3–4 cm (1¼–1½ inches) thick	direct/indirect	200–220°C (400–425°F)	10–14 minutes	50–54°C (122–129°F)	
Tomahawk steak	3–4 cm (1¼–1½ inches) thick	direct/indirect	200–220°C (400–425°F)	15–16 minutes	50–52°C (122–126°F)	
Rump/sirloin steak	2.5–3 cm (1–1¼ inches) thick	direct/indirect	200–220°C (400–425°F)	10–12 minutes	49–52°C (120–126°F)	
Rib eye steak/entrecôte	3–4 cm (1¼–1½ inches) thick	direct/indirect	200–230°C (400–450°F)	10–12 minutes	49–52°C (120–126°F)	
Filet mignon/fillet steak	4–5 cm (1½–2 inches) thick	direct/indirect	200–220°C (400–425°F)	12–15 minutes	52–54°C (126–129°F)	
Beef fillet, cooked whole	1.2–1.5 kg (2 lb 10 oz–3 lb 5 oz)	direct/indirect	180–200°C (350–400°F)	16–20 minutes	49–52°C (120–126°F)	
Hip-bone steak	3–4 cm (1¼–1½ inches) thick	direct/indirect	200–220°C (400–425°F)	12–15 minutes	49–52°C (120–126°F)	
Flank steak	1.5–2 cm (about ¾ inch) thick	direct	220–230°C (425–450°F)	8–10 minutes	52–54°C (126–129°F)	
Skirt steak	1.5–2 cm (about ¾ inch) thick	direct	220–240°C (425–475°F)	6–8 minutes	49–52°C (120–126°F)	
Flat iron	2.5–3 cm (1–1¼ inches) thick	direct/indirect	200–220°C (400–425°F)	12–15 minutes	52–54°C (126–129°F)	
Hanging tender	2.5–3 cm (1–1¼ inches) thick	direct/indirect	220–240°C (425–475°F)	8–10 minutes	49–52°C (120–126°F)	
Roast beef, on the bone	2.8–3.5 kg (6 lb 2 oz–7 lb 12 oz)	direct/indirect	140–160°C (275–325°F)	3–3½ hours	52–54°C (126–129°F)	
Roast beef, boneless	1.5–2 kg (3 lb 5 oz–4 lb 8 oz)	indirect	140–160°C (275–325°F)	2½–3 hours	52–54°C (126–129°F)	
Prime rib of beef, on the bone	2–2.5 kg (4 lb 8 oz–5 lb 8 oz)	indirect	140–160°C (275–325°F)	2–2½ hours	50–54°C (122–129°F)	
Prime rib of beef, boneless	1.6–2 kg (3 lb 8 oz–4 lb 8 oz)	indirect	140–160°C (275–325°F)	1–1½ hours	52–54°C (126–129°F)	
Beef brisket, packer cut	5.5–7.3 kg (12–16 lb)	indirect	110–125°C (225–260°F)	12–14 hours	93–98°C (199–208°F)	
Tri-tip	4.5–5 cm (1¾–2 inches) thick	direct/indirect	120–140°C (250–275°F)	1½–2 hours	54–56°C (129–133°F)	
Picanha rump cap	5–8 cm (2–3¼ inches) thick	indirect	140–160°C (275–325°F)	35–40 minutes	54–56°C (129–133°F)	
Minced beef/burgers	3 cm (1¼ inches) thick	direct	180–200°C (350–400°F)	8–10 minutes	54–56°C (129–133°F)	
Bacon bomb/meat balls	5–8 cm (2–3¼ inches) thick	indirect	140–160°C (275–325°F)	30–45 minutes		65–68°C (149–154°F)
Meat skewers	3 cm (1¼ inch) cubes	direct	180–200°C (350–400°F)	12–15 minutes		
Beef short ribs	2–2.5 kg (4 lb 8 oz–5 lb 8 oz)	indirect	120–125°C (250–260°F)	8–10 hours		90–95°C (194–203°F)
Teres major, butcher's cut	600–800 g (1 lb 5 oz–1 lb 12 oz)	direct/indirect	200–230°C (400–450°F)	12–15 minutes	52–54°C (126–129°F)	

VEAL	SIZE/WEIGHT	METHOD	COOKING TEMP	COOKING TIME	MEDIUM
Veal saddle steak	2–2.5 cm (¾–1 inch) thick	direct/indirect	180°C (350°F)	8–10 minutes	52–54°C (126–129°F)
Veal cutlet	2–2.5 cm (¾–1 inch) thick	direct/indirect	180°C (350°F)	10–12 minutes	52–54°C (126–129°F)
Veal fillet	4–4.5 cm (1½–1¾ inches) thick	direct/indirect	180°C (350°F)	12–15 minutes	48–52°C (118–126°F)
Saddle of veal, on the bone	2–2.3 kg (4 lb 8 oz–5 lb)	indirect	120–140°C (250–275°F)	2½–3 hours	52–54°C (126–129°F)
Saddle of veal, boneless	1.5–2 kg (3 lb 5 oz–4 lb 8 oz)	indirect	120–140°C (250–275°F)	2–2½ hours	52–54°C (126–129°F)
Veal steak	3–3.5 cm (about 1¼ inches) thick	direct/indirect	180–200°C (350–400°F)	12–14 minutes	53–55°C (127–131°F)
Veal topside	1.2–1.5 kg (2 lb 10 oz–3 lb 5 oz)	indirect	140–160°C (275–325°F)	35–45 minutes	52–54°C (126–129°F)
Veal mince/sausage meat	3 cm (1¼ inches) thick	direct/indirect	160–180°C (325–350°F)	8–10 minutes	54–56°C (129–133°F)

PORK

Breed & sustainability

I like to know where the food I put on my barbecue comes from, and breed and sustainability are important considerations. There doesn't have to be meat on the table every day, but when there is, I only choose the best to ensure a successful barbecue. With just a few simple steps, a sustainably reared and breed-appropriate piece of pork almost cooks itself on the barbecue and tastes great. Meat that's been pre-packed or comes from a discount supermarket requires so much work that nobody enjoys it. You can improve the meat and achieve acceptable results by adding herbs and spices, but the inherent flavour is lacking. People who live in the countryside have an advantage as they often know a farmer they can trust. But if that's not the case for you, look for a butcher you trust and build up a relationship with them.

When is it done?

Perfectly cooked pork should, in my opinion, still have an even, light pink colour, but then I only barbecue it when I have a fantastic piece of meat to start with. I rarely go higher than a core temperature of 65–68°C (149–154°F) for such a short cooking time, but that is a matter of personal preference.

The following table is for guidance only. The cooking times and temperatures below are approximate as they will be affected by a number of factors, including the quality, cut and thickness of the meat. External factors such as wind, air pressure and outside temperature also play an important role when cooking with a gas barbecue.

The core temperature of perfectly grilled meat should be measured, not estimated. Cook **smaller cuts such as steaks and chops** over a direct heat for the time indicated in the table or until the desired degree of doneness, turning once during that time, and if necessary finishing over an indirect heat. During the resting phase, the core temperature will increase a little, depending on the heat. The resting phase is usually 3–5 minutes. Cook **roasts or thicker cuts** over indirect heat for the duration indicated in the table or until the desired core temperature is reached. During the resting phase, the temperature increases more than it does with smaller cuts of meat, depending on the size, weight and heat. The resting phase is usually 12–15 minutes but can be up to 2 hours. During the resting phase, the fibres relax and the meat juices are evenly distributed. You can leave the meat to rest in a cool box, for example, to keep it warm.

PORK	SIZE/WEIGHT	METHOD	COOKING TEMP	COOKING TIME	MEDIUM	DONE
Pork fillet	450–600 g (1 lb–1 lb 5 oz)	direct/indirect	160–180°C (325–350°F)	15–18 minutes	58–62°C (136–144°F)	
Fillet medallions	3–4 cm (1¼–1½ inches) thick	direct/indirect	180–200°C (350–400°F)	6–8 minutes	58–62°C (136–144°F)	
Chops	3–3.5 cm (about 1¼ inches) thick	direct/indirect	180–200°C (350–400°F)	10–12 minutes	54–58°C (129–136°F)	
Pork loin roast, on the bone	1.4–2.3 kg (3–5 lb)	indirect	120–140°C (250–275°F)	1½–2 hours	56–58°C (133–136°F)	
Pork loin roast, boneless	1.1–1.4 kg (2 lb 6 oz–3 lb)	indirect	150–160°C (300–325°F)	1–1½ hours	54–56°C (129–133°F)	
Pork sausages, raw	100–120 g (3½–4¼ oz)	direct/indirect	160–180°C (325–350°F)	12–15 minutes		70–72°C (158–162°F)
Pork sausages, pre-boiled	100–120 g (3½–4¼ oz)	direct/indirect	160–180°C (325–350°F)	8–10 minutes		70–72°C (158–162°F)
Minced pork/patties	3 cm (1¼ inches) thick	direct/indirect	180–200°C (350–400°F)	10–12 minutes		72–76°C (162–169°F)
Baby back ribs	650–900 g (1 lb 7 oz–2 lb)	indirect	115–125°C (240–260°F)	3½–4 hours		85–90°C (185–194°F)
Spare ribs	1.8–2 kg (4 lb–4 lb 8 oz)	indirect	115–125°C (240–260°F)	7–8 hours		84–92°C (183–198°F)
Thick ribs	2–2.5 kg (4 lb 8 oz–5 lb 8 oz)	indirect	125–130°C (260–265°F)	5–6 hours		82–85°C (180–185°F)
Roast side of pork	1.4–1.8 kg (3–4 lb)	indirect	220–240°C (425–475°F)	45–50 minutes	66–68°C (151–154°F)	
Pork belly	1.2–1.6 kg (2 lb 10 oz –3 lb 8 oz)	indirect	160–180°C (325–350°F)	1–1½ hours		74–76°C (165–169°F)
Back of suckling pig	1.4–1.8 kg (3–4 lb)	indirect	150–160°C (300–325°F)	35–40 minutes	54–56°C (129–133°F)	
Leg of suckling pig, on the bone	2.5–2.8 kg (5 lb 8 oz–6 lb 2 oz)	indirect	150–160°C (300–325°F)	2–2½ hours		72–75°C (162–167°F)
Leg of suckling pig, boneless, rolled	1.5–2 kg (3 lb 5 oz–4 lb 8 oz)	indirect	160–180°C (325–350°F)	1–1½ hours		68–72°C (154–162°F)
Pork jowl	450–600 g (1 lb–1 lb 5 oz)	indirect	160–180°C (325–350°F)	45–55 minutes		76–78°C (169–172°F)
Shoulder/neck, boneless, rolled	2–5.5 kg (4 lb 8 oz–12 lb)	indirect	130–150°C (265–300°F)	4–4½ hours		72–76°C (162–169°F)
Collar steak	2–2.5 cm (¾–1 inch) thick	direct	200–220°C (400–425°F)	8–12 minutes	56–58°C (133–136°F)	76–78°C (169–172°F)
Collar chops	2.5–3 cm (1–1¼ inches) thick	direct	200–220°C (400–425°F)	10–12 minutes	58–62°C (136–144°F)	74–78°C (165–172°F)
Roast pork collar	1.4–1.8 kg (3–4 lb)	indirect	140–160°C (275–325°F)	2–2½ hours		74–76°C (165–169°F)
Pulled pork	2–2.5 kg (4 lb 8 oz–5 lb 8 oz)	indirect	125–135°C (260–275°F)	10–11 hours		88–96°C (190–205°F)
Secreto steak	300–500 g (10½ oz–1 lb 2 oz)	direct/indirect	180–200°C (350–400°F)	8–12 minutes	52–54°C (126–129°F)	
Spider steak/tile meat	120–150 g (4¼–5½ oz)	direct	200–220°C (400–425°F)	5–6 minutes		
Meat skewers	3 cm (1¼ inch) cubes	direct/indirect	180–200°C (350–400°F)	12–14 minutes		
Pork knuckle	800 g–1.2 kg (1 lb 12 oz–2 lb 10 oz)	indirect	180°C (350°F)	1–1½ hours		82–85°C (180–185°F)
Pork cheeks	80–120 g (2¾–4¼ oz)	indirect	125–135°C (260–275°F)	2½–3 hours		88–92°C (190–198°F)
Pluma	400–500 g (14 oz–1 lb 2 oz)	direct	160–180°C (325–350°F)	12–15 minutes	58–60°C (136–140°F)	

LAMB & GAME

Lamb

Lamb is a very special meat. It should be bright red and finely fibrous, with white fat. Any solid and excess fat, such as on the loin, leg or shoulder, should be removed before barbecuing to minimize the risk of flare-ups when cooking over a direct heat. The animals are usually less than a year old when they are slaughtered, so even the muscle meat from the leg or shoulder can be used to cut steaks for quick cooking. Leg meat is also suitable for making skewers or cooking whole.

Venison

Whether it's red deer or fallow deer, venison is lean, spicily tender and free from medication and hormones, as the animals are raised in the wild. The fat content is much lower than that of farmed animals. Deer feed on leaves, grasses, herbs and nuts – in other words, the best that nature has to offer. Seasonality and regionality are important criteria for me when buying game. Some red deer, for example, are raised in large herds and usually grow one-third larger than other deer. Regardless of whether it is meat from the leg, shoulder or back, when prepared perfectly, venison is suitable for grilling quickly as steaks, or more slowly on the bone as a joint.

When is it done?

Lamb: I prefer to barbecue tender, fast-cooking cuts to medium, with a core temperature of between 52 and 58°C (126–136°F). For meat from older animals or more aged meat in joints, I prefer a core temperature of 65°C (149°F) or higher.

Local game: This is something I rarely eat, but when I do, I always know exactly where it's from so I aim to achieve a core temperature of between 55 and 75°C (131–167°F). If you cook game frequently, aim for a core temperature of over 72°C (162°F) and grill the meat thoroughly.

The following table is for guidance only. The cooking times and temperatures below are approximate as they will be affected by a number of factors, including the quality, cut and thickness of the meat. External factors such as wind, air pressure and outside temperature also play an important role when cooking with a gas barbecue.

The core temperature of perfectly grilled meat should be measured, not estimated. Cook **smaller cuts such as steaks and chops** over a direct heat for the time indicated in the table or until the desired degree of doneness, turning once during that time, and if necessary finishing over an indirect heat. During the resting phase, the core temperature will increase a little, depending on the heat. The resting phase is usually 3–5 minutes. Cook **roasts or thicker cuts** over indirect heat for the duration indicated in the table or until the desired core temperature is reached. During the resting phase, the temperature increases more than it does with smaller cuts of meat, depending on the size, weight and heat. The resting phase is usually 12–15 minutes but can be up to 2 hours. During the resting phase, the fibres relax and the meat juices are evenly distributed. You can leave the meat to rest in a cool box, for example, to keep it warm.

LAMB	SIZE/WEIGHT	METHOD	COOKING TEMP	COOKING TIME	MEDIUM	DONE
Lamb chops	2.5 cm (1 inch) thick	direct/indirect	180°C (350°F)	8–10 minutes	52–54°C (126–129°F)	
Rack of lamb	500–600 g (1 lb 2 oz –1 lb 5 oz)	direct/indirect	160–180°C (325–350°F)	15–18 minutes	52–54°C (126–129°F)	
Lamb loin	2–2.5 kg (4 lb 8 oz–5 lb 8 oz)	indirect	140–160°C (275–325°F)	25–30 minutes	49–52°C (120–126°F)	
Leg of lamb, on the bone	2.5–3 kg (5 lb 8 oz–6 lb 8 oz)	indirect	140–160°C (275–325°F)	1–1½ hours	55–58°C (131–136°F)	
Leg of lamb, boneless, rolled	1.4–1.8 kg (3–4 lb)	indirect	140–160°C (275–325°F)	45–50 minutes	55–58°C (131–136°F)	
Knuckle, boneless, flat	1.5–1.7 kg (3 lb 5 oz –3 lb 12 oz)	indirect	140–160°C (275–325°F)	45–50 minutes	55–58°C (131–136°F)	
Knuckle, boneless, rolled	1.7–2 kg (3 lb 12 oz–4 lb 8 oz)	indirect	140–160°C (275–325°F)	1–1½ hours	55–58°C (131–136°F)	
Lamb mince/burgers	3 cm (1¼ inches) thick	direct/indirect	180–200°C (350–400°F)	12–14 minutes		65–68°C (149–154°F)

GAME	SIZE/WEIGHT	METHOD	COOKING TEMP	COOKING TIME	MEDIUM	DONE
Venison loin, boneless	400–600 g (14 oz–1 lb 5 oz)	direct/indirect	160–180°C (325–350°F)		55–57°C (131–135°F)	
Venison backstrap, on the bone	2.5–3 kg (5 lb 8 oz–6 lb 8 oz)	indirect	140–160°C (275–325°F)	35–40 minutes	54–56°C (129–133°F)	
Haunch of venison	1.8–2 kg (4 lb–4 lb 8 oz)	indirect	140–160°C (275–325°F)	1–1½ hours	72–75°C (162–167°F)	
Meat skewers, using venison shoulder	2–3 cm (¾–1¼ inch) cubes	direct/indirect	160–180°C (325–350°F)	15–18 minutes		68–72°C (154–162°F)
Venison fillet, red, fallow or roe deer	80–120 g (2¾–4¼ oz)	direct	180–200°C (350–400°F)	4–6 minutes	56–58°C (133–136°F)	
Saddle of venison, boneless	300–400 g (10½–14 oz)	direct/indirect	160–180°C (325–350°F)	6–8 minutes	58–60°C (136–140°F)	
Saddle of venison, on the bone	1.8–2.2 kg (4–5 lb)	indirect	140–150°C (275–300°F)	1–1½ hours	58–60°C (136–140°F)	
Leg of venison	1–1.2 kg (2 lb 4 oz–2 lb 10 oz)	indirect	150–160°C (300–325°F)	50–55 minutes		72–75°C (162–167°F)
Wild boar back, boneless	350–480 g (12 oz–1 lb 1 oz)	direct/indirect	180–200°C (350–400°F)	12–15 minutes	62–64°C (144–147°F)	
Leg of wild boar, on the bone	2.8–3.25 kg (6 lb 2 oz–7 lb)	indirect	240°C (475°F)	2–2½ hours		76–78°C (169–172°F)
Leg of wild boar, boneless	2.5–2.8 kg (5 lb 8 oz–6 lb 2 oz)	indirect	140°C (275°F)	1½–2 hours		74–76°C (165–169°F)
Roast boar, from the hip	1.2–1.4 kg (2 lb 10 oz–3 lb)	direct/indirect	160–180°C (325–350°F)	45–50 minutes	62–64°C (144–147°F)	

POULTRY

Quality not quantity

There is a world of difference between a cheap factory-farmed chicken and a bird that has been raised in a breed-appropriate way. Factory-farmed birds, which are usually found in supermarkets, cook quickly and are relatively tender, but have little to offer in terms of taste. When they're cooked on the barbecue, covered in oily marinades, ready-made seasoning mixes or sauces, you can no longer taste the actual chicken.

Free-range chickens or those raised organically and fed in a specific way are usually worth their higher price. These birds have access to open air and get plenty of exercise, which results in firmer and tastier meat. Often these chickens come from old breeds, which are less likely to have a plump breast or regular shape but have much more flavour.

A chicken should have taut, undamaged skin that looks neither too tight or too loose, without any dry patches. However, as the skin usually only provides information about how a bird was fed rather than about its actual quality, it is advisable to focus on the smell. If the chicken smells strange, don't buy it, let alone cook it and eat it.

Even when properly slaughtered and refrigerated, poultry can be contaminated with salmonella. Bring home fresh poultry as quickly as possible, keeping it cool, and put it in the coldest part of the refrigerator. Poultry should not be washed before cooking or barbecuing, as this will spread any bacteria around the kitchen. The key thing is to cook the poultry thoroughly, so bacteria won't stand a chance of surviving.

When is it done?

Poultry should generally be cooked through. The core temperature is measured at the thickest part and should be 70–80°C (158–176°F). When checking the temperature, do not allow the thermometer probe to touch the bone, as it retains heat during barbecuing and becomes hotter than the surrounding meat. The following applies to all poultry: do not simply estimate the core temperature but measure it with a temperature probe. If you don't have a thermometer, simply cut halfway into the meat after the cooking time specified in the recipe: the meat is cooked when clear juices run out and the meat on the bone is no longer pink.

The following table is for guidance only. The cooking times and temperatures below are approximate as they will be affected by a number of factors, including the quality, cut and thickness of the meat. External factors such as wind, air pressure and outside temperature also play an important role when cooking with a gas barbecue.

The core temperature of perfectly grilled meat should be measured, not estimated. Cook **smaller cuts such as steaks and chops** over a direct heat for the time indicated in the table or until the desired degree of doneness, turning once during that time, and if necessary finishing over an indirect heat. During the resting phase, the core temperature will increase a little, depending on the heat. The resting phase is usually 3–5 minutes. Cook **roasts or thicker cuts** over indirect heat for the duration indicated in the table or until the desired core temperature is reached. During the resting phase, the temperature increases more than it does with smaller cuts of meat, depending on the size, weight and heat. The resting phase is usually 12–15 minutes but can be up to 2 hours. During the resting phase, the fibres relax and the meat juices are evenly distributed. You can leave the meat to rest in a cool box, for example, to keep it warm.

POULTRY	SIZE/WEIGHT	METHOD	COOKING TEMP	COOKING TIME	MEDIUM	DONE
Whole chicken	1–1.2 kg (2 lb 4 oz–2 lb 10 oz)	indirect	180–200°C (350–400°F)	50–60 minutes		76–80°C (169–176°F)
Chicken breast, on the bone with skin	180–230 g (6¼–8 oz)	direct/indirect	180–200°C (350–400°F)	15–20 minutes		72–76°C (162–169°F)
Chicken breast, boneless and skinless	180–230 g (6¼–8 oz)	direct/indirect	180–200°C (350–400°F)	15–18 minutes		72–74°C (162–165°F)
Chicken leg	230–260 g (8–9¼ oz)	direct/indirect	160–180°C (325–350°F)	35–40 minutes		76–78°C (169–172°F)
Chicken drumsticks	120–140 g (4¼–5 oz)	direct/indirect	160–180°C (325–350°F)	25–30 minutes		76–78°C (169–172°F)
Chicken breast fillet	60–80 g (2¼–2¾ oz)	direct	180–200°C (350–400°F)	5–8 minutes		72–74°C (162–165°F)
Chicken mince/patties	160–200 g (5½–7 oz), 3 cm (1¼ inches) thick	direct/indirect	180–200°C (350–400°F)	12–15 minutes		74–76°C (165–169°F)
Chicken wings	80–100 g (2¾–3½ oz)	indirect	160–180°C (325–350°F)	20–25 minutes		76–78°C (169–172°F)
Spatchcock chicken	1–1.2 kg (2 lb 4 oz–2 lb 10 oz)	direct/indirect	180–200°C (350–400°F)	40–45 minutes		76–80°C (169–176°F)
Poussin	350–450 g (12 oz–1 lb)	direct	180–200°C (350–400°F)	30–35 minutes		72–74°C (162–165°F)
Whole turkey breast, boneless and skinless	1.5–1.8 kg (3 lb 5 oz–4 lb)	direct/indirect	160–180°C (325–350°F)	50–65 minutes		72–76°C (162–169°F)
Turkey breast, on the bone with skin	1.7–2 kg (3 lb 12 oz–4 lb 8 oz)	direct/indirect	160–180°C (325–350°F)	55–70 minutes		74–78°C (165–172°F)
Turkey breast skewers	3 cm (1¼ inch) cubes	direct/indirect	180°C (350°F)	12–15 minutes		74–76°C (165–169°F)
Turkey leg	450–680 g (1 lb–1 lb 8 oz)	direct/indirect	160–180°C (325–350°F)	55–65 minutes		76–80°C (169–176°F)
Whole turkey	4.5–6 kg (10 lb–13 lb 4 oz)	indirect	160–180°C (325–350°F)	2½–3½ hours		76–80°C (169–176°F)
Duck breast, boneless with skin	220–250 g (8–9 oz)	direct/indirect	200–220°C (400–425°F)	12–15 minutes	52–54°C (126–129°F)	
Duck leg	350–400 g (12–14 oz)	direct/indirect	160–180°C (325–350°F)	35–40 minutes		70–74°C (158–165°F)
Whole duck	1.7–2 kg (3 lb 12 oz –4 lb 8 oz)	indirect	160°C (325°F)	1½–2 hours		70–74°C (158–165°F)
Goose breast, on the bone with skin	1.2–1.5 kg (2 lb 10 oz–3 lb 5 oz)	direct/indirect	140–150°C (275–300°F)	2–2½ hours		74–78°C (165–172°F)
Goose breast, boneless and skinless	1.2–1.5 kg (2 lb 10 oz–3 lb 5 oz)	direct/indirect	140–150°C (275–300°F)	1½–2 hours		74–76°C (165–169°F)
Whole goose	5–7 kg (11 lb–15 lb 7 oz)	indirect	140–150°C (275–300°F)	4–4½ hours		88–92°C (190–198°F)
Goose leg	800 g–1 kg (1 lb 12 oz–2 lb 4 oz)	direct/indirect	140–160°C (275–325°F)	3–3½ hours		88–92°C (190–198°F)
Guinea fowl breast, on the bone with skin	160–180 g (5½–6¼ oz)	direct	180–200°C (350–400°F)	12–15 minutes		72–74°C (162–165°F)
Whole guinea fowl	900 g–1.2 kg (2 lb–2 lb 10 oz)	indirect	160–180°C (325–350°F)	45–50 minutes		72–74°C (162–165°F)
Whole pheasant	900 g–1.2 kg (2 lb–2 lb 10 oz)	indirect	180–200°C (350–400°F)	45–50 minutes		72–74°C (162–165°F)

FISH & SEAFOOD

Wild or farmed?

When buying fish, the first decision is whether to buy wild fish or fish that has been farmed, because wild fish can cost three times as much.

Wild capture is the term used to describe fish that have been caught on a line or with nets. These fish feed, grow and live in mostly cold waters, making their flesh firm, leaner and more nutritious. The disadvantage of wild fish is that trawlers used to harvest some species usually result in a considerable amount of by-catch.

Certified aquaculture can be a sustainable way to raise farmed fish. Various types of fish are raised this fairly natural way, kept in sufficiently large tanks and fed partly with algae and mussels. Feed such as fishmeal or the use of medication such as antibiotics are not allowed.

Conventional aquaculture is a kind of underwater factory farming. When buying fresh or prepared fish such as fish fillets, keep an eye out for the appropriate labels and designations of origin to avoid this fish.

Choosing fish for the barbecue

Firm fish and seafood are particularly suitable as they retain their shape when cooked on a barbecue. Fish with more delicate flesh can also be cooked on a barbecue, but they will require a little more attention or the right accessories, such as a fish basket or a plank.

Cooking fish on a barbecue

- **Clean the grate:** A clean grate prevents fish fillets or steaks sticking on any leftover residue.
- **Oil the fish:** Coat fish fillets with a thin layer of oil but do not oil the grate. This prevents fish sticking to the grate.
- **Use intense heat:** Fish will come off the grate when its underside is caramelized and a thin crust has developed.
- **Cook on a plank:** Skinless or marinated fish fillets should, if possible, be cooked on a plank. It's straightforward, easy to manage and gives the fish a nice smoky note.
- **Focus on timing:** If possible, always grill fish fillets with the skin on, and cook the first side for 2–3 minutes longer than the second. This makes it easier to remove the fish from the grill and also gives it a nice pattern.

When is it done?

Under no circumstances should fish be grilled for too long. It has to come off the barbecue before the protein oozes out in big white bubbles and the meat falls apart into flakes. I prefer to cook fish with a core temperature of 52–54°C (126–129°F); however, most people like their fish almost cooked through, so the core temperature can be adjusted accordingly. If the fish fillet is too thin to use a thermometer, you can judge the level of doneness by the colour of the flesh. It should not be translucent or glassy at the core.

The following table is for guidance only. The cooking times and temperatures below are approximate as they will be affected by a number of factors, including the quality, cut and thickness of the fish. External factors such as wind, air pressure and outside temperature also play an important role when cooking with a gas barbecue. The most important rule of thumb when grilling fish is to cook it for 3–4 minutes per 1 cm (½ inch) of thickness.

The core temperature of perfectly grilled fish should always be measured, not estimated. **Fish fillets or steaks** should be grilled over a direct heat for the time indicated in the table or until the desired degree of doneness, turning once during that time and if necessary finishing over an indirect heat. During the resting phase, the core temperature will increase a little, depending on the heat. The resting phase is usually 1–2 minutes. Grill **whole fish or fish in a crust** over an indirect heat for the time indicated in the table or until the required core temperature is reached. During the resting phase, the temperature increases more than it does with fish fillets, depending on the size, weight and heat. The resting phase is usually 12–15 minutes, and up to 30 minutes for fish cooked in a salt crust. During the resting phase, the fibres relax and the juices are evenly distributed. You can leave the fish to rest in a cool box, for example, to keep it warm.

FISH	SIZE/WEIGHT	METHOD	COOKING TEMP	COOKING TIME MEDIUM-RARE		DONE
Fish fillets, with skin (sea bream, trout, sole, pike perch)	5 mm–1 cm (¼–½ inch) thick	direct, skin side	170–180°C (340–350°F)	6–8 minutes		58–64°C (136–147°F)
Fish fillets, with skin (char, sea bass, red perch)	1–2.5 cm (½–1 inch) thick	direct, skin side	170–180°C (340–350°F)	8–10 minutes		58–64°C (136–147°F)
Fish fillets, with skin (halibut, turbot, salmon)	2–3 cm (¾–1¼ inches) thick	direct, skin side	170–180°C (340–350°F)	10–12 minutes		58–64°C (136–147°F)
Fish fillets, without skin (pollock, Victoria perch, scalloped perch)	1–1.5 cm (½–¾ inch) thick	indirect	170–180°C (340–350°F)	6–8 minutes		58–64°C (136–147°F)
Salmon steaks	2–3 cm (¾–1¼ inches) thick	direct/indirect	170–180°C (340–350°F)	10–12 minutes		58–64°C (136–147°F)
Salmon fillet	2.5–3 cm (1–1¼ inches) thick	direct/indirect	160–180°C (325–350°F)	10–12 minutes		58–65°C (136–149°F)
Swordfish steak	3 cm (1¼ inches) thick	direct/indirect	160–180°C (325–350°F)	10–12 minutes		62–65°C (144–149°F)
Tuna steak	3 cm (1¼ inches) thick	direct	240–260°C (475–500°F)	6–8 minutes	42–46°C (108–115°F)	
Monkfish tail, whole	1.4–1.6 kg (3 lb–3 lb 8 oz)	indirect	160–180°C (325–350°F)	20–25 minutes		62–65°C (144–149°F)
Monkfish loin	600–700 g (1 lb 5 oz–1 lb 9 oz)	direct/indirect	180–200°C (350–400°F)	12–15 minutes		62–65°C (144–149°F)
Monkfish fillet	120–140 g (4¼–5 oz), 2–2.5 cm (¾–1 inch) thick	direct/indirect	180–200°C (350–400°F)	8–10 minutes		62–65°C (144–149°F)
Monkfish medallions	3 cm (1¼ inches) thick	direct	180–200°C (350–400°F)	6–8 minutes		62–65°C (144–149°F)
Cod loin	500–800 g (1 lb 2 oz–1 lb 12 oz)	direct/indirect	160–180°C (325–350°F)	12–15 minutes		58–60°C (136–140°F)
Cod medallions	3 cm (1¼ inches) thick	direct	180–200°C (350–400°F)	6–8 minutes		58–60°C (136–140°F)
Red perch loin	500–700 g (1 lb 2 oz–1 lb 9 oz)	direct/indirect	160–180°C (325–350°F)	10–12 minutes		54–56°C (129–133°F)
Whole fish (sea bream, sea bass, red snapper, trout)	1.2–1.5 kg (2 lb 10 oz–3 lb 5 oz)	direct/indirect	160–180°C (325–350°F)	20–25 minutes		60–64°C (140–147°F)
Fish skewers, firm fish (salmon, monkfish, tuna, swordfish)	3 cm (1¼ inch) cubes	direct/indirect	160–170°C (325–340°F)	12–15 minutes		60–64°C (140–147°F)
Fish mince, (fishcakes, balls, salmon bombs)	3–5 cm (1¼–2 inches) thick	direct/indirect	160–180°C (325–350°F)	10–12 minutes		65–68°C (149–154°F)

SEAFOOD	SIZE/WEIGHT	METHOD	COOKING TEMP	COOKING TIME	MEDIUM
Lobster tail, detached and pre-cooked	800–900 g (1 lb 12 oz–2 lb)	direct	180–200°C (350–400°F)	5–6 minutes	56–58°C (133–136°F)
Lobster, whole	800–900 g (1 lb 12 oz–2 lb)	direct	180–200°C (350–400°F)	18–20 minutes	56–58°C (133–136°F)
King prawns and langoustine, with shell	120–150 g (4¼–5½ oz)	direct	160–180°C (325–350°F)	6–8 minutes	
King prawns and langoustine, without shell	80–120 g (2¾–4¼ oz)	direct	160–180°C (325–350°F)	5–6 minutes	
Scallops	2.5–5 cm (1–2 inches) thick	direct	180–200°C (350–400°F)	4–6 minutes	56–60°C (133–140°F)
Oysters		direct	160–180°C (325–350°F)	3–6 minutes	
Octopus tentacles, pre-cooked	2–3 cm (¾–1¼ inches) thick	direct	200–220°C (400–425°F)	12–15 minutes	

VEGETABLES

Regional & seasonal

Choose the best-quality vegetables while they are in season and selling at a fair price. Look for local products as they will be riper, more sustainable and taste much better than those that have had to travel half way across the world to get to you.

Preparing veg for the barbecue

Prepare vegetables that you are planning to barbecue so that as large a surface area as possible can come into contact with the hot grate. The more direct the contact, the more the sugar in the vegetables can caramelize and the better the taste.

Only the best oil will do

Coat vegetables with a fine layer of oil so that they do not stick to the grate during cooking. Neutral oils such as sunflower oil and rapeseed oil work well as they do not hide the individual flavour of each vegetable. Use just enough oil to lightly coat the surface, no more. After cooking, you can then finish the vegetables with herbs, garlic oils or a seasoning mix.

Cooking veg

Fine or sliced vegetables such as courgettes and asparagus are usually cooked at a medium temperature. I like it when vegetables still have a bit of bite after grilling. Grilling caramelizes the sugars, releasing the natural sweetness.

Firm vegetables such as celery, root vegetables and potatoes benefit from a longer rest period after grilling – place them in a bowl, cover the bowl with clingfilm and leave the vegetables to sweat for 8–15 minutes, depending on the variety. This ensures they are cooked through thoroughly, making them as tender as butter.

The vegetable pieces should be cut to a similar thickness so that they cook evenly on the barbecue. When grilling vegetable skewers, make sure that only vegetables of a similar structure, such as courgette and aubergine, are used on the same skewer so they cook at the same speed.

The following table is for guidance only. The cooking times and temperatures below are approximate as they will be affected by a number of factors, including the quality, age and thickness of the vegetables. External factors such as wind, air pressure and outside temperature also play an important role when cooking with a gas barbecue.

The cooking temperature for most vegetables should be 140–200°C (275–400°F). Take care to turn the pieces of vegetable if they start to get too dark in one place. Otherwise, the following applies: move as little as possible.

VEGETABLES	SIZE/WEIGHT	METHOD	COOKING TEMP	COOKING TIME	DONE
Aubergines, sliced	1 cm (½ inch) thick	direct	160–180°C (325–350°F)	5–8 minutes	
Cauliflower, sliced	2–3 cm (¾–1¼ inches) thick	direct	180–200°C (350–400°F)	10–12 minutes	
Fennel, sliced	5 mm (¼ inch) thick	direct	160–180°C (325–350°F)	4–6 minutes	
Mushrooms, whole or halved, depending on size	3–5 cm (1¼–2 inches) thick	direct	150–160°C (300–325°F)	8–10 minutes	
Spring onions	1–1.5 cm (½–¾ inch) diameter	direct	140–160°C (275–325°F)	6–8 minutes	
Potatoes, whole and floury	6–8 cm (2½–3¼ inches) diameter	indirect	180–200°C (350–400°F)	30–50 minutes	92–95°C (198–203°F)
Potatoes, small and waxy	3–5 cm (1¼–2 inches) diameter	indirect	160–180°C (325–350°F)	30–35 minutes	92–95°C (198–203°F)
Potatoes, sliced	1–1.5 cm (½–¾ inch) thick	direct	150–160°C (300–325°F)	12–15 minutes	
Garlic bulb, wrapped in baking parchment and foil	whole	indirect	150–160°C (300–325°F)	40–45 minutes	
Butternut squash & other squashes, halved	about 400 g (14 oz)	indirect	150–160°C (300–325°F)	40–60 minutes	
Pumpkin wedges	3–5 cm (1¼–2 inches) thick	direct/indirect	160–180°C (325–350°F)	20–25 minutes	
Vegetable kebabs	2–3 cm (¾–1¼ inch) cubes	direct/indirect	150–160°C (300–325°F)	12–15 minutes	
Corn cobs, whole and pre-cooked		direct	150–160°C (300–325°F)	15–20 minutes	
Root vegetables, whole (carrots, turnips, parsnips)	1–3 cm (½–1¼ inches) diameter	direct	180–200°C (350–400°F)	8–10 minutes	
Peppers, whole		direct	150–160°C (300–325°F)	12–17 minutes	
Peppers, sliced	5 mm (¼ inch) thick	direct	150–160°C (300–325°F)	6–8 minutes	
Asparagus	1–2 cm (½–¾ inch) diameter	direct	160–180°C (325–350°F)	6–10 minutes	
Celery sticks	2–3 cm (¾–1¼ inches) thick	direct	180–200°C (350–400°F)	10–12 minutes	
Large mushrooms, whole (Portobello)	3–5 cm (1¼–2 inches) diameter	direct	150–160°C (300–325°F)	10–15 minutes	
Sweet potatoes	6–8 cm (2½–3¼ inches) diameter	indirect	160–180°C (325–350°F)	45–60 minutes	95–98°C (203–208°F)
Sweet potatoes, sliced	1–2 cm (½–¾ inch) thick	direct	150–160°C (300–325°F)	12–15 minutes	
Tomatoes, halved	2–3 cm (¾–1¼ inches) thick	direct	150–160°C (300–325°F)	6–8 minutes	
Tomatoes, whole	6–8 cm (2½–3¼ inches) diameter	direct	150–160°C (300–325°F)	8–12 minutes	
Courgettes, halved	2–3 cm (¾–1¼ inches) thick	direct/indirect	160–180°C (325–350°F)	6–8 minutes	
Courgettes, sliced	1–2 cm (½–¾ inch) thick	direct	160–180°C (325–350°F)	3–5 minutes	
Onions, sliced	2–3 cm (¾–1¼ inches) thick	direct	160–180°C (325–350°F)	6–8 minutes	
Onions, whole with skin	6–8 cm (2½–3¼ inches) diameter	indirect	160–180°C (325–350°F)	20–35 minutes	

FRUIT

Sweet fruit from the barbecue

The rules for grilling vegetables on a barbecue also apply to grilling fruit. Choose ripe but firm fruit for best results, taking care to use seasonal, local produce when possible. Many types of fruit become even sweeter and juicier on the barbecue as the heat intensifies their flavour. Avoid leaving them in one spot for too long or they may burn, but do aim for a good level of caramelization to concentrate the sugars.

A little oil goes a long way

Just as with vegetables, I like to use a neutral, high-quality vegetable oil when cooking fruit, such as sunflower or rapeseed oil, as these oils do not affect the fruit's natural flavour. Use just a thin film of oil on fruit with a high sugar content to prevent them sticking to the grate.

The grand finale

Warm fruit from the grill can be the perfect end to a successful barbecue and fruity desserts are quick and easy to prepare. Combined with ice cream or sorbet or made into a crumble, barbecued fruits can make a fantastic dessert.

The following table is for guidance only. The cooking times and temperatures below are approximate as they will be affected by a number of factors, including the quality, ripeness and thickness of the fruit. External factors such as wind, air pressure and outside temperature also play an important role when cooking with a gas barbecue.

The cooking temperature for most fruit should be 160–180°C (325–350°F). Take care to turn the pieces of fruit if they start to get too dark in one place. For very watery fruit, such as watermelon skewers or steaks, you will need temperatures of 220–250°C (425–485°F) so that the watermelon caramelizes rather than boils in its own juices.

FRUIT	SIZE/WEIGHT	METHOD	COOKING TEMP	COOKING TIME
Pineapple, sliced (fibrous core removed)	2–3 cm (¾–1¼ inches) thick	direct	160–180°C (325–350°F)	10–12 minutes
Apples, whole	8–10 cm (3¼–4 inches) diameter	indirect	160–180°C (325–350°F)	30–35 minutes
Apples, halved	3–5 cm (1¼–2 inches) thick	direct	160–180°C (325–350°F)	12–15 minutes
Apricots, halved and pitted		direct	160–180°C (325–350°F)	6–8 minutes
Bananas, halved		direct	160–180°C (325–350°F)	6–8 minutes
Bananas, whole		direct/indirect	180–200°C (350–400°F)	8–10 minutes
Pears, whole	6–8 cm (2½–3¼ inches) diameter	indirect	160–180°C (325–350°F)	30–35 minutes
Pears, halved	3–5 cm (1¼–2 inches) thick	direct	160–180°C (325–350°F)	12–15 minutes
Figs, with a cross cut in the top		indirect	160–180°C (325–350°F)	3–5 minutes
Strawberries		direct	160–180°C (325–350°F)	3–5 minutes
Nectarines/peaches, halved	3–5 cm (1¼–2 inches) thick	direct	160–180°C (325–350°F)	8–10 minutes
Watermelon steaks	2–3 cm (¾–1¼ inches) thick	direct	220–250°C (425–480°F)	6–8 minutes

THE 11 COMMANDMENTS
for a successful gas barbecue

1 Keep a spare gas bottle
We have seen how to tell how much gas is left in the bottle (see page 15), but to be on the safe side, always have a spare gas bottle to hand. Cooking can often take longer than expected, and you want to be sure there is enough gas for slow-cooked dishes.

2 Choose the right size gas bottle
The two most common bottle sizes in the UK are 5 kg and 13 kg. If you have a gas barbecue with three or more burners, it is better to choose the larger size so that your cooking capabilities match the size of your barbecue.

3 Read through new recipes in advance
Once you have purchased the ingredients for a new recipe, it is a good idea to take time to have a careful read through the preparation method before you start cooking. You'll see exactly if and when the barbecuing technique or temperature changes, allowing you to plan properly.

4 Keep all your accessories to hand
All accessories should be ready and waiting, near the barbecue. This way you will be more relaxed as you are cooking, allowing you more time to focus on your guests. After all, beer tastes better when you've been able to keep a cool head.

5 Never cook on a cold barbecue with a dirty grate
Your gas barbecue should always be preheated for 12–15 minutes, depending on the required cooking temperature. A preheated and clean grate will prevent food sticking right from the start. In addition, thanks to the build-up of heat under the lid during preheating, dishes such as pizza will be ready in good time.

6 Season the food at the right time
Do you season with salt before or after cooking? This is a philosophy in its own right! I think the best results are achieved by salting meat beforehand. However, when grilling with high direct heat, you should only season your food with spices such as pepper, cumin or paprika shortly before the end of the cooking time or after grilling, so that they do not burn and become bitter. However, when using a dry marinade or rub, the surface is moist and the food is usually cooked over a low to medium heat, which prevents the spices burning.

7 Be flexible with your heat zones
Multiple heat zones allow for flexibility when cooking on a gas barbecue. You'll have more space on the grate, for example, if you use the warming rack to continue cooking a piece of meat over indirect heat. This means you can cook a range of different foods at the same time, and the heat of each burner can be adjusted individually to get the right set-up for your meal.

8 Don't overload the barbecue
If your barbecue is too full, you will have to juggle different cooking techniques needed for each ingredient. A fully packed grate will also reduce the heat under the lid, making cooking temperatures lower than you want. This in turn affects the food being cooked, which will no longer brown and caramelize to perfection.

9 Don't keep opening that lid!
To ensure a consistent and constant cooking temperature, keep the barbecue lid closed as much as possible. This keeps the heat and smoke flavour under the lid and also prevents flare-ups. When checking food on the barbecue, only open the lid as far as necessary – never open it wide. This also saves on gas and keeps the cooking time down, as the barbecue does not need constant heating.

10 Don't just guess, measure
You should only be putting your hands to your face if something has gone wrong during the cooking process – this is not a proven method for determining the level of doneness of a piece of meat! Use a temperature probe instead. If you are trying a new recipe or are relatively new to cooking on a barbecue, a good thermometer is your best friend (see page 34).

11 Try out new ideas
Barbecuing today has a much wider scope than ever before. The accessories available allow us to maximize the performance of our barbecue and try a wide range of different recipes and techniques. These days, a gas barbecue can be used for grilling, smoking, braising, baking, roasting and much, much more.

Weber's barbecue bible **TIPS**

SEASONINGS

Why should I season meat with just salt before searing?

Spices such as pepper, cumin and paprika burn and become bitter over a medium to high direct heat. Therefore, these delicate spices should only be added after the food has been removed from the barbecue or while cooking with indirect heat.

When should I salt meat?

I believe that food absorbs salt better before being cooked on the barbecue than after. The medium to high heat experienced during barbecue cooking causes the sugars in the protein to caramelize, which seals the meat fibres and creates a beautiful crust. If you try seasoning your meat with salt after it's been grilled, you'll see that it just rolls off. Salting cooked meat once you have sliced it is a different matter, though, because the cut surfaces are able to absorb salt.

What is the difference between a seasoning mix and a rub or dry marinade?

While they are all basically the same thing, seasoning mixes and rubs are used differently. A seasoning mix is a mixture of various dry spices, combined with salt and/or sugar as needed. It's used to season food immediately before, during or after cooking. If the food is marinated with dry spices for several hours or days before cooking, it's known as a rub.

Does marinating make meat, fish or vegetables more tender?

The answer is a resounding yes! But only in combination with salt, for example, in a rub, brine or wet marinade, or an acidic ingredient (vinegar, lemon juice, buttermilk) in a wet or oily marinade. Only salt and acid can change the proteins in food in such a way that they can penetrate and thus make the food more tender. While on the barbecue, the meat will stay juicy and take on the flavour of the marinade. Long marinating times can noticeably shorten the cooking time, but only with large food items such as a beef brisket (pastrami) or a whole pork neck (pulled pork).

What's the best way to prepare a spice mix? And how long will it keep in an airtight container?

When grinding spice mixes/rubs by hand using a pestle and mortar, I would always start with the harder spices such as peppercorns. You can also prepare spice mixes, especially larger quantities, quite easily with a food processor. Your creations will keep for 2–3 weeks in an airtight container, stored in a dry and dark place. After that, they won't go off but they will start to lose their flavour.

What type of mortar is best for making spice mixes?

A large stone mortar with a rough interior surface is best. To ensure that the ingredients stay inside the mortar when grinding, simply make a tear in the middle of a piece of kitchen paper and place it over the pestle like a lid. This keeps all the ingredients inside the mortar.

Should a spice mix be ground coarsely or finely?

The larger the piece of meat, the coarser the rub should be, so that the dry marinade can be absorbed slowly and doesn't just remain on the surface. For smaller food items or shorter marinating times, the seasoning mix should be finely ground.

How do I get the best results when marinating?

It is best to vacuum-pack food while marinating – that is to say, sealed airtight. However, if you don't have a vacuum-packer to hand, you can use a large plastic bag instead, which you can seal airtight with the aid of a hand-held vacuum pump. Another option when using dry marinades is to wrap the food tightly in clingfilm. When using wet marinades, place the food in a casserole dish or bowl that is just big enough to contain it and remember to turn the food occasionally.

THE RIGHT TEMPERATURE

When does meat need to be brought up to room temperature before cooking and when does it not?

It depends on the marbling of the meat, the type of feed given to the animal and, of course, the size of the cut. I like to bring lower-fat and smaller pieces of meat which require a relatively short barbecue time up to room temperature to keep the temperature difference as low as possible during cooking. This is gentler on the meat and it will be juicier. For example, a 3–5 cm (1¼–2 inch) thick beef steak with an initial temperature of 3–5°C (37–41°F) will have a core temperature of 12–18°C (54–64°F) after it has been left for 15–25 minutes at a room temperature of 20–24°C (68–75°F).

Fine meats such as Wagyu beef or those heavily marbled with fat, on the other hand, are less suited to bringing up to room temperature. The fat would ooze out immediately during cooking because the meat does not contain enough protein to bind it. This could potentially result in a grease fire on the barbecue. Foods that spoil quickly such as poultry and fish should also be kept in the refrigerator until cooking.

If you do bring your meat up to room temperature before cooking, cook it without delay and do not refrigerate it again.

It also helps to bring the seasoning mix for larger pieces up to room temperature too, so that it can work on the meat better.

How do I get the food to room temperature?

Prepare the food to be barbecued as required, marinating or seasoning if necessary, wrap it in baking parchment and keep in the refrigerator. When you are getting ready to barbecue, simply take the food out of the refrigerator and cover it with clingfilm to protect it from insects while it comes up to temperature.

SLICING

How should you slice meat after grilling?

Meat is always cut across the grain. It feels more tender in the mouth because the meat fibres have been severed. However, some cuts tempt you to slice them incorrectly because of their texture – a prime example of this is skirt steak. But regardless of the level of doneness and cooking technique used, simply look for the parallel lines of muscle fibre in the meat and cut across them, against the grain.

SPICE MIXES
FOR 1 KG (2 LB 4 OZ) FOOD

① Basic spice mix

MAKES ABOUT 6 TABLESPOONS:
1 teaspoon coriander seeds, 1 teaspoon onion powder, 1 tablespoon dried herbes de Provence, 2 tablespoons coarse sea salt, 1 tablespoon sugar, 1 tablespoon sweet paprika, 1 teaspoon hot paprika — Grind all of the ingredients finely in a mortar. Great with BEEF, PORK, POULTRY, GAME and LAMB.

② Curry spice mix

MAKES ABOUT 5 TABLESPOONS:
½ stalk lemon grass, ½ star anise, 1 tablespoon coriander seeds, 1 teaspoon lemon pepper, 1 tablespoon curry powder, 1 teaspoon onion powder, 1 tablespoon brown sugar, 1 teaspoon coarse sea salt — Slice the lemon grass in fine rings and chop. Grind the remaining ingredients roughly in a mortar and mix together with the lemon grass. This spice mix works well with POULTRY, FISH, VEGETABLES and LIGHT MEAT.

③ Espresso & pepper spice mix

MAKES ABOUT 3 TABLESPOONS:
1 tablespoon espresso coffee beans, 1 tablespoon freshly ground black pepper, 1 teaspoon Java pepper, 1 teaspoon dried thyme, 1 teaspoon coarse sea salt, 1 teaspoon brown sugar — Grind all of the ingredients roughly in a mortar. Great with BEEF, PORK, FIRM-FLESHED FISH and POULTRY.

④ Pepper & chilli spice mix

MAKES ABOUT 3 TABLESPOONS:
1 teaspoon dried chilli flakes, ½ teaspoon caraway seeds, 1 tablespoon brown sugar, 1 teaspoon coarse sea salt, 1 tablespoon sweet paprika, 1 teaspoon hot paprika — Grind all the ingredients roughly in a mortar. Great with BEEF, PORK, FIRM-FLESHED FISH and POULTRY.

⑤ Herb mix

MAKES ABOUT 4 TABLESPOONS:
½ teaspoon lemon pepper, ½ teaspoon black peppercorns, 1 tablespoon coriander seeds, 2 tablespoons dried herbes de Provence, 1 teaspoon fennel seeds, 1 teaspoon coarse sea salt — Grind all of the ingredients roughly in a mortar. Great with BEEF, PORK, FIRM-FLESHED FISH and POULTRY.

⑥ Spice mix for beef

MAKES ABOUT 3 TABLESPOONS:
1½ teaspoons coarse sea salt, ½ teaspoon brown sugar, 1 teaspoon black peppercorns, 1½ teaspoons coriander seeds, ½ teaspoon fennel seeds, ½ teaspoon garlic powder, 1 tablespoon sweet paprika — Grind all the ingredients roughly in a mortar. Great with RED MEAT, STEAKS and MEAT SKEWERS.

⑦ Vanilla & pepper spice mix

MAKES ABOUT 6 TABLESPOONS:
Seeds from ½ vanilla pod, 2 tablespoons Tellicherry peppercorns (or black peppercorns), 1 tablespoon coriander seeds, 1 tablespoon mustard seeds, 2 tablespoons coarse sea salt
— Grind all the ingredients finely in a mortar. Great with BEEF, PORK, POULTRY, GAME and VEGETABLES.

⑧ BBQ spice mix for poultry

MAKES ABOUT 4 TABLESPOONS:
1 tablespoon coriander seeds, 1 teaspoon black peppercorns, ½ teaspoon ground cinnamon, ½ star anise, ½ tonka bean (optional), 1 tablespoon sweet paprika, 1 teaspoon brown sugar, 1 teaspoon coarse sea salt
— Grind all the ingredients finely in a mortar. Great with POULTRY such as CORN-FED CHICKEN, CHICKEN, DUCK, GOOSE, TURKEY, PHEASANT, QUAIL and GUINEAFOWL.

⑨ Five-spice mix

MAKES ABOUT 5 TABLESPOONS:
1 tablespoon black peppercorns, 1 tablespoon coriander seeds, 8 cloves, 1 tablespoon aniseed, 2 tablespoons ground cinnamon
Grind all the ingredients finely in a mortar.
— Great with VEGETABLES, SWEET POTATOES, POULTRY, BEEF, LAMB and HEARTY CUTS OF PORK.

⑩ Potato & vegetable spice mix

MAKES ABOUT 3 TABLESPOONS:
1 tablespoon fine sea salt, ½ teaspoon white sugar, ½ teaspoon curry powder, 1 tablespoon sweet paprika, 1 teaspoon onion powder, ½ teaspoon dried lemon peel, 1 teaspoon dried parsley
— Mix all the ingredients in a bowl. Great for FRENCH FRIES, POTATO DISHES, VEGETABLES and MUSHROOMS. Perfect for seasoning and marinating.

⑪ Texas-style spice mix

MAKES ABOUT 7 TABLESPOONS:
1 tablespoon coarse sea salt, 2 tablespoons brown sugar, 1 teaspoon garlic granules, 1½ tablespoons onion powder, ½ teaspoon chilli powder, 2 tablespoons hot paprika
— Grind all the ingredients roughly in a mortar. Great with BEEF, PORK, POULTRY, CORN ON THE COB and VEGETABLES.

⑫ Bread seasoning mix

MAKES ABOUT 4 TABLESPOONS FOR 2 KG (4 LB 8 OZ) BREAD DOUGH:
1 tablespoon coriander seeds, 1 tablespoon fennel seeds, 1 teaspoon black peppercorns, 3 cloves, ¼ star anise, 1 teaspoon caraway seeds, 1 large pinch of ground cinnamon
— Grind all the ingredients finely in a mortar. Great for BREAD, BAGUETTES and other SAVOURY BAKED GOODS.

⑬ Fish & seafood seasoning mix

MAKES ABOUT 4 TABLESPOONS:
1 teaspoon coarse sea salt, 1 tablespoon coriander seeds, 1 tablespoon fennel seeds, 1 teaspoon black peppercorns, 1 tablespoon dried parsley, 1 teaspoon dried basil, 1 teaspoon dried coriander leaves
— Grind all the ingredients finely in a mortar. Great with FISH and SEAFOOD, VEGETABLES and VEAL.

MARINADES & GLAZES
FOR 1 KG (2 LB 4 OZ) FOOD

① Sour cherry marinade with red onions

MAKES ABOUT 350 ML (12 FL OZ):
1 jar or can pitted sour cherries in their juice or black cherries in syrup (about 350 g/12 oz), *drained (for sour cherries, reserve the juice; for black cherries, add 125 ml/4 fl oz apple juice),* 2 red onions, *sliced,* 2 garlic cloves, *crushed,* 4 tablespoons soy sauce, 1 tablespoon finely chopped thyme
— Put all the ingredients for the marinade in a casserole dish with plenty of room for the meat, and mix with a whisk. Turn the meat in the marinade until it is covered all over, then cover with baking parchment. Leave to marinate in the refrigerator for at least 1 hour and up to 24 hours. After marinating, pat the meat dry and leave it to come up to room temperature. Great with BEEF STEAKS, ROASTS, GAME and LAMB.

② Honey glaze with soy sauce & garlic

MAKES ABOUT 250 ML (9 FL OZ):
4 tablespoons clear honey, 4 tablespoons maple syrup, 1½ tablespoons mustard, juice of 1 orange, 3 tablespoons soy sauce, ½ teaspoon ground coriander
— Whisk all the ingredients together in a small bowl. During a short cooking time, keep brushing the meat on the barbecue with the glaze until it is all used up. Keep an eye on the heat. For large pieces of meat, start brushing on the glaze about 15 minutes before the end of the cooking time. Great for BEEF STEAKS, CUTS of PORK or VEAL, CHICKEN BREASTS and SKEWERS.

③ Lemon marinade with parsley

MAKES ABOUT 250 ML (9 FL OZ):
1 red onion, *finely diced,* 4 garlic cloves, *finely diced,* 1 red pepper, *cored, deseeded and finely diced,* zest and juice of 2 unwaxed lemons, 50 g (1¾ oz) parsley, *chopped,* 1 teaspoon fine sea salt, 8 tablespoons olive oil
— Put all the ingredients for the marinade in a casserole dish with plenty of room for the food, and mix with a whisk. Turn the food in the marinade until it is evenly coated all over. Cover with baking parchment and leave to marinate in the refrigerator for at least 1 hour or up to 24 hours. After marinating, pat the food dry and leave to come up to room temperature. Great for POULTRY, FISH, CHEESE, VEGETABLES and LIGHT MEAT such as VEAL or PORK.

④ Asian-inspired marinade

MAKES ABOUT 200 ML (7 FL OZ):
1 walnut-sized piece of ginger, *peeled and grated,* 1 jalapeño, *finely diced,* 2 stalks lemon grass, *very finely chopped,* 2 teaspoons sesame seeds, 2 tablespoons brown sugar, 5 tablespoons soy sauce, 5 teaspoons light sesame oil or olive oil
— Put all the ingredients for the marinade in a casserole dish with plenty of room for the food, and whisk together. Turn the food in the marinade until it is evenly coated all over. Cover with baking parchment and leave to marinate in the refrigerator for at least 30 minutes or up to 24 hours. After marinating, pat the food dry. Great for VEGETABLES, FISH, POULTRY, SHELLFISH and PORK DISHES.

⑤ Herb oil marinade

MAKES ABOUT 200 ML (7 FL OZ), FOR MARINATING OR BRUSHING:
1 garlic clove, *finely chopped,* 2 sprigs of rosemary, *leaves finely chopped,* 2 sprigs of thyme, *leaves finely chopped,* 40 g (1½ oz) mixed herbs (tarragon, flat-leaf parsley, chives, chervil, salad burnet or cress), *leaves finely snipped,* zest and juice of 1 unwaxed lemon, 1 teaspoon fine sea salt, 5 tablespoons oil or olive oil, ½ teaspoon freshly ground black pepper
— In a casserole dish with plenty of room for the food, mix the garlic and herbs with the lemon zest and juice, sea salt and oil, and season with pepper. Turn the food in the marinade until it is evenly coated all over. Cover with baking parchment and leave to marinate in the refrigerator for at least 1 hour or up to 24 hours. After marinating, pat the food dry and leave it to come up to room temperature. About 10 minutes before the end of the cooking time, brush the food with the rest of the marinade. Great for PORK, VEAL, LAMB, VEGETABLES, FISH and CHEESE.

⑥ Pot roast marinade

MAKES ABOUT 700 ML (1¼ PINTS):
250 g (8 oz) small shallots, *halved,* 4 garlic cloves, 250 g (8 oz) baby carrots, *trimmed,* 1 bunch of spring onions, 500 ml (17 fl oz) full-bodied red wine, 50 ml (2 fl oz) red wine vinegar, 1 spice bag* (containing 4 cloves, 1 teaspoon allspice, 1 stick of cinnamon, 1 tablespoon coriander seeds, 1 star anise), 2 tablespoons coarse sea salt, 1 teaspoon brown sugar
— Put the ingredients for the marinade in a casserole dish with plenty of room for the food, and mix with a whisk. Turn the food in the marinade until it is evenly coated all over. Cover with baking parchment and

* Reusable tea bags, sturdy kitchen paper, coffee filter papers or even tea balls all make good spice bags.

leave to <u>marinate in the refrigerator for at least 1 hour or up to 24 hours</u>. After marinating, pat the food dry and leave it to come up to room temperature. Great with BEEF STEAKS, ROASTING BEEF JOINTS, GAME and LAMB.

⑦ Bourbon glaze

MAKES ABOUT 400 ML (14 FL OZ): 2 red onions, *sliced*, 2 garlic cloves, *crushed*, 4 tablespoons maple syrup, juice of ½ lemon, 150 ml (¼ pint) beef stock, 200 ml (7 fl oz) Bourbon, ½ teaspoon fine sea salt
— Put all the ingredients in a heatproof dish, place over low to medium heat on the barbecue and simmer to reduce by half while you are cooking the meat. Strain the liquid through a sieve into a bowl. About 10 minutes before the end of the cooking time, start brushing the glaze over the meat on the grill until it is all used up. Great for BEEF, LAMB, GAME or SMOKED MEATS.

⑧ Mop sauces

FOR 1–1.5 KG (2 LB 4 OZ–3 LB 5 OZ) FOOD

ORANGE MOP SAUCE MAKES ABOUT 175 ML (6 FL OZ): 100 ml (3½ fl oz) orange juice, 5 teaspoons white balsamic vinegar, 1 tablespoon brown sugar, 1 tablespoon Worcestershire sauce

BEER & WHISKY MOP SAUCE MAKES ABOUT 175 ML (6 FL OZ): 100 ml (3½ fl oz) lager, 5 teaspoons whisky, juice of 1 lemon, 1 tablespoon clear honey

PASSION FRUIT MOP SAUCE MAKES ABOUT 175 ML (6 FL OZ): 100 ml (3½ fl oz) passion fruit juice, 3–4 teaspoons honey, 2 tablespoons soy sauce

GRAPE MOP SAUCE MAKES ABOUT 175 ML (6 FL OZ): 100 ml (3½ fl oz) green or purple grape juice, juice of 1 lime, 2 tablespoons Worcestershire sauce, 1 tablespoon maple syrup

BEER MOP SAUCE MAKES ABOUT 250 ML (6 FL OZ): 150 ml (¼ pint) alcohol-free beer, 50 ml (2 fl oz) apple cider vinegar, 50 ml (2 fl oz) apple juice

— Mix all the ingredients together in a bowl or put them in a spray bottle and shake well. These sauces are great for dishes that need longer on the grill, such as BRISKET, RIBS, PULLED PORK, WHOLE BIRDS and LARGE ROASTING JOINTS.

⑨ Craft beer marinade

MAKES ABOUT 350 ML (12 FL OZ): 4 garlic cloves, *finely chopped*, 250 ml (8 fl oz) light or dark craft beer, juice of 2 lemons, 4 tablespoons maple syrup, 1 tablespoon coarse sea salt, 1 red pepper, *cored, deseeded and diced*, 200 g (7 oz) tomato ketchup (optional)
— Put all the ingredients for the marinade in a casserole dish with plenty of room for the meat, and whisk together. Turn the meat in the marinade until it is evenly coated all over. Cover with baking parchment and leave to <u>marinate in the refrigerator for at least 1 hour or up to 24 hours</u>. After marinating, pat the food dry and leave to come up to room temperature. Great with BEEF STEAKS, ROASTING BEEF JOINTS, GAME and LAMB.

Tip: While the food is on the barbecue, reduce the craft beer marinade by half over a direct heat, stir in 200 g (7 oz) tomato ketchup and add 1 teaspoon smoked paprika, if you like. Serve as a sauce with the meat.

SPICE PASTES
FOR 1 KG (2 LB 4 OZ) FOOD

① Tomato & chilli spice paste

MAKES ABOUT 250 ML (9 FL OZ):
2 garlic cloves, 1 white onion, *diced*,
50 g (2 oz) sun-dried tomatoes, *diced*,
2 hot red chillies, *diced*, 1 tablespoon
tomato purée, 1 teaspoon coarse sea salt,
1 tablespoon tomato ketchup
— Blitz all the ingredients in a food
processor to make a smooth paste.

② Herb & garlic paste

MAKES ABOUT 250 ML (9 FL OZ):
4 garlic cloves, 1–2 shallots, *diced*, 30 g
(1 oz) mixed herbs (such as tarragon,
flat-leaf parsley, cress, chives, salad
burnet), *leaves and stalks torn*, zest and
juice of 1 unwaxed lemon, 1 teaspoon
coarse sea salt, ½ teaspoon freshly
ground black pepper
— Blitz all the ingredients in a food
processor to make a smooth paste.

③ Roasting joint spice paste

MAKES ABOUT 6–8 TABLESPOONS:
2 tablespoons mustard seeds,
1 tablespoon black peppercorns,
1 teaspoon fine sea salt, 2 tablespoons
mustard, 1 tablespoon freshly grated
horseradish (or from a jar), 1 teaspoon
Worcestershire sauce
— Grind all the dried spices in a mortar
and mix in the mustard, horseradish and
Worcestershire sauce.

④ Onion spice paste

MAKES ABOUT 300 ML (½ PINT):
4 garlic cloves, 1 onion, *diced*, 1 teaspoon
fine sea salt, 15 g (½ oz) tarragon, *leaves
and stalks torn*, 4 tablespoons olive oil,
2 tablespoons coarsely ground pepper,
2 tablespoons rosemary leaves,
2 tablespoons thyme leaves
— Blitz all the ingredients in a food
processor to make a smooth paste.

TIP: Spice pastes are perfect
for marinating barbecued food
of all kinds – everything
from steaks and rolled roasts
to cheese, fish and poultry. If
you are brushing the paste on
the food before cooking, as a
marinade, the barbecue
temperature should not be too
high or the paste will burn.
So if you want to barbecue a
steak that has been marinated
in a paste, simply wipe off
the paste before putting it on
the grill. Alternatively, you
could spread the paste on the
steak after it has been cooked,
or serve it alongside.

SAUCES, DIPS & MORE

① Sweet chilli sauce

MAKES ABOUT 400 ML (14 FL OZ):
1 onion, *diced*, 4 garlic cloves, *finely sliced*, 2 red chillies, *diced*, 6 tablespoons clear honey, 3 tablespoons soy sauce, 200 ml (7 fl oz) water, 2 tablespoons tomato purée, 1 large pinch of ground coriander, sea salt, chilli powder
— Put the diced onion in a pan with the garlic, chillies and honey and cook over a medium heat until soft and translucent. Add the tomato purée, sauté for 1–2 minutes, then deglaze the pan with the soy sauce and measured water. Simmer the sauce for 2–3 minutes, then season with coriander, salt and chilli powder. Stir in a little cornflour paste to thicken the sauce, if you like.

② White onion BBQ sauce

MAKES ABOUT 400 ML (14 FL OZ):
100 ml (3½ fl oz) agave syrup, 2 onions, *diced*, 100 g (3½ oz) canned pears, *diced*, 1 tablespoon dried herbes de Provence, *coarsely ground*, 1 tablespoon fennel seeds, *coarsely ground*, 50 ml (2 fl oz) white balsamic vinegar, 50 ml (2 fl oz) elderflower cordial, sea salt, freshly ground black pepper
— Heat the agave syrup in a pan, add the diced onions and pears and cook until soft and translucent. Add the remaining ingredients, then reduce over a medium heat until syrupy. Season with salt and pepper to taste.

③ Classic BBQ sauce

MAKES ABOUT 400 ML (14 FL OZ):
4 tablespoons maple syrup, 2 onions, *diced*, 2 garlic cloves, *diced*, 1 tablespoon tomato purée, 1 teaspoon sweet paprika, 1 teaspoon onion powder, 150 ml (¼ pint) malt beer, 25 ml (1 fl oz) balsamic vinegar, sea salt, freshly ground black pepper, 25 g (1 oz) sugar beet leaves, 50 g (2 oz) tomato ketchup
— Heat the maple syrup in a pan, add the diced onions and garlic and cook until soft and translucent. Stir in the tomato purée, add the paprika and onion powder, cook briefly, then deglaze the pan with the malt beer. Pour in the vinegar, then reduce over a medium heat until syrupy. Season with salt and pepper to taste, then stir in the sugar beet leaves and the ketchup.

For a *bacon version*, fry 150 g (5 oz) diced bacon in a dry pan until crispy, drain on kitchen paper and stir into the finished BBQ sauce.

④ Spicy tomato glaze

MAKES ABOUT 500 ML (18 FL OZ):
100 g (3½ oz) clear honey, 2 onions, *diced*, 2 garlic cloves, *diced*, 1 tablespoon tomato purée, 300 g (10 oz) very ripe tomatoes, *diced*, 250 g (8 oz) tomato passata, 50 g (2 oz) sugar, 100 ml (3½ fl oz) raspberry vinegar, generous pinch of ground coriander, chilli powder, sea salt
— Heat the honey in a pan, add the diced onion and garlic and cook until soft and translucent. Stir in the tomato purée, add the tomatoes and passata and reduce by about half over a medium heat. Meanwhile, in a separate pan, reduce the sugar and vinegar to form a syrupy mixture and stir it into the tomato sauce. Strain the reduced tomato sauce through a sieve, then add the coriander and season the glaze with chilli and sea salt to taste.

For a *hotter version*, simply add a few drops of Tabasco.

For a *curry sauce*, add 150 ml (¼ pint) beef stock, 2 tablespoons tomato ketchup and 1 teaspoon curry powder after reducing down the glaze.

SAUCES, DIPS & MORE continued

⑤ Basic mayonnaise

MAKES ABOUT 250 ML (9 FL OZ):
1 egg, 1 teaspoon mustard (medium hot), juice of ½ lemon, ¼ teaspoon fine sea salt, freshly ground black pepper, 200 ml (7 fl oz) rapeseed or sunflower oil
— Put the egg, mustard and lemon juice in a mixing bowl, add the salt and season with pepper to taste. Use a stick blender to process the mixture, adding the oil drop by drop at first, and then in a steady stream. Keep in the refrigerator until ready to use. The mayonnaise will keep for up to 3 days in an airtight container in the refrigerator.

For *saffron mayonnaise*, infuse 6–8 saffron threads in the lemon juice for at least 20 minutes. This will unleash its flavour, smell and colour. You can then continue with the recipe as above.

For *garlic mayonnaise*, add 4 garlic cloves to the bowl with the egg, mustard and lemon juice and continue with the recipe as above.

⑥ Chipotle sauce

MAKES ABOUT 300 ML (½ PINT):
1 onion, *finely diced,* 2 garlic cloves, *finely diced,* 3 chipotle chillies in adobo sauce, 1 tablespoon olive oil, 1 egg, 1 teaspoon mustard (medium hot), juice of ½ lemon, 200 ml (7 fl oz) sunflower oil, 2 tablespoons clear honey, 1 teaspoon sweet paprika, sea salt, freshly ground black pepper
— Put the diced onion, garlic and chillies in a pan with the olive oil and sweat over a medium heat for 2–3 minutes, then leave to cool. Put the cooled mixture in a mixing bowl with the egg, mustard and lemon juice, then process with a stick blender until smooth. Add the oil drop by drop, then in a steady stream. Add the honey and paprika to the sauce and season with salt and pepper to taste.

⑦ BBQ mayonnaise

MAKES ABOUT 250 ML (9 FL OZ):
100 ml (3½ fl oz) mayonnaise, 100 ml (3½ fl oz) BBQ sauce, 1–2 tablespoons bacon lardons fried in a dry pan until crisp, zest of 1 unwaxed lime, freshly ground black pepper
— Mix all the ingredients together and keep in the refrigerator until ready to use.

⑧ Sweet & sour mango sauce

MAKES ABOUT 350 ML (12 FL OZ):
1 ripe mango, 2 yellow peppers, *cored, deseeded and diced,* 1 teaspoon grated ginger, 4 tablespoons clear honey, juice of ½ lemon, 50 ml (2 fl oz) olive oil, fine sea salt
— Peel the mango and cut the flesh away from the stone. Use a stick blender to process the mango flesh, peppers, ginger, honey and lemon juice until smooth, first adding the oil drop by drop, then in a steady stream. Season the sauce with salt to taste.

⑨ Brown butter*

MAKES ABOUT 250 G (9 OZ):
250 g (8 oz) butter, zest and juice of ½ unwaxed lime, ¼ teaspoon fine sea salt, cayenne pepper
— Melt half the butter in a pan over a medium heat. Stir until the whey begins to caramelize and brown on the base of the pan. Remove from the heat immediately and continue stirring for a few minutes. Transfer the butter to a metal bowl and refrigerate until it cools down to room temperature or below. Then use a handheld mixer to beat it with the remaining butter for a few minutes until thick and creamy. Add the lime zest and juice and season with cayenne pepper to taste. Great with grilled fish, vegetables and as a spread on bread, brown butter can be made well in advance.

* Brown butter has a distinctive nutty flavour due to the caramelized whey.

⑩ **Herby steak butter**

MAKES ABOUT 250 G (9 OZ):
200 g (7 oz) soft unsalted butter,
4 tablespoons beef or veal gravy,
4 tablespoons finely chopped mixed
herbs (such as parsley, chives, cress,
borage, chervil, salad burnet, sorrel),
zest and juice of ½ lime, fine sea salt,
freshly ground black pepper
— Put the butter in a bowl and beat using
a handheld mixer for a few minutes until
thick and creamy. Stir in the gravy, herbs,
zest and juice and season well with sea
salt and black pepper.

TIP: You can, of course, add
the combination of herbs of
your choice to tailor the butter
to your personal taste.

⑪ **Smashed avocado**

MAKES ABOUT 400 G (14 OZ):
2 ripe avocados, zest and juice of
½ unwaxed lemon, 1 tomato, *finely
diced*, 1 shallot, *finely diced*, 4 sprigs of
fresh coriander, *leaves roughly chopped*,
2 tablespoons soy sauce, fine sea salt,
freshly ground black pepper
— Cut the avocados in half lengthways,
remove the stones, scoop out the flesh with
a spoon and transfer it to a bowl. Add the
lemon zest and juice and mash the
avocados roughly with a fork. Mix in the
diced tomatoes and shallots, stir in the
coriander and soy sauce, then season the
smashed avocado with salt and pepper. If
you are not a fan of coriander, you can use
flat-leaf parsley instead.

TIP: You can tell an avocado
is ripe if the stalk end lifts
away slightly when you press
the fruit. Avocados are
climacteric fruit – they carry
on ripening after harvesting.

⑫ **Tomato & anchovy dip
with capers**

MAKES ABOUT 250 G (9 OZ):
2 shallots, *finely diced*, 8 anchovy fillets,
finely chopped, 2 tablespoons capers,
finely chopped, 100 g (3½ oz) sun-dried
tomatoes, *finely chopped*, 1 tablespoon
tomato purée, 1 tablespoon tomato
ketchup, 4 tablespoons finely chopped
flat-leaf parsley, 1 tablespoon clear
honey, fine sea salt, freshly ground
black pepper
— Mix all the ingredients together in a bowl
and season with sea salt and black pepper.

Cocktail sauce

MAKES ABOUT 500 ML (18 FL OZ):
150 ml (¼ pint) orange juice, 50 ml (2 fl oz)
brandy, 1 egg, 1 teaspoon mustard,
1 teaspoon tomato purée, 1 tablespoon
balsamic vinegar, fine sea salt, freshly
ground black pepper, 200 ml (7 fl oz)
sunflower oil, 50 g (2 oz) tomato ketchup,
1 teaspoon freshly grated horseradish (or
from a jar)
— Put the orange juice and brandy in a pan
over a low to medium heat. Reduce by half,
then leave to cool. Put the cold reduction
in a mixing bowl with the egg, mustard,
tomato purée and vinegar and season with
salt and pepper to taste. Use a
stick blender to process
the mixture, adding the
oil drop by drop at
first, and then in
a steady stream.
Finally, stir in
the ketchup and
horseradish (not
illustrated).

TOP
ELEVEN

CLASSIC BABY BACK RIBS

Baby back ribs are not the same thing as spare ribs. These small, slightly curved pork ribs are cut from the rib ends between the back and the belly.

SERVES 4

1–1.5 kg (2 lb 4 oz–3 lb 5 oz) baby back ribs (loin ribs)

Basic spice mix (see page 52)

Classic BBQ sauce (see page 57, or ready-made)

MOP SAUCE

150 ml (¼ pint) apple juice

25 ml (1 fl oz) cider vinegar

1 tablespoon brown sugar

2 tablespoons soy sauce

EQUIPMENT

1 smoker box

1 handful dry fruitwood chips for smoking (such as applewood)

1–2 handfuls fruitwood chips for smoking (such as applewood), *soaked for at least 30 minutes*

1 spare rib rack

PREPARATION
10 minutes, plus
at least 30 minutes
marinating

COOKING TIME
3 hours 30 minutes–4 hours

off   max.   max.

COOKING METHOD
Direct/indirect heat

RESTING TIME
10–15 minutes

1 Remove the silvery skin from the bone side of the ribs. To do this, slide a metal skewer under the skin along the bone until the halfway point, lift up the skin, grasp it with a piece of kitchen towel and pull it away. If you find that you're cutting into solid fat, which tends to happen towards the tip of the ribcage, leave the skin on. Alternatively, slide the back of a small spoon under the skin along the rib meat until midway through, lift up the skin, grasp it with a piece of kitchen towel and pull it away.

2 Make the spice mix. Rub the ribs all over with the spice mix, including the edges and sides. Cover with baking parchment and put in the refrigerator to marinate for at least 30 minutes. Meanwhile, take the grate out. Fill the smoker box with the dry chips, place it on the flavorizer bars over a high direct heat (220–240°C/425–475°F), close the lid and burn for 6–8 minutes.

3 Place an aluminium tray on the flavorizer bars over an indirect heat to catch any liquid from the ribs. Re-insert the grate, place the smoker box on the grate and add 1 handful of soaked chips to it. Reduce the temperature to a low heat (115–130°C/240–265°F). Put the ribs on the rack over the tray, close the lid and grill and smoke for about 1 hour, gradually topping up the smoker box with the remaining wood chips.

4 To make the mop sauce, mix the apple juice with the vinegar, sugar and soy sauce. Take the ribs off the grill, place them on two sheets of butcher's paper and brush them all over with the sauce until it has all been used up. (Alternatively, you can wrap the sauce-coated ribs in baking parchment, followed by a layer of kitchen foil.)

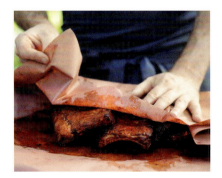

5 Wrap the ribs in the paper so that they are completely enclosed. Place them over an indirect heat, close the lid and grill for 1 hour 30 minutes–2 hours. For the final third of the grilling time, carefully unwrap the ribs. Reserve any cooking juices in the paper and mix them with the BBQ sauce.

6 Put the ribs on the grate and brush them generously with the BBQ sauce, then put them back on the rack. Put them over an indirect heat, close the lid and continue grilling for about 1 hour, brushing repeatedly with the BBQ sauce until it is all used up. At the end, the core temperature of the ribs should be 85–90°C (185–194°F).

BABY BACK RIBS

FLAVOUR UPGRADE

Spicy tomato ribs

Make the Texas-style spice mix (see page 53). To make a mop sauce, mix 100 ml (3½ fl oz) orange juice with 25 ml (1 fl oz) white balsamic vinegar, 1 tablespoon brown sugar and 1 tablespoon Worcestershire sauce. Make the Spicy tomato glaze (see page 57). Prepare, smoke and grill the ribs as described on page 63.

Smoky pepper ribs

Make the Espresso & pepper spice mix (see page 52). To make a mop sauce, mix together 100 ml (3½ fl oz) lager, 25 ml (1 fl oz) whisky, juice of 1 lemon and 1 tablespoon clear honey. Make the White onion BBQ sauce (see page 57). Prepare, smoke and grill the ribs as described on page 63.

Fruity honey ribs

Make the Herb mix (see page 52). To make a mop sauce, mix together 100 ml (3½ fl oz) passion fruit juice, 25 ml (1 fl oz) clear honey and 2 tablespoons soy sauce. Make the Sweet & sour mango sauce (see page 58). Prepare, smoke and grill the ribs as described on page 63.

Sweet bacon ribs

Make the Pepper & chilli spice mix (see page 52). To make a mop sauce, mix together 100 ml (3½ fl oz) white grape juice, the juice of 1 lime, 2 tablespoons Worcestershire sauce and 1 tablespoon maple syrup. Make the Classic BBQ sauce (see page 57) with bacon. Prepare, smoke and grill the ribs as described on page 63.

STONE-BAKED PIZZA

There's nothing better than stone-baked pizza. If you don't have a proper pizza peel, shape the dough on a floured baking tray and slide it on to the stone from there.

SERVES 4

DOUGH

½ cake (20 g/¾ oz) fresh yeast or 10 g (¼ oz) fast-action dried yeast

250 ml (9 fl oz) lukewarm water

1 teaspoon sugar

500 g (1 lb 2 oz) plain flour, plus extra for dusting

10 g (¼ oz) salt

3 tablespoons olive oil, plus extra for serving

TOPPING

20 shell-on prawns (size 8/12)

200 g (7 oz) tomato passata

1 teaspoon cornflour

1 tablespoon dried herbes de Provence

sea salt and freshly ground black pepper

1 red onion, *finely diced*

2–3 tablespoons capers

20 anchovy fillets

1 handful baby spinach

EQUIPMENT

1 pizza peel

1 pizza stone

 **PREPARATION**
15 minutes, plus
35–40 minutes
marinating

 **COOKING TIME**
6–8 minutes per pizza

 **COOKING METHOD**
Direct/indirect heat

1 To make the dough, crumble the yeast into the lukewarm water, add the sugar and stir until the yeast and sugar have completely dissolved. Sieve the flour into a large mixing bowl, add the salt and olive oil, then pour in the yeast water and knead the ingredients together by hand to form a soft dough.

2 Cover the bowl with clingfilm and leave the dough at room temperature to rise for 35–40 minutes or until it has doubled in size.

3 Prepare the grill for a high direct and indirect heat (220–240°C/ 425–475°F). Place the pizza stone over direct heat and preheat for 12–15 minutes until very hot.

4 Meanwhile, start preparing the ingredients for the topping by peeling and deveining the prawns. Rinse the prawns under cold running water and then pat dry. In a blender, blitz the tomato passata and herbs until smooth, then season with salt and pepper to taste.

5 Shape the dough into 4 balls of equal size. Put the dough balls on a surface dusted with the cornflour and use your hands or a rolling pin to push them out into circles 25–30 cm (10–12 inches) wide and 2–3 mm (about ⅛ inch) thick, leaving them a little thicker around the edge.

6 Spread the tomato sauce evenly over the bases and arrange the prawns, diced onion, capers and anchovies on top. Using a floured pizza peel, slide the pizzas on to the preheated stone, one at a time, then close the lid and bake for 6–8 minutes until crispy. To serve, top with a little spinach, drizzle over olive oil to taste and season with salt and pepper.

PIZZA

FLAVOUR UPGRADE

BBQ steak pizza

Make the dough as described on page 67.
Rub 200 g (7 oz) flank steak with oil and season
with salt. Place the steak over a high direct heat
(220–240°C/425–475°F) and grill for about
1 minute, turning once (core temperature
38–42°C/100–108°F). Take off the grill and leave
to rest for 3–5 minutes. Spread the pizza bases
with 125 ml (4 fl oz) Classic BBQ sauce (see page
57). Alternatively, you could use a ready-made
version. Cut the steak into strips and arrange them
on the pizza bases. Top with 1 red onion, cut into
wedges, 1 yellow and 1 red pepper, sliced, 2 sliced spring
onions and 100 g (3½ oz) grated Cheddar cheese and bake
the pizzas as described on page 67.

Crispy triple cheese pizza

Make the dough as described on page 67. Fry 150 g (5½ oz)
minced beef in 2 tablespoons hot oil and season with salt and
freshly ground black pepper. Stir in 150 g (5½ oz) tomato
passata and 1 teaspoon dried herbes de Provence, then leave
the mixture to cool. Spread the minced beef sauce over the
pizza bases, arrange 50 g (1¾ oz) halved mixed cherry
tomatoes on top and scatter over 100 g (3½ oz) mixed grated
cheese (such as Cheddar, Emmental and mozzarella). Bake the
pizzas as described on page 67. Top with some chopped
flat-leaf parsley, if liked, and serve.

Chicken doughnut pizzas

Make the dough as described on page 67. Rub 200 g (7 oz) corn-fed chicken breasts with oil and season with salt. Place the chicken over a high direct heat (220–240°C/425–475°F) and grill for about 1 minute, turning once. Take the chicken off the grill, dust with curry powder and leave to rest for 3–5 minutes. To make the sauce, blend 150 g (5½ oz) tomato passata with 1 peeled garlic clove and 1 teaspoon dried herbes de Provence, then season with salt and freshly ground black pepper. Roll out the dough and use a round cutter to make 16 mini pizza bases, each about 12 cm (4½ inches) across. Using a 3 cm (1¼ inch) diameter cutter, cut out the middles of the bases to make a doughnut shape. Spread the pizza bases with the tomato sauce and top with the diced grilled chicken, 4 tablespoons drained sweetcorn (from a can), 1 diced red onion, ½ diced yellow pepper and 50 g (1¾ oz) grated Emmental cheese. Grill the doughnut-shaped pizzas on the stone in batches of 4, as described on page 67. If you like, top with 1 shredded pak choi before serving.

Mediterranean pizza

Make the dough as described on page 67. To make the sauce, blend 150 g (5½ oz) tomato passata with 1 peeled garlic clove and 1 teaspoon dried herbes de Provence, then season with salt and freshly ground black pepper. Spread the tomato sauce over the pizza bases and top with 50 g (1¾ oz) sun-dried tomatoes, 100 g (3½ oz) crumbled feta cheese, 150 g (5½ oz) mixed pitted olives and 1 red onion cut into wedges. Bake the pizzas as described on page 67. Drizzle with olive oil and scatter over finely chopped flat-leaf parsley.

WEBER'S CLASSIC BEEFBURGER

It's an unbeatable formula: tomato ketchup, lettuce, gherkins, sliced tomatoes and a succulent burger, topped with mustard and onions.

SERVES 4

BURGERS

800 g (1 lb 12 oz) minced beef (ideally freshly minced)

2–3 tablespoons Basic spice mix (see page 52)

1 tablespoon mustard

1 teaspoon Worcestershire sauce

1–2 tablespoons olive oil

TOPPING

1 red onion

2 tomatoes

2 gherkins

1 handful of salad leaves

4 slices Cheddar cheese

75 ml (2½ fl oz) tomato ketchup

4 teaspoons mustard

4 brioche buns

2 tablespoons melted butter

EQUIPMENT

1 burger press

PREPARATION
15 minutes

COOKING TIME
8–10 minutes

max. max. max.

COOKING METHOD
Direct heat

RESTING TIME
3–5 minutes

1 Preheat the grill for a direct medium to high heat (200–220°C/ 400–425°F). Mix the minced beef thoroughly with the spice mix, mustard and Worcestershire sauce.

2 Divide the minced beef into 4 equal balls, rub each with olive oil all over and use the burger press to form them into patties. Place each of the patties between two layers of baking parchment.

3 For the topping, peel and dice the onion. Wash the tomatoes, pat them dry and cut them into thin slices. Slice the gherkins finely. Remove any wilted salad leaves, wash the good ones and spin dry. Slice the buns in half.

4 Place the patties over direct heat on the grate, close the lid and grill for 3–4 minutes.

5 Turn the patties, place 1 slice of cheese on each and grill for 5–6 minutes until done. At the end, the core temperature should be 54–56°C (129–133°F).

6 Shortly before the end of the grilling time, brush the cut surfaces of the brioche buns with melted butter, place them on the grate, cut sides down, and grill briefly until a grill pattern forms on them. Take the patties and buns off the grate. Assemble the burgers (see tip) and serve warm.

TIP: The order is crucial when assembling this burger! It goes like this: start by spreading the lower halves of the buns with tomato ketchup, then add (1) salad leaves, (2) gherkins and (3) tomatoes. Now add the patties, top with mustard and chopped onion and finish with the top halves of the buns.

BURGERS

FLAVOUR UPGRADE

Smoked chilli burger

Mix 800 g (1 lb 12 oz) minced pork with 2–3 tablespoons Thai chilli sauce, 2 tablespoons teriyaki sauce and 1 tablespoon chopped chives, then season with 1 teaspoon sea salt and a pinch of chilli powder. Shape the mixture into patties as described on page 71 and place them on a smoking plank. Prepare a smoker box with 2 handfuls of dry applewood chips (see page 22). As soon as smoke begins to form, put the patties on the smoking plank over a low to medium indirect heat (150–160°C/300–325°F), close the lid and cook for 15–20 minutes until the core temperature is 65–68°C (149–154°F).

Meanwhile, reduce 50 g (1¾ oz) clear honey with 40 ml (1½ fl oz) white balsamic vinegar for the topping. Slice 1 pointed pepper, 8 kumquats, 1 stick of celery and 1 onion, add them to the honey and vinegar mixture and bring to the boil. Remove from the heat and leave to infuse for 10 minutes. To serve, spread the lower halves of the toasted buns with Basic mayonnaise with saffron (see page 58) and top each one with 1 patty and the vegetables.

Double meat burger

Prepare the patties as described on page 71 and grill them with cheese. Rub 400 g (14 oz) flank steak (1–2 cm/½–¾ inch thick) all over with 1 teaspoon oil and season with sea salt. Put the steak over high to very high direct heat (240–260°C/475–500°F), close the lid and grill for 4–6 minutes, turning once, until the core temperature is 54–56°C (129–133°F). Remove from the grill, season with freshly ground black pepper and leave to rest for 3–5 minutes. Then cut into slices across the grain. Spread the lower halves of the brioche buns with Classic BBQ sauce (see page 57), then top each one with 2 slices of tomato, 1 patty and the flank steak slices. Top with more BBQ sauce and 1 tablespoon chopped spring onions each, then finish with the top halves of the buns.

Chicken cheeseburger

Place 2–3 unpeeled red onions over a medium to high indirect heat (180–200°C/350–400°F), close the lid and grill for 20–30 minutes, turning occasionally. Transfer to a bowl, cover with clingfilm and rest for 10 minutes. Peel the onions and slice them into rings. Mix 800 g (1 lb 12 oz) minced chicken with 1 teaspoon finely diced jalapeño, 1 teaspoon grated ginger, 2 finely chopped garlic cloves and 1 teaspoon chopped coriander leaves. Shape the mixture into 4 patties as described on page 71. Place the patties over a medium to high direct heat (180–200°C/350–400°F) and grill for 12–15 minutes, turning once, until the core temperature is 74–76°C (165–169°F). After turning the patties, place 1 slice of mature Cheddar cheese on top of each one. Toast the buns as described, spread the lower halves with Garlic mayonnaise (see page 58), then add onion rings and 1 slice of Cheddar on each and leave the cheese to melt for 2–3 minutes. Put the patties on the lower halves of the buns, top with the remaining onion rings and the bun tops.

Quinoa & avocado burger

Cook 100 g (3½ oz) quinoa according to packet instructions and leave to cool. Mix the quinoa with 100 g (3½ oz) grated courgette, ½ grated avocado, 100 g (3½ oz) grated potato, 3 tablespoons breadcrumbs and 1 tablespoon chopped flat-leaf parsley and season with salt and freshly ground black pepper. Using your hands, shape the mixture into 4 patties.

Cut ½ courgette into round slices about 1 cm (½ inch) thick. Cut ½ avocado and ½ red onion into thin batons. Put 3–4 tablespoons oil on a preheated plancha, add the patties and sliced courgettes over a medium direct heat (160–180°C/325–350°F), close the lid and grill for 8–10 minutes, turning once and removing the courgette slices when cooked. Season with salt and pepper. Mix 150 g (5½ oz) soured cream with 3–4 tablespoons defrosted frozen peas and 2 tablespoons finely chopped parsley. Season to taste with salt and pepper. Spread the toasted buns with a little of the pea-flavoured soured cream, top with some pak choi, grilled courgette, the patties, the avocado and onion pieces and a little more of the pea cream, then finish with the top halves of the buns.

BEER CAN CHICKEN

Instead of a beer can, which can't withstand high heat, we recommend using a heat-resistant poultry roaster which catches the fat and juices for this chicken dish.

SERVES 4

1 corn-fed chicken
(about 1 kg/2 lb 4 oz)

4 tablespoons milk

1 teaspoon coarse sea salt

BBQ spice mix for poultry
(see page 53)

200 ml (7 fl oz) lager

15 g (½ oz) herbes de
Provence (such as
thyme, bay leaves,
rosemary)

EQUIPMENT

1 deluxe poultry roaster

PREPARATION
10 minutes, plus
15 minutes marinating

 COOKING TIME
45–50 minutes

 COOKING METHOD
Indirect heat

RESTING TIME
3–5 minutes

1 Prepare the grill for a medium to high indirect heat (180–200°C/ 350–400°F). Rub the chicken with half the milk inside and out, then season with the sea salt. Cover with baking parchment and put in the refrigerator to marinate for about 15 minutes. Make the spice mix.

2 Put about 50 ml (2 fl oz) beer and some of the herbs in the liquid compartment of the poultry roaster, then put the cap on top.

3 Pat the chicken dry, then slide it over the poultry roaster so that it is flush with the top edge of the cone.

4 Cover the neck opening of the chicken with the cap so that the liquid doesn't evaporate too quickly while the chicken cooks.

5 Put the remaining herbs and any remaining beer in the drip tray. Place the chicken on the poultry roaster over an indirect heat, close the lid and cook for about 30 minutes.

6 Brush the chicken with the remaining milk, sprinkle with the spice mix, then grill for 15–20 minutes until done; the core temperature should be 76–80°C (169–176°F). Wearing BBQ gloves, take the poultry roaster off the grill and leave the chicken to rest for 3–5 minutes. Remove the cap, take the chicken off the roaster, carve it and serve warm.

TIP: Who's for chicken? This dish once involved inserting a beer can into the chicken, which was then placed upright on the grate. However, this is best avoided as contaminants from the paint on the can can transfer to the meat when heat is applied.

BEER CAN CHICKEN

FLAVOUR UPGRADE

Tomato chicken

To make the marinade, blitz 2 tomatoes, 1 peeled garlic clove, 1 teaspoon tomato purée, 1 tablespoon Worcestershire sauce, ½ teaspoon sea salt, 1 teaspoon sweet paprika, 2 tablespoons maple syrup and 4 tablespoons olive oil until smooth. Rub the chicken all over with the marinade, then cover and transfer to the refrigerator to marinate for at least 4 hours. Take it out of the marinade (reserving any excess), pat dry and cook on the poultry roaster (with the beer and herbs) as described on page 75. About 5 minutes before the end of the cooking time, brush with 2–3 tablespoons of the reserved marinade and season with black pepper.

Soy chicken

To make the marinade, thoroughly mix together 25 ml (1 fl oz) soy sauce, 1 teaspoon grated ginger, ¼ teaspoon ground star anise, 1 tablespoon agave syrup, the juice of ½ lemon and 100 ml (3½ fl oz) chicken stock. Rub the chicken all over with the marinade, then cover and transfer to the refrigerator to marinate for at least 4 hours. Take it out of the marinade (reserving any excess), pat dry and cook on the poultry roaster (with the beer and herbs) as described on page 75.* About 5 minutes before the end of the cooking time, brush with 1–2 tablespoons of the reserved marinade and season with freshly ground black pepper.

* If the chicken is cooked on a normal poultry roaster, it should be set over a heatproof drip tray. Put the herbs and beer in the tray, and it will catch the meat juices while the chicken cooks.

Smoked chicken

To make the marinade, blend 4 peeled garlic cloves, the juice of 1 lemon, 1 tablespoon brown sugar, 50 ml (2 fl oz) whisky, 50 ml (2 fl oz) dark beer, ½ teaspoon sea salt and 1 teaspoon coarsely ground black peppercorns until smooth. Rub the chicken all over with the marinade, then cover and transfer to the refrigerator to marinate for at least 4 hours. To smoke the chicken, leave 1–2 handfuls of hickory wood chips to soak for at least 30 minutes. Burn a handful of dry hickory chips in a smoker box (see page 22).

Take the chicken out of the marinade (reserving any excess), pat dry and grill and smoke on the poultry roaster (with the beer and herbs) as described on page 75, gradually topping up the smoker box with soaked chips. About 5 minutes before the end of the cooking time, brush with 1–2 tablespoons of the reserved marinade and season with freshly ground black pepper.

FLAVOUR BOOSTER

For best results, marinate the chicken in a vacuum pack or a large resealable freezer bag. You could also put it in a large bowl and cover it with clingfilm, but in this case you'll have to remember to turn it occasionally. Ideally, leave the chicken to marinate in the refrigerator for several hours or overnight. While marinating, it absorbs the liquid that it will later lose as it grills, so this makes the chicken especially flavoursome and keeps it succulent.

Sweet BBQ chicken

To make the marinade, mix 100 ml (3½ fl oz) beetroot juice with the juice of 1 lemon, 1 tablespoon chopped rosemary, ¼ teaspoon ground coriander and ½ teaspoon sea salt. Rub the chicken all over with the marinade, then cover and put in the refrigerator to marinate for at least 4 hours. Take it out of the marinade, pat dry and cook on the poultry roaster (with the beer and herbs) as described on page 75. About 5 minutes before the end of the cooking time, brush the chicken with 1–2 tablespoons Classic BBQ sauce (see page 57).

SALMON ON A PLANK
with honey-mustard glaze & herbs

SERVES 6–8

1 whole boneless salmon
   fillet (1–1.2 kg/2 lb 4 oz–
   2 lb 10 oz) with skin

1–2 tablespoons olive oil

½ teaspoon coarse sea salt

freshly ground black pepper

**HONEY-MUSTARD
GLAZE**

1 bunch of dill (about
   10 g/¼ oz)

3 tablespoons acacia honey

3 tablespoons mild tarragon
   mustard

zest and juice
   of ½ unwaxed orange

1 pinch of ground coriander

40 g (1½ oz) mixed herbs
   (such as parsley, chives,
   chervil, cress)

EQUIPMENT

1 cedarwood smoking plank

PREPARATION
15 minutes, plus at least 1 hour soaking and 15–20 minutes marinating

 COOKING TIME
20–25 minutes

 COOKING METHOD
Indirect heat

RESTING TIME
3–5 minutes

1 Soak the smoking plank for at least 1 hour or overnight (preferably weighted down). Rub the flesh side of the salmon fillet with oil and season with sea salt. Cover with baking parchment and put in the refrigerator to marinate for 15–20 minutes.

2 To make the glaze, rinse the dill, shake it dry and chop finely. Mix with the remaining glaze ingredients. Before cooking, brush the flesh side of the salmon fillet with a little glaze.

3 Prepare the grill for a high to very high direct and indirect heat (240–260°C/475–500°F). Rinse the herbs, shake them dry, discard any wilted leaves and finely chop the good ones.

4 Place the smoking plank over a direct heat, close the lid and char for 6–8 minutes. As soon as it is beginning to sizzle and is smoking slightly, turn the board and prepare the grill for a medium indirect heat (160–180°C/325–350°F).

5 Place the salmon on the board, glazed size up, then place it over an indirect heat, close the lid and cook for about 10 minutes. Then brush again with the glaze, scatter over the herbs and continue cooking for 10–15 minutes or until the core temperature is 58–64°C (136–147°F).

6 Take the plank with the salmon off the grill, season with black pepper and leave on the plank to rest for 3–5 minutes before serving.

TIP: Salmon is one of the most popular fish, along with cod and tuna. Always check the quality of your salmon. Try to buy the best organic salmon, wild salmon or salmon from a sustainable fishery.

PLANK-GRILLED SALMON

FLAVOUR UPGRADE

Caipirinha-style

SERVES 4: Mix together 1 sprig of finely chopped mint, the zest and juice of 2 unwaxed limes, 3 tablespoons brown sugar and 1 teaspoon sea salt until the sugar and salt have completely dissolved. Place 4 salmon fillets (skin on, about 200 g/7 oz each) in a large dish, pour over the liquid, cover and transfer to the refrigerator to marinate for 15–20 minutes. Meanwhile, wash 1 unwaxed lime with hot water, rub dry and cut into slices. Pat the salmon fillets dry, lay the lime slices on top, transfer to the smoking plank and proceed as described on page 79.

With an avocado crust

SERVES 4: Rub 4 salmon fillets (skin on, about 200 g/7 oz each) with 1–2 tablespoons olive oil and season with sea salt. Cover with baking parchment and put in the refrigerator to marinate for 15 minutes. To make the avocado crust, blend the flesh of ½ avocado with 1 tablespoon soy sauce, the juice of ½ lime and 1 tablespoon untoasted sesame oil until smooth, then season the creamy mixture to taste with salt and dried chilli flakes. Pat the salmon fillets dry, spread them with the avocado cream, sprinkle each one with 1–2 tablespoons panko breadcrumbs and cook on the smoking plank as described on page 79.

With Baja sauce

SERVES 4: Rub 4 salmon fillets (skin on, about 200 g/7 oz each) with 1–2 tablespoons olive oil and season with sea salt. Cover with baking parchment and put in the refrigerator to marinate for 15 minutes. To make the sauce, mix 4 tablespoons mayonnaise with 2 tablespoons soured cream, 2 tablespoons finely chopped sun-dried tomatoes and 2 tablespoons sliced spring onions, then season with salt and freshly ground black pepper. Pat the salmon fillets dry, spread with the sauce and cook on the smoking plank as described on page 79.

Texas-style

SERVES 4: Make the Texas-style spice mix (see page 53). Rub 4 salmon fillets (skin on, about 200 g/7 oz each) with 1–2 tablespoons olive oil and season with the spice mix. Cover with baking parchment and put in the refrigerator to marinate for 15 minutes. Mix 100 g (3½ oz) crème fraîche with 2 tablespoons finely chopped chives and season with salt and freshly ground black pepper. Cook the salmon fillets on the smoking plank as described on page 79. Add a dollop of chive cream to each salmon fillet before serving.

MEDITERRANEAN BBQ VEGETABLES

These vegetables are bursting with flavour – perfectly finished off with that wonderful grilled taste. They're delicious on their own or served alongside meat, fish or cheese.

SERVES 4–6

AUBERGINES & COURGETTES

3 Japanese aubergines

1 standard aubergine

1 each small yellow and small green courgette

sea salt

4–5 tablespoons olive oil

TOMATOES & PEPPERS

150 g (5½ oz) mixed cherry tomatoes (red, green and yellow)

½ each yellow, red and green pepper

2 garlic cloves

1 tablespoon dried herbes de Provence

3–4 tablespoons olive oil

1–2 tablespoons clear honey

juice of ½ lemon

Potato & vegetable spice mix (see page 53)

basil leaves to serve (optional)

olive oil to taste (optional)

EQUIPMENT

1 vegetable basket

PREPARATION
15 minutes, plus
15–30 minutes marinating

 COOKING TIME
15–20 minutes

 COOKING METHOD
Direct/indirect heat

 RESTING TIME
3–5 minutes

1 Wash the Japanese aubergines and cut them in half lengthways. Wash and trim the aubergine and courgettes and cut them into slices 15 mm (about ¾ inch) thick. Wash and halve the tomatoes. Trim and wash the peppers, then cut them into pieces. Peel and finely chop the garlic. Mix the tomatoes, peppers and garlic in a bowl with the herbs, oil, honey and lemon juice.

2 Prepare the grill for a medium to high direct and indirect heat (200–220°C/400–425°F). Put the vegetable basket over an indirect heat and preheat for 5–6 minutes. Make the vegetable seasoning mix.

3 Season the cut sides of the Japanese aubergines and the aubergine and courgette slices with salt to taste and drizzle over olive oil.

4 Place the sliced vegetables over a direct heat, close the lid and grill for 6–8 minutes, turning once.

5 Meanwhile, place the tomatoes and peppers in the vegetable basket, close the lid and grill for 5–6 minutes, turning occasionally.

6 Take the cooked aubergines and courgettes off the grill, leave to cool slightly and cut into chunks of equal size. Transfer the vegetables from the basket to a clean bowl, add the aubergine and courgette pieces and mix with the seasoning mix. Scatter over fresh basil and drizzle over olive oil to serve.

LESS WATER = MORE FLAVOUR

Aubergines and courgettes have a very high water content. To really bring out the flavour when they are grilled, salt the sliced vegetables lightly, leave them to stand for 30 minutes, then pat them dry and grill. This works especially well if you're planning on pickling the vegetables.

BBQ VEGETABLES

FLAVOUR UPGRADE

Bright beetroot
with lime vinaigrette

Put 600 g (1 lb 5 oz) mixed raw beetroot (candy cane, yellow and red beetroot) over a medium to high indirect heat (180–200°C/350–400°F), close the lid and cook for 25 minutes. Rub 2 slices of swede, 15 mm (about ¾ inch) thick, with 1 tablespoon oil, then season with salt, place over an indirect heat, close the lid and cook for 20 minutes, turning once. Mix ½ bunch of radishes, leaves intact, with 1 tablespoon oil and add to the indirect heat zone 10 minutes before the end of the cooking time.

Meanwhile, mix the zest and juice of 1 unwaxed lime with 2 tablespoons maple syrup, 1 tablespoon mild mustard and 4–5 tablespoons olive oil and season the vinaigrette with salt and pepper. Transfer the grilled vegetables to a bowl that fits all of them comfortably, cover with clingfilm and leave to sweat for 20 minutes. Then peel, cut into pieces and mix with the vinaigrette. The beetroot can be enjoyed lukewarm as a salad or served hot as a vegetable side dish.

Rustic cabbage with honey

Cut 400 g (14 oz) trimmed white cabbage and 400 g (14 oz) trimmed red cabbage, stalks intact, into 2 cm (¾ inch) thick slices. Rub all over with 2–3 tablespoons oil and season with sea salt to taste. Place over a high direct heat (220–240°C/425–475°F), close the lid and grill for 15–20 minutes, turning occasionally.

Meanwhile, mix the zest and juice of 2 unwaxed limes with 4 tablespoons clear honey, 1 tablespoon mild mustard and 4–5 tablespoons olive oil and season the vinaigrette with salt and freshly ground black pepper. Transfer the grilled cabbage to a bowl, cover with clingfilm and leave to sweat for 20 minutes. Then remove the stalks, cut the cabbage into pieces and mix with the vinaigrette. The cabbage can be served lukewarm as a salad or hot as a vegetable side dish.

Asparagus with baby spinach & Parmesan

Trim 500 g (1 lb 2 oz) green and white asparagus and slice it diagonally into 4–5 cm (1¾–2 inch) long pieces. Peel 1 red onion and slice it into rings.

Put 50 g (1¾ oz) butter in a cast iron GBS pan and melt over a medium to high direct heat (180–200°C/350–400°F). Add the asparagus and onion, close the lid and cook for 4–5 minutes. Then dust with ½ teaspoon icing sugar and deglaze the pan with the zest and juice of 1 unwaxed orange. Pour in 100 ml (3½ fl oz) vegetable stock, close the lid and continue cooking for 6–8 minutes. To serve, mix in 100 g (3½ oz) trimmed baby spinach, season the vegetables with salt and freshly ground black pepper and scatter over 50 g (1¾ oz) grated Parmesan cheese.

Mushrooms with vanilla pepper

Trim and clean 600 g (1 lb 5 oz) mixed mushrooms (seasonal, such as button mushrooms, enoki, shiitake, king oyster) and roughly chop them into chunks. Wash, trim and dice 1 tomato. Peel 1 red onion and cut it into strips. Peel and finely dice 2 garlic cloves.

Melt 50 g (1¾ oz) butter in a cast iron GBS pan over a medium to high direct heat (180–200°C/350–400°F), add the mushrooms, close the lid and cook for 4–6 minutes. Add the onion, garlic and diced tomato, close the lid and cook for a further 4–5 minutes. Remove from the grill, season the mushrooms with salt and vanilla pepper to taste, then add 1 teaspoon chopped thyme leaves and 1 tablespoon finely chopped flat-leaf parsley for even more flavour.

SHISH KEBABS
with peppers

Shish kebabs are great for grilling, as this method of cooking unleashes the full umami flavours.

SERVES 4–6

SKEWERS

800 g (1 lb 12 oz) pork neck

1–2 tablespoons oil

Basic spice mix
  (see page 52)

3 red onions

1 red, 1 yellow and 1 green
  pepper

400 g (14 oz) streaky bacon
  rashers

SAUCE

3 garlic cloves

2 red jalapeño peppers

5–6 tablespoons maple
  syrup

2–3 bay leaves

1 tablespoon brown sugar

3 tablespoons tomato purée

400 ml (14 fl oz) chicken
  stock

2 tablespoons
  Worcestershire sauce

EQUIPMENT

4–6 bamboo or
  wooden skewers,
  *soaked for at least
  30 minutes*

1 GBS cast iron griddle

 **PREPARATION**
20 minutes, plus
30 minutes marinating

 COOKING TIME
50–55 minutes

off   max.   max.
 COOKING METHOD
Direct/indirect heat

RESTING TIME
3–5 minutes

1 Cut the pork into 4 cm (1¾ inch) chunks, put them in a bowl and mix with the oil and three-quarters of the spice mix. Cover and put in the refrigerator to marinate for at least 30 minutes.

2 Meanwhile, peel the onions and slice them into wedges 15 mm (about ¾ inch) thick. Quarter, trim and wash the peppers and cut them into chunks. Slice the bacon diagonally into pieces. Prepare the grill for a direct medium to high heat (200–220°C/400–425°F).

3 Meanwhile, thread the pork, bacon, onion and peppers on to the skewers, alternating the ingredients. Set any remaining vegetables to one side.

4 Place the skewers over a direct heat, close the lid and grill for 6–8 minutes, turning occasionally. Put the GBS cast iron griddle over a direct heat and preheat for 8–10 minutes.

5 To make the sauce, peel and crush the garlic. Deseed the jalapeño and cut it into 1 cm (½ inch) pieces. Pour the maple syrup into the griddle, add the garlic, jalapeño, remaining vegetables and the bay leaves, close the lid and cook for 5 minutes. Sprinkle with the sugar, stir in the tomato purée and deglaze with the stock. Bring the sauce to a boil and season with the remaining spice mix.

6 Prepare the grill for a low to medium indirect heat (140–160°C/275–325°F). Lay the skewers in the sauce and cook for 40–45 minutes over indirect heat until done, turning occasionally. At the end, the core temperature of the meat should be 86–90°C (187–194°F). Take the griddle off the grill and leave the kebabs to rest for 3–5 minutes before serving.

SKEWERS & KEBABS

Pork & onion kebabs

Peel 2 onions and cut them into wedges. Cut 600 g (1 lb 5 oz) pork loin into 5 mm (¼ inch) thick slices. Mix the meat with 4 grated garlic cloves, the zest and juice of 1 unwaxed lemon, 2 tablespoons dried thyme, 2 tablespoons dried rosemary, 1 teaspoon sea salt, 1 teaspoon sweet paprika, the onion and 50 ml (2 fl oz) olive oil. Cover and put in the refrigerator to marinate for at least 1 hour.

Preheat the grill for a medium to high indirect heat, (180–200°C/350–400°F). Take the pork and onions out of the marinade, thread on to 4–6 double-pronged skewers, place over an indirect heat, close the lid and cook for 15–18 minutes, turning every so often, until the core temperature is 58–62°C (136–144°F). Take off the grill and leave to rest for 3–5 minutes.

Pork skewers with thyme & tomato

Peel and chop 4 onions. Wash, trim and dice 2 tomatoes. Cut 600 g (1 lb 5 oz) pork neck into 3 cm (1¼ inch) cubes, then mix with 2 tablespoons chopped thyme, 1 tablespoon tomato purée, 4 tablespoons white wine vinegar, 5 bay leaves, 1 teaspoon sea salt, the onions and tomatoes, and 4–5 tablespoons oil. Season with ½ teaspoon cayenne pepper, cover and put in the refrigerator to marinate for at least 4 hours.

Prepare the grill for a medium to high direct heat (170–190°C/340–375°F). Peel 2 onions and cut them into wedges. Take the meat out of the marinade, wipe dry and thread the pieces of meat on to 4–6 metal skewers, alternating with the onion wedges. Put the skewers over a direct heat, close the lid and grill for 20–25 minutes, turning once, until the core temperature is 76–78°C (169–172°F). Take off the grill and leave to rest for 3–5 minutes.

Italian-style beef skewers

Preheat the grill for a medium to high indirect heat (180–200°C/350–400°F). Peel 2 red onions and slice into wedges. Cut 500 g (1 lb 2 oz) beef fillet into 1 cm (½ inch) thick slices and mix with 1 finely chopped garlic clove, 2 tablespoons clear honey, 1 tablespoon dried thyme, 1 teaspoon balsamic vinegar and 1 teaspoon sea salt. Wash and trim 2–3 plum tomatoes and cut into slices 15 mm (about ¾ inch) thick. Wash 1 bunch of basil, shake dry and remove the leaves. Cut 80 g (2¾ oz) Parmesan cheese into 5 mm (¼ inch) chunks. Thread the onion wedges, beef, tomatoes, basil leaves and Parmesan on to double-pronged skewers, alternating the ingredients. Put the skewers over an indirect heat, close the lid and cook for 8–10 minutes, turning once, until the core temperature of the meat is 54–56°C (129–133°F). Take off the grill and leave to rest for 3–5 minutes.

Beef & lambs koftas

Prepare the grill for a medium to high indirect heat (180–200°C/350–400°F). Peel and finely chop 1 onion and 2 garlic cloves. Finely chop ½ bunch of flat-leaf parsley, including the stalks. Thoroughly mix together 400 g (14 oz) minced beef, 200 g (7 oz) minced lamb, 1 teaspoon ras el hanout, 1 teaspoon sweet paprika, ½ teaspoon harissa, 1 teaspoon sea salt, the chopped onion and garlic and the parsley. Shape the mixture into 4–6 even- sized sausage shapes and thread each on a double-pronged skewer. Brush with 1–2 tablespoons olive oil, place over an indirect heat, close the lid and cook for 8–10 minutes, turning occasionally, until the core temperature is 76–78°C (169–172°F). Remove from the grill and serve.

THE PERFECT STEAK

When it comes to grilled steak, it's all about high-quality meat, the cut, the right grilling method and your preferred degree of doneness.

SERVES 4

4 rib eye steaks (about 300 g/10½ oz each and 3–4 cm/1¼–1½ inches thick)

1–2 tablespoons olive oil

1 teaspoon coarse sea salt

freshly ground black pepper

TIP: Top-quality meat guarantees the perfect steak, regardless of the cut. Every cut has its own advantages, so feel free to choose from T-bone, tomahawk, flank, sirloin and rib eye.

PREPARATION
5 minutes

COOKING TIME
10–12 minutes

off   max.   max.

COOKING METHOD
Direct/indirect heat

RESTING TIME
3–5 minutes

1 Take the steaks out of the refrigerator and pat them dry.

2 Rub the steaks all over with oil and scatter evenly all over with salt.

3 Cover the steaks with baking parchment and leave them to stand for about 15 minutes to come up to room temperature.

3 Prepare the grill for a medium to high direct and indirect heat (220–240°C/425–475°F). Place the steaks over a direct heat, close the lid and grill for 4–6 minutes, turning once.

5 Place them in the indirect heat zone and continue cooking for about 6 minutes until they reach a core temperature of 49–52°C (120–126°F).

6 Use tongs to lift the steaks on to a chopping board, season all over with pepper, then leave to rest for 3–5 minutes before serving.

HOW TO GET THE PERFECT STEAK

Always choose top-quality meat. The better quality the meat, the less extra prep or added ingredients it will require. Opt for meat that has been sustainably produced and wet-aged, dry-aged or a combination of both. You can also distinguish between the way in which the cows were reared. With *grain-fed beef*, the animals have been fed on grain and corn as well as the usual hay. This gives the meat a superior marbling, so it is richer in fat. *Grass-fed beef* comes from cattle fed with grass and hay, resulting in a better muscle structure and slightly leaner meat.

THE PERFECT STEAK – 4 DEGREES OF DONENESS

Rare

Prepare the steak as described on page 91. The optimal core temperature for rare is 35°C (95°F).

Medium-rare

Prepare the steak as described on page 91. The optimal core temperature for medium-rare is 41°C (106°F).

Medium

Prepare the steak as described on page 91. The optimal core temperature for medium is 54°C (129°F).

Well done

Prepare the steak as described on page 91. The optimal core temperature for well done is 63°C (145°F).

THE PERFECT SAUSAGE

Grilled sausages are always a treat – and there's a variety for everyone. Whether you like them as they are, or with mustard, ketchup or BBQ sauce, feel free to make them your own.

TIP: Soaking the sausages in milk for 10-15 minutes before grilling will reduce the risk of them bursting. Only drain them slightly before putting them on the grill. If you like your sausages especially crispy on the outside, brush them thinly with maple syrup for the final 1-2 minutes of the grilling time. This works especially well with plain pork sausages.

Sausages made with finely ground meat

Fresh sausages made with finely ground meat aren't always easy to cook. If you put them on too high a heat, they'll burst or burn. Instead, put the uncooked sausages in a saucepan of water with flavoursome ingredients (such as seasonings, stock vegetables) at 70–80°C (158–176°F) and poach for 8–20 minutes (the cooking time will depend on the size and type of sausage). Take the sausages out of the broth, pat them dry, place them over a medium to high direct heat (200–220°C/400–425°F), close the lid and grill for 4–6 minutes, turning once. *Examples include Rhineland-style bratwurst, curry sausage, Thuringian sausage and veal frankfurters.*

Smoked sausages with cheese

Smoked parboiled sausages with cheese are pre-cooked, so you simply need to warm up or grill until crisp on the outside. If you put them on too high a heat at first, the cheese will run out or they may go brown too quickly. To avoid this, start by putting the sausages on a low to medium indirect heat (140–160°C/275–325°F), close the lid and grill for 5–6 minutes, turning once. Then increase the temperature to a medium to high heat (180–200°C/350–400°F), close the lid and grill for a further 3–4 minutes, turning once. *Examples include cheese kranskies, Bern-style sausages and cheese-and-beef sausages.*

PREPARATION
For sausages containing fine sausagemeat: 8–20 minutes

COOKING TIME
4–10 minutes

COOKING METHOD
Direct/indirect heat

Sausages made with coarsely ground meat

Rustic-style sausages tend to contain coarsely ground (sometimes cured) fresh meat with seasonings. As these sausages are uncooked, they need to be grilled shortly before serving in the same way as sausages made with finely ground meat. If you put them on too high a heat to start with, the sausages will go dark very quickly, may burst and won't cook all the way through. To avoid this, start by putting them on a low to medium indirect heat (140–160°C/275–325°F), close the lid and grill for 4–5 minutes, turning once. Then increase the temperature to medium to high (180–200°C/350–400°F), close the lid and grill for a further 5–6 minutes, turning once. *Examples include Frankish-style bratwurst, grilling sausages, pork sausages and wild boar sausages.*

Sausages with a high fat content

Sausages with a high fat content have a tendency to catch fire on a gas grill. If you place them over a direct heat at too high a temperature, they will burst and the fat will spatter everywhere, drip on to the flavorizer bars and catch fire. To avoid this, place a drip pan with a little water on the flavorizer bars under the area where the sausages will be grilling. Then place the sausages over the drip pan on a medium indirect heat (160–180°C/325–350°F), close the lid and grill for 8–10 minutes, turning once. *Examples include merguez, salsiccia and chorizo.*

THE PERFECT SAUSAGE

FLAVOUR UPGRADE

Sausage skewers
with Gouda

SERVES 4: Cut 4 uncooked rustic sausages into 2 cm (¾ inch) chunks. Cut 200 g (7 oz) mild Gouda cheese into 2 cm (¾ inch) chunks. Thread the pieces of sausage and cheese alternately on to wooden skewers that have been soaked for at least 30 minutes and wrap each skewer with 2–3 bacon rashers. Make sure that the cheese is completely covered. Put the skewers over a medium indirect heat (160–180°C/325–350°F), close the lid and grill for 12–15 minutes, turning once, until the core temperature is 76–80°C (169–176°F).

Grilled sausages
with Tex Mex topping

SERVES 4: Grill 20 small sausages as described on page 94–5. To make the topping, mix 1 handful of crumbled tortilla chips with 4 tablespoons sweetcorn and kidney beans (from a can), 4 tablespoons mixed diced peppers, 2 tablespoons chopped flat-leaf parsley and 6 tablespoons grated Emmental cheese. Place the sausages in a preheated griddle pan and scatter the topping over them. Place over an indirect heat, close the lid and grill for 2–3 minutes.

Sausage 'fatties'

SERVES 4: Turn the sausagemeat from 500 g (1 lb 2 oz) veal sausages out of their casings and mix with 2–3 tablespoons finely chopped flat-leaf parsley, 1 tablespoon finely diced jalapeños and 100 g (3½ oz) finely diced Cheddar cheese. Shape the mixture into 4 oval shapes, place each one on 5–6 slightly overlapping bacon rashers and roll up. Place over a medium indirect heat (160–180°C/325–350°F), close the lid and grill for 20–25 minutes until the core temperature is 76–80°C (169–176°F). Brush with 3–4 tablespoons BBQ sauce 10 minutes before the cooking time is up. If you like, you could also smoke the fatties with hickory wood chips in a smoker box while grilling.

Burnt end smoked cheese sausages

SERVES 4: Cut 4 smoked parboiled sausages with cheese into 2 cm (¾ inch) pieces. Put 200 g (7 oz) sliced red onion and 4 peeled garlic cloves in a GBS cast iron griddle, place it over a low to medium direct heat (140–150°C/275–300°F), close the lid and cook for 6–8 minutes. Add the sausage pieces, cook briefly, then deglaze the griddle with 200 ml (7 fl oz) Classic BBQ sauce (see page 57). Season to taste with the juice of ½ lemon, 2 tablespoons maple syrup and freshly ground black pepper.

Currywurst

SERVES 4: Grill 4 fine parboiled sausages as described on page 94. Cut the sausages into pieces, pour over the Spicy tomato glaze (see page 57) and top with 1 diced onion and a sprinkle of curry powder.

Wild dog

SERVES 4: Cook 200 g (7 oz) sliced onions in 25g (1 oz) clear honey, 25 ml (1 fl oz) white balsamic vinegar and ½ teaspoon turmeric over a medium heat until soft, then season to taste with salt and freshly ground black pepper. Grill 4 wild boar sausages as described on page 95. Split 4 hot dog rolls in half lengthways, and toast for 2–3 minutes. Fill each hot dog roll with 2–3 tablespoons pickled red cabbage, 1 wild boar sausage, 1 tablespoon diced pickled gherkins and one-quarter of the onions.

PORK CHOPS
with BBQ cabbage

SERVES 4

4 dry-aged pork chops
(about 300 g/10½ oz
each and 3–3.5 cm/
1¼–1½ inches thick)

1–2 tablespoons oil

coarse sea salt

freshly ground
black pepper

Herb oil marinade
(see page 54; optional)

BBQ CABBAGE

½ small pointed cabbage
(about 400 g/14 oz)

1 white onion

1 tablespoon clarified butter

1 teaspoon sweet
paprika

generous pinch of ground
caraway

50 ml (2 fl oz) chicken stock

3–4 tablespoons Classic
BBQ sauce (see page 57)

EQUIPMENT

1 GBS cast iron griddle

PREPARATION
15–20 minutes

COOKING TIME
10–12 minutes

COOKING METHOD
Direct/indirect heat

RESTING TIME
3–5 minutes

1 Prepare the grill for a medium to high direct and indirect heat (180–200°C/350–400°F). Rub the chops with oil and season on both sides with coarse sea salt.

2 Cover with baking parchment, put in the refrigerator and leave to marinate for 10–15 minutes.

3 Meanwhile, make the herb oil marinade. To make the BBQ cabbage, trim and quarter the cabbage, remove the stalk and shred the leaves. Peel and finely slice the onion.

4 Place the pork chops over an indirect heat, fatty edge down, close the lid and grill for 5–6 minutes.

5 Then place the chops over a direct heat, cut side down, close the lid and grill for 5–6 minutes, turning once. After turning, season with pepper and drizzle over a little herb oil marinade. Close the lid and grill for 4–5 minutes until done and the core temperature reaches 54–58°C (129–136°F). Take them off the grill and leave to rest for 3–5 minutes before serving.

6 Melt the clarified butter in the preheated GBS griddle over medium direct heat (160–180°C/325–350°F). Add the onion and shredded cabbage and sweat for 4–5 minutes until soft and translucent. Season with paprika, caraway, salt and pepper, then pour in the stock. Close the lid and bring to a boil for 4–5 minutes, then stir in the BBQ sauce. Arrange the chops and cabbage on plates and serve warm.

3 PRIME CUTS

Neck chops have the highest fat content and are cut from the topmost neck area on the back. **Middle chops** and **rib chops** are taken from the middle part of the back and are leaner. The bones here are usually longer, so they are sometimes called tomahawk chops (shown here). The leanest kind are **loin or fillet chops**. When grilling, you should make sure that these aren't allowed to dry out too much.

PORK CHOPS

With Espresso & pepper spice mix

Make the Espresso & pepper spice mix (see page 52). Prepare and grill the chops as described on page 99. After turning, scatter half of the spice mix over the chops and grill until done. Slice the chops and serve with the remaining spice mix.

With honey & soy sauce

Prepare and grill the chops as described on page 99. Mix 3 tablespoons clear honey with 1 teaspoon mild mustard and 2 tablespoons soy sauce. After turning, keep brushing the chops with the glaze until it is all used up.

With prawns & tomatoes

Prepare and grill the chops as described on page 99. Cut 4 large peeled prawns into 1 cm (½ inch) pieces and mix with 1 diced garlic clove, 1 tablespoon diced shallot and 2 tablespoons diced sun-dried tomatoes. Season the mixture with sea salt and freshly ground black pepper. After turning, spoon the mixture on to the chops and grill until done.

With bacon & onions

Prepare and grill the chops as described on page 99. Mix 50 g (1¾ oz) diced bacon or ham with 1 diced red onion, ½ teaspoon chopped thyme and 40 g (1½ oz) grated mozzarella cheese and season with sea salt and freshly ground black pepper. After turning, carefully spoon the mixture on to the chops and grill until done.

ROAST HAM & CRACKLING
in a hop broth

SERVES 6–8

1 cured roasting ham
(1.5–1.8 kg/3 lb 5 oz–4 lb)

BROTH

4 onions

15 g (½ oz) fresh herbes de
Provence (thyme, bay
leaves, sage, rosemary)

250 ml (9 fl oz) veal stock

600 ml (1 pint) lager
(such as Pils)

Herb & garlic spice paste,
see page 56

1 tablespoon mild Dijon
mustard

EQUIPMENT

1 ceramic BBQ
casserole dish or
ovenproof baking dish

PREPARATION
15 minutes

COOKING TIME
45–50 minutes

COOKING METHOD
Indirect heat

RESTING TIME
8–10 minutes

1 Prepare the grill for a high indirect heat (220–240°C/425–475°F). Using a knife, score the rind of the ham in a criss-cross pattern with the cuts 5 mm–1 cm (¼–½ inch) apart, being careful not to cut into the meat itself. The more evenly you score the rind, the crispier the crackling will be later on.

2 To make the broth, peel and quarter the onions. Rinse the herbs, shake them dry and discard any wilted leaves.

3 Put the onions and herbs in the dish and place the ham in the centre on top.

4 Place the dish over an indirect heat, pour in the veal stock and half the lager, close the lid and cook for 25 minutes. Then pour in the remaining lager, close the lid and continue to cook for 20–25 minutes until done. At the end, the core temperature should be 65–68°C (149–154°F).

5 Meanwhile, make the spice paste. Take the dish off the grill, lift the roast ham out of the broth and transfer it to a chopping board to rest for 8–10 minutes.

6 Brush the sides of the meat with 1 tablespoon mild mustard and add the spice paste on top.

TIP: To get a crispy crackling, the ham doesn't need any seasoning, just a nice, even cut and high heat. You can pep up the ham with spice pastes, rubs and sauces once it's finished cooking.

ROAST PORK

FLAVOUR UPGRADE

Crispy pork belly

SERVES 4: Using a sharp knife, score the rind of a slab of pork belly (1.2–1.5 kg/2 lb 10 oz–3 lb 5 oz) in even cuts 1 cm (½ inch) apart, without cutting into the meat itself. Then turn the pork belly over and butterfly it (see page 173) so that it is double the size. Scatter the Texas-style spice mix (see page 53) over the meat side. Spoon 400 g (14 oz) sausagemeat on top. Roll up the pork belly so that the rind is on the outside, then tie tightly with soaked kitchen string. Place over a medium indirect heat (160–180°C/325–350°F) and grill for 1 hour–1 hour 30 minutes until the core temperature is 74–76°C (165–169°F). Take off the grill and leave to rest for 8–10 minutes.

Grilled pork knuckle

SERVES 4: Using a sharp knife, score the rind of 2 pork knuckles (650–800 g/1 lb 7 oz–1 lb 12 oz each) in a diamond pattern with cuts 1–2 cm (½–¾ inch) apart, then season all over with sea salt. To make the broth, put 2 peeled and halved onions, 2 peeled garlic cloves, 200 g (7 oz) diced tomatoes, 400 ml (14 fl oz) veal stock and some fresh herbes de Provence (such as thyme, bay leaves, sage, rosemary) in a ceramic BBQ casserole dish. Put the pork knuckles in the casserole dish with the bone side down so that the rind is on top, then place over a medium to high indirect heat (180–200°C/350–400°F), close the lid and grill for 1 hour–1 hour 30 minutes, topping up with a little more broth if necessary, until the meat has a core temperature of 82–85°C (180–185°F). Take the casserole dish off the grill, lift the pork knuckles out of the broth and transfer to a chopping board to rest for 8–10 minutes.

Suckling pig loin with sea salt

SERVES 4: Make the Pepper & chilli spice mix (see page 52). Using a sharp knife, score the rind of a slab of suckling pig loin (1–1.2 kg/2 lb 4 oz–2 lb 10 oz) crossways with cuts 1 cm (½ inch) apart, without cutting into the meat itself. Rub the meaty side with 1 tablespoon oil and sprinkle with the spice mix. Spread 400 g (14 oz) sea salt over the rind, place the suckling pig loin over a medium to high indirect heat (180–200°C/350–400°F), with the rind side up, close the lid and grill for 35–40 minutes until the core temperature is 54–56°C (129–133°F). Remove from the grill, leave to rest for 6–8 minutes, then remove the sea salt before serving.

Secreto

SERVES 4: Rub 4 pieces of secreto with fat* (200–250 g/7–9 oz each and 2 cm/¾ inch thick) with 1 tablespoon oil and season with sea salt. Place the meat on the grill, fatty side down, over a medium to high direct heat (180–200°C/350–400°F), close the lid and grill for 4–6 minutes. Then turn and continue grilling for 4–6 minutes until the core temperature is 52–54°C (126–129°F). Take off the grill, season with pepper and leave to rest for 3–5 minutes.

* This special cut of pork, which is still relatively unknown outside Spain, is called 'secreto' because it lies hidden between the back muscle and the back fat. This area is rarely under strain, so the meat is coarse-textured yet tender.

BEEF & VEAL

STEAKS

Hefty porterhouse beef steaks are cut from the short loin, so they have a larger fillet section than a T-bone, which is a flatter cut. Club steaks have a bone in, too, but don't contain any part of the fillet.

Tip: In these recipes, steaks are done medium rare – in other words, pinkish red. Of course, you're free to decide how you'd like your steak and can cook it accordingly. For more about steaks and specific levels of doneness, see pages 90-93.

*Sour cherries are available online, but if you struggle to find them, you can use a drained can of black cherries instead, along with 125 ml (4 fl oz) apple juice to replace the syrup.

PREPARATION
5–10 minutes, plus
30 minutes marinating

 COOKING TIME
10–14 minutes

 off max. max.
COOKING METHOD
Direct/indirect heat

 RESTING TIME
3–5 minutes

(a) Porterhouse steak with cherries

SERVES 4–6

1 jar of pitted sour cherries* in their juice (350 g/12 oz), 2 red onions, 2 garlic cloves, 4 tablespoons soy sauce, 1 tablespoon finely chopped thyme, 2 porterhouse steaks (about 600 g/1 lb 5 oz each and 3–4 cm 1¼–1½ inches thick), 1–2 tablespoons oil for rubbing, 1 tablespoon coarse sea salt, freshly ground black pepper

1 Drain the sour cherries in a sieve, reserving the juice. Peel and roughly chop the onions and garlic. Mix the cherry juice with the onions, garlic, soy sauce and thyme. Place the steaks in the marinade, cover with baking parchment and marinate for about 30 minutes at room temperature. Prepare the grill for a medium to high direct and indirect heat (200–220°C/400–425°F).

2 Take the steaks out of the marinade, pat them dry and rub them all over with oil, then season with coarse sea salt. Transfer to a direct heat, close the lid and grill for 4–6 minutes, turning once. Place them in the indirect heat zone and continue cooking for 6–8 minutes until they reach a core temperature of 50–54°C (122–129°F).

3 Pour the marinade into a pan, place it on the side burner over a medium heat and reduce for 8–10 minutes until syrupy. Stir in the cherries.

4 Take the steaks off the grill, season on both sides with pepper, then leave to rest for 3–5 minutes before serving. Detach the meat from the bones, cut into 1 cm (½ inch) thick slices across the grain, spoon the preserved cherries over the top and serve warm.

(b) T-bone steaks with beef powder rub

SERVES 4–6

2 T-bone steaks (about 600 g/1 lb 5 oz each and 3–4 cm/1¼– 1½ inches thick), Spice mix for beef (see page 52), 1–2 tablespoons oil for rubbing, sea salt flakes, olive oil to taste

1 Pat the steaks dry, rub them all over with oil and scatter one-third of the spice mix evenly over both sides. Cover with baking parchment and marinate for 30 minutes at room temperature.

2 Prepare the grill for a medium to high direct and indirect heat (200–220°C/400–425°F).

3 Place the steaks over a direct heat, close the lid and grill for 4–6 minutes, turning once. Transfer to an indirect heat, close the lid and continue cooking for 6–8 minutes until they reach a core temperature of 54–56°C (129–133°F)

4 Use the grill tongs to lift the cooked steaks on to a chopping board and scatter over the remaining spice mix. Leave them to rest for 3–5 minutes before serving.

5 Detach the meat from the bones and cut across the grain into 1 cm (½ inch) thick slices. Season the cut sides with sea salt flakes and drizzle over olive oil to taste.

(c) Honey-glazed club steaks

SERVES 4–6

2 club steaks (about 500 g/1 lb 2 oz each and 3–4 cm/1¼–1½ inches thick), 1–2 tablespoons oil for rubbing, 1 tablespoon coarse sea salt, freshly ground black pepper, sea salt flakes

GLAZE

4 tablespoons clear honey, 4 tablespoons maple syrup, 1½ tablespoons mustard, 3 tablespoons soy sauce, ½ teaspoon ground coriander

1 Pat the steaks dry, rub them all over with oil and scatter coarse sea salt evenly over both sides. Cover with baking parchment and leave for about 20 minutes. to come up to room temperature.

2 Prepare the grill for a medium to high direct and indirect heat (200–220°C/400–425°F). Meanwhile, beat the ingredients for the glaze thoroughly together with a whisk.

3 Place the steaks over a direct heat, close the lid and grill for 4–6 minutes, turning once. Transfer to an indirect heat, close the lid and continue cooking for 4–6 minutes, brushing every so often with the glaze until it is all used up. At the end, the core temperature of the steaks should be 54–56°C (129–133°F).

4 Using the grill tongs, lift the steaks on to a chopping board and season on both sides with pepper. Leave to rest for 3–5 minutes.

5 Detach the meat from the bones and cut across the grain into 1 cm (½ inch) thick slices. Season the cut sides with sea salt flakes to taste and serve warm.

BONE-IN PRIME ROAST RIB

Top-quality cuts like this prime rib are especially easy to cook, as it's much easier to maintain the constant low temperature that they require.

PREPARATION
10 minutes, plus
1 hour marinating

COOKING TIME
2–2 hours 30 minutes

COOKING METHOD
Indirect heat

RESTING TIME
30 minutes

1 Cut any excess fat off the prime rib and tie the meat with kitchen string. Season all over with the 2 teaspoons coarse sea salt and the black pepper and brush evenly with the seasoning paste. Cover with baking parchment and marinate for about 1 hour at room temperature.

2 Meanwhile, prepare the grill for a low to medium indirect heat (140–160°C/275–325°F).

3 Place the prime rib over an indirect heat, close the lid and grill for 2–2 hours 30 minutes until the core temperature reaches 50–55°C (122–131°F).

4 Take the roasted meat off the grill, transfer to a chopping board and leave to rest for 30 minutes.

5 Before serving, remove the kitchen string, detach the meat from the bones and cut across the grain into 1 cm (½ inch) thick slices. Season the cut sides with sea salt flakes to taste and serve warm.

SERVES 6–8

1 prime rib on the bone (2–2.5 kg/4 lb 8 oz–5 lb 8 oz)

2 teaspoons coarse sea salt

1½ teaspoons coarsely ground black pepper

2–3 x Onion spice paste (see page 56)

sea salt flakes

EQUIPMENT

kitchen string, *pre-soaked in water*

TIP: Why is it worth trussing meat with kitchen string? The answer's simple: it helps it retain its shape, and it also allows for a more even finish. There are different techniques for trussing the meat. One of them, involving loops, is shown on page 173.

Smoked craft beer
ROAST BEEF

The intense, nutty and wonderfully smoky flavour of hickory wood goes especially well with this beef marinated in craft beer, and enriches its unique taste.

SERVES 4–6

1 boneless side of beef (1–1.5 kg/2 lb 4 oz–3 lb 5 oz), ready to cook, without fat or sinews

1–2 tablespoons oil

1 tablespoon coarse sea salt

sea salt flakes

freshly ground black pepper

MARINADE

4 garlic cloves, *finely sliced*

200 ml (7 fl oz) craft beer

juice of 2 lemons

4 tablespoons maple syrup

1 tablespoon coarse sea salt

1 red chilli, *deseeded*

200 g (7 oz) tomato ketchup

EQUIPMENT

1 smoker box

1–2 handfuls of dry hickory wood chips for smoking

2–3 handfuls of hickory wood chips for smoking, *pre-soaked in water for at least 30 minutes*

1 large aluminium drip tray

PREPARATION
5 minutes, plus at least
1 hour marinating

 COOKING TIME
45 minutes

 COOKING METHOD
Indirect heat

 RESTING TIME
10 minutes

1 Place the beef in a large dish. Put the ingredients for the marinade into a bowl and mix them together with a whisk. Pour the marinade over the beef and turn it in the marinade until it is evenly coated all over. Cover with baking parchment and put in the refrigerator to marinate for at least 1 hour.

2 Take the beef out of the marinade, pat it dry, rub it all over with a little oil and season with coarse sea salt. Leave it to stand for 30 minutes to allow it to come up to room temperature.

3 Meanwhile, strain the marinade through a sieve into a bowl.

4 Take out the grill racks. Fill the smoker box with the dry chips, place it on the flavorizer bars over a high direct heat (220–240°C/425–475°F), close the lid and burn for 6–8 minutes. Pour 500 ml (18 fl oz) water into an aluminium bowl, place it on the flavorizer bars and replace the grill racks. Place the smoker box on the grill rack and top it up with some of the pre-soaked wood chips.

5 Meanwhile, prepare the grill for a medium indirect heat (180–200°C/350–400°F). Place the beef over an indirect heat, close the lid and grill and smoke for about 45 minutes until the meat reaches a core temperature of 52–54°C (126–129°F). Top up the smoker box with pre-soaked wood chips from time to time.

6 During the grilling time, brush the beef with the marinade every 15 minutes until it is all used up. Take the cooked beef off the grill, put it on a chopping board and leave to rest for 10 minutes. Cut the meat into 1 cm (½ inch) thick slices across the grain and season the cut surfaces with sea salt flakes and pepper to taste.

ROAST BEEF

FLAVOUR UPGRADE

Texas-style roast beef

Pat the beef dry, tie it into shape with pre-soaked kitchen string (see page 173), rub it all over with 1–2 tablespoons oil and scatter the Texas-style spice mix (see page 53) evenly over all sides. Cover with baking parchment and marinate for 30 minutes at room temperature. Meanwhile, prepare the grill (see Step 5 on page 113), then place the beef over an indirect heat and grill for 45 minutes.

Mix 50 ml (2 fl oz) orange juice with 50 ml (2 fl oz) maple syrup. About 10 minutes before the grilling time is up, keep brushing the beef with this glaze until it is all used up. Take the cooked beef off the grill, transfer it to a chopping board and leave to rest for 10 minutes. Remove the kitchen string and cut the beef across the grain into 1 cm (½ inch) thick slices. Season the cut surfaces with sea salt and freshly ground black pepper to taste.

Roast beef with onions

Pat the beef dry and tie with pre-soaked kitchen string (see page 173). Brush the beef on all sides with the wet ingredients for the Roasting joint spice paste (see page 56), then scatter over the dry spices for the paste. Cover with baking parchment and marinate for 30 minutes at room temperature. Meanwhile, prepare the grill for a high direct heat (220–240°C/425–475°F). Pat 1 pre-soaked cedarwood plank dry, place it over a direct heat, close the lid and char on one side for 2–3 minutes. As soon as it is beginning to sizzle and is smoking slightly, turn the plank and prepare the grill (see Step 5 on page 113.)

Arrange 2 onions cut into wedges and the roughly chopped leaves and stalks of 4 sprigs of flat-leaf parsley over the charred side of the smoking plank and place the beef on top. Place the beef on the plank over an indirect heat, close the lid and cook for 30–35 minutes until the core temperature reaches 52–54°C (126–129°F). Take the meat off the grill and leave to rest for 10 minutes. Remove the kitchen string and cut the beef across the grain into 1 cm (½ inch) thick slices. Season the cut surfaces with sea salt flakes and freshly ground black pepper to taste. Serve warm with the onions and parsley.

Marinated pot roast

Prepare the Pot roast marinade (see page 54), cover the beef with it (see Step 1 on page 113), put in the refrigerator and marinate for at least 1 hour (or ideally overnight). Take the beef out of the marinade, pat it dry and tie with pre-soaked kitchen string (see page 173). Rub all over with 1–2 tablespoons oil and season on all sides with 1 tablespoon coarse sea salt. Leave the beef to stand for 30 minutes to come up to room temperature. Take the spice bag out of the marinade and pour the liquid off. Pat the marinated vegetables dry.

Prepare the grill for a medium direct and indirect heat (180–200°C/350–400°F). Place the beef over a direct heat, close the lid and grill on all sides for 2–3 minutes each until a grill pattern forms on the meat. Transfer the beef to an indirect heat, close the lid and continue cooking for about 25 minutes until it reaches a core temperature of 49–52°C (120–126°F). About 15 minutes before the cooking time is up, put the vegetables in a GBS cast iron griddle along with 1 tablespoon butter, place it over a direct heat, close the lid and cook, stirring occasionally, until tender but still firm to the bite. Take the cooked beef off the grill and leave to rest for 5 minutes. Remove the kitchen string and cut the beef across the grain into 1 cm (½ inch) thick slices. Season the cut surfaces with sea salt flakes and freshly ground black pepper. Serve the roast beef warm, with the vegetables alongside.

Roast beef
with herbs & hay

Roughly chop 80 g (2¾ oz) mixed herbs (such as rosemary, thyme, lavender, oregano). Truss the beef with pre-soaked kitchen string (see page 173), rub it with 1–2 tablespoons oil and season with 1 tablespoon sea salt and 1 tablespoon coarsely ground black pepper. Turn the beef in the herbs. Put 1–2 large handfuls of organic hay in a fireproof baking dish big enough to fit the beef and place the beef on top. Cover the beef with another large handful of hay, then leave to stand for 30 minutes to come up to room temperature. Prepare the grill for a medium indirect heat (160–180°C/325–350°F).

Place the beef in the dish over an indirect heat, close the lid and cook for about 45 minutes until the core temperature reaches 52–54°C (126–129°F). Take the dish off the grill and leave the meat to rest for 10 minutes. Remove the hay and kitchen string. Cut the meat into 1 cm (½ inch) thick slices across the grain and season the cut surfaces with sea salt flakes and freshly ground black pepper to taste.

TOMAHAWK STEAK
with BBQ potato mash

PREPARATION
10 minutes

COOKING TIME
about 1 hour

off   max.   max.

COOKING METHOD
Direct/indirect heat

RESTING TIME
6–8 minutes

1 Prepare the grill for a medium indirect heat (180–200°C/350–400°F). Scrub the potatoes thoroughly under cold running water and pat dry. Place the potatoes on the grill over an indirect heat, close the lid and cook for about 40 minutes until soft. About 15 minutes before the potatoes have finished cooking, add the unpeeled onions over an indirect heat, close the lid and cook until soft.

2 Meanwhile, pat the steak dry, rub it all over with oil and scatter coarse sea salt over all sides. Cover with baking parchment and leave to stand for about 25 minutes to come up to room temperature.

3 Remove the cooked potatoes and onions from the barbecue. Prepare the grill for a high direct heat (220–240°C/425–475°F). Put the steak over a direct heat, close the lid and grill for 2–3 minutes on each side. Then transfer to a medium indirect heat (180–200°C/350–400°F), close the lid and continue cooking for 12–14 minutes until it reaches a core temperature of 50–52°C (122–126°F).

4 Meanwhile, cut the warm potatoes in half and spoon the flesh onto the GBS cast iron griddle. Halve and peel the onions and cut them into strips. Mix the butter, onions and spice mix with the potatoes. About 10 minutes before the steaks have finished cooking, put the potatoes over an indirect heat, close the lid and leave them to warm, crushing from time to time with a wooden spoon.

5 Take the steak and griddle off the grill. Place the steak on a chopping board and scatter over the finely chopped herbs, then leave to rest for 6–8 minutes. Meanwhile, wash the parsley, shake it dry and chop the leaves and stalks roughly. Detach the steak meat from the bone and cut it across the grain into 1 cm (½ inch) thick slices. Season the cut surfaces with sea salt flakes and pepper to taste. Sprinkle the potato mash with parsley. Serve warm with the potato mash.

SERVES 4

POTATOES

6–8 floury potatoes

2 onions

50 g (1¾ oz) butter

2 tablespoons Potato & vegetable spice mix (see page 53)

6 sprigs of flat-leaf parsley

1 tomahawk steak (1–1.5 kg/2 lb 4 oz– 3 lb 5 oz and 3–4 cm/ 1¼–1½ inches thick)

1–2 tablespoons oil for rubbing

1 tablespoon coarse sea salt

2 tablespoons finely chopped mixed herbs (such as rosemary, thyme, sage)

freshly ground black pepper

sea salt flakes

EQUIPMENT

1 GBS cast iron griddle

TIP: The Potato & vegetable spice mix is ideal for seasoning vegetables of all sorts. Put the remaining seasoning mix in an airtight container and store it in a dark, dry place. It will keep its flavour for several weeks.

Simple grilled
RUMP STEAK

Superlative meat, a few seasonings and a little olive oil – the perfect ingredients for a truly great steak. Sometimes that's all you need.

PREPARATION
5 minutes

COOKING TIME
10–12 minutes

COOKING METHOD
Direct/indirect heat

RESTING TIME
3–5 minutes

SERVES 4–6

2 rump steaks (about 400 g/14 oz each and 2.5–3 cm/ 1–1¼ inches thick)

1–2 tablespoons oil for rubbing

2 teaspoons coarse sea salt

2 teaspoons coarsely ground black pepper

a few sprigs of rosemary and thyme

2 garlic cloves, *peeled and halved*

sea salt flakes

freshly ground black pepper

olive oil

1 Pat the steaks dry, rub them all over with oil and scatter coarse sea salt and pepper evenly over all sides. Cover with baking parchment and leave to stand for about 15 minutes to come up to room temperature.

2 Prepare the grill for a medium to high direct and indirect heat (200–220°C/400–425°F).

3 Place the steaks over a direct heat, close the lid and grill on each side for 2–3 minutes, then arrange the herbs and halved garlic cloves on top. Transfer the steaks to an indirect heat, close the lid and continue cooking for about 6 minutes until they reach a core temperature of 49–52°C (120–126°F).

4 Take the steaks off the grill, transfer to a chopping board and leave to rest for 3–5 minutes. Cut the meat across the grain into 1 cm (½ inch) thick slices. Season the cut sides with sea salt flakes and pepper to taste, and drizzle over a little olive oil.

TIP: If you ever fancy taking this exquisite steak up yet another notch, I heartily recommend the Herby steak butter on page 59, and, of course, the toppings on the following two pages.

RUMP STEAK

With rocket & Parmesan

Trim and wash 80 g (2¾ oz) rocket, then shake it dry. Wash 150 g (5½ oz) mixed cherry tomatoes (red, green and yellow), pat them dry and cut in half. Cut the flesh of 1 avocado into slices about 15 mm (¾ inch) thick. Slice 50 g (1¾ oz) Parmesan cheese into shavings. Roughly chop 2 tablespoons shelled walnuts. Put all the ingredients in a large bowl, add 2 tablespoons capers and mix together.

To make the vinaigrette, mix 2 tablespoons white balsamic vinegar thoroughly with 2 tablespoons clear honey, sea salt flakes and freshly ground black pepper. Using a whisk, mix in 3–4 tablespoons olive oil, first drop by drop and then in a steady stream. Dress the salad with the vinaigrette and arrange on plates. Place the warm steak slices on top and serve.

With broccoli & saffron mayonnaise

Put a GBS cast iron griddle or plancha over a high direct heat (200–230°C/400–450°F), close the lid and preheat for 8–10 minutes. Meanwhile, trim 300 g (10½ oz) tenderstem broccoli. Blanch the broccoli, then refresh in cold water and pat dry. Peel and finely dice 1 red onion. Trim, wash and finely dice 1 red pepper. Put 1 tablespoon oil in the hot griddle and fry 3 tablespoons bacon lardons until crisp. Add the prepared vegetables and cook for 5–6 minutes.

Meanwhile, mix 2 tablespoons clear honey with 2 tablespoons white balsamic vinegar and season to taste with sea salt flakes and freshly ground black pepper. Take the griddle off the grill and mix the vegetables into the honey and vinegar mixture. Arrange the warm steak slices and vegetables on plates, top with a spoonful of Basic mayonnaise with saffron (see page 58) and serve.

With pak choi & peppers

Put a GBS cast iron griddle or plancha over a high direct heat (220–230°C/400–450°F), close the lid and preheat for 8–10 minutes. Meanwhile, trim and wash 250 g (9 oz) pak choi, pat it dry and cut into rough lengths. Trim and wash 1 red and 1 orange or yellow pepper, pat them dry and cut into strips. Peel 1 red onion and slice it into wedges. Put 2 tablespoons groundnut oil on the griddle, add the pak choi, pepper and onion and cook for 5–6 minutes. Remove the vegetables from the grill.

In a large bowl, mix 2 tablespoons clear honey with the juice of ½ lime and 2 tablespoons ponzu (citrus-seasoned soy sauce) and season with sea salt flakes and chilli powder to taste. Add the warm vegetables and mix with the dressing. Arrange the warm steak slices and vegetables on plates, scatter over 4 tablespoons peanuts and some roughly chopped coriander leaves, and serve.

With pomegranate & feta

Half-fill a metal bowl with water. Cut 1 pomegranate in half crossways and hold one half over the bowl, with the cut side down. Beat the top of the pomegranate half with a wooden spoon until all the seeds have fallen into the water. Do the same with the other half. Use a slotted spoon to skim off any white membranes that float to the surface and discard them. Pour off the water, catching the pomegranate seeds in a sieve.

Crumble 200 g (7 oz) feta cheese into a bowl with 80 g (2¾ oz) baby spinach leaves and 100 g (3½ oz) raspberries. Mix these ingredients with 4 tablespoons toasted pine nuts and the pomegranate seeds. Add 4 tablespoons olive oil and season everything with sea salt flakes and freshly ground black pepper to taste. Arrange the warm steak slices on plates, top with the pomegranate and feta mixture and serve.

TERES MAJOR
with mac 'n' cheese

Mac 'n' cheese is traditionally made with short pasta, but it works just as well with the long macaroni we have used here.

PREPARATION
10 minutes

COOKING TIME
40 minutes

off   max.   max.

COOKING METHOD
Direct/indirect heat

RESTING TIME
3–5 minutes

1 Pat the steaks dry, rub them all over with oil and scatter the coarse sea salt evenly over both sides. Cover with baking parchment and leave to stand for about 25 minutes to allow them to come up to room temperature.

2 Meanwhile, start making the mac 'n' cheese by cooking the macaroni according to the packet instructions until al dente, then draining. Prepare the grill for a medium to high direct and indirect heat (180–200°C/350–400°F).

3 Grease the ceramic dish with 1 tablespoon butter. Toss the cooked macaroni with the cream, milk, Worcestershire sauce, paprika and the cheeses, season with sea salt and pepper to taste, and arrange in an even layer in the dish. Scatter the softened butter and breadcrumbs loosely over the macaroni. Place over an indirect heat, close the lid and cook for 20–25 minutes. Take the dish off the grill and cover with baking parchment, then with kitchen foil.

4 Prepare the grill for a high direct and indirect heat (200–230°C/400–450°F). Transfer the steaks to a direct heat, close the lid and grill for 3–4 minutes, turning once. Then place them over indirect heat, close the lid and continue cooking for 4–6 minutes until they reach a core temperature of 52–54°C (126–129°F).

5 Use tongs to lift the steaks on to a chopping board and leave to rest for 3–5 minutes before serving.

6 Cut the meat across the grain into 1 cm (½ inch) thick slices. Season the cut sides with sea salt flakes and pepper to taste, and drizzle over olive oil. Scatter the parsley over the mac 'n' cheese and serve in the dish alongside the steaks.

SERVES 4–6

2 teres major steaks (about 400 g/14 oz each and 2–3 cm/¾–1¼ inches thick), *well trimmed*

1–2 tablespoons oil for rubbing

2 teaspoons coarse sea salt

sea salt flakes

freshly ground black pepper

olive oil

MAC 'N' CHEESE

200 g (7 oz) macaroni

1 tablespoon butter

200 g (7 oz) cream

200 ml (7 fl oz) milk

2 tablespoons Worcestershire sauce

½ teaspoon sweet paprika

40 g (1½ oz) Parmesan cheese, *grated*

40 g (1½ oz) Alpine-style cheese such as Comté, or Gruyere, *grated*

100 g (3½ oz) Cheddar cheese, *grated*

freshly ground black pepper

50 g (1¾ oz) butter, softened

75 g (2¾ oz) breadcrumbs

1 tablespoon finely chopped flat-leaf parsley

EQUIPMENT

1 ceramic BBQ dish

TIP: Teres major has been a major rediscovery in recent years. This tender cut of beef is especially high in quality and comes from the rear shoulder. If your butcher isn't familiar with this cut, ask for a bistro filet or petite tender, which are alternative names for it.

RIB EYE STEAK
with stuffed sweet potatoes

Many people believe rib eye, which comes from the upper rib section, to be the ultimate steak cut.

PREPARATION
10 minutes

COOKING TIME
about 1 hour

COOKING METHOD
Direct/indirect heat

RESTING TIME
3–5 minutes

1 Prepare the grill for a medium to high indirect heat (180–200°C/ 350–400°F).

2 Scrub the sweet potatoes thoroughly under cold running water, then pat dry. Place them on the barbecue over an indirect heat, close the lid and cook for 45–50 minutes until soft.

3 Pat the steaks dry, rub them all over with oil and scatter evenly over both sides with coarse sea salt. Cover with baking parchment and leave to stand for about 25 minutes to come up to room temperature.

4 Remove the cooked sweet potatoes from the barbecue and cut them in half lengthways. Scoop out all the flesh and put it in a medium-sized bowl, leaving the skins intact. Mix with the spring onions, cream cheese, grated cheese, zest and juice of the lemon and the Five-spice mix, then season with sea salt. Carefully spoon equal amounts of the mixture into 4 of the hollowed-out potato halves.

5 Prepare the grill for a high direct and indirect heat (200–230°C/ 400–450°F). Place the steaks on a direct heat, close the lid and grill for 3–4 minutes, turning once. Then place them over indirect heat with the stuffed sweet potatoes, close the lid and continue cooking for 6–8 minutes until the steaks reach a core temperature of 49–52°C (120–126°F).

6 Remove the steaks from the barbecue, transfer to a chopping board and leave to rest for 3–5 minutes before serving.

7 Cut the steaks across the grain into 1 cm (½ inch) thick slices. Season the cut sides with sea salt flakes and pepper to taste, and drizzle over olive oil. Tear the chervil leaves, scatter them over the sweet potatoes and serve with the steaks.

SERVES 4

SWEET POTATOES

3 sweet potatoes (about 200 g/7 oz each)

2 spring onions, *finely sliced*

100 g (3½ oz) cream cheese

50 g (1¾ oz) Cheddar cheese, *grated*

50 g (1¾ oz) Emmental cheese, *grated*

zest and juice of ½ unwaxed lemon

1 teaspoon Five-spice mix (see page 53)

sea salt

a few sprigs of chervil, *washed and shaken dry*

2 rib eye steaks (about 500 g/1 lb 2 oz each and 3–4 cm/1¼–1½ inches thick)

1–2 tablespoons oil for rubbing

2 teaspoons coarse sea salt

sea salt flakes

freshly ground black pepper

olive oil

TIP: What's the different between entrecôte and rib eye? There isn't one! Both names refer to the same cut. Grilling and BBQs are extremely popular in the US, and the terms used there are finding their way into our own grilling vocabulary.

Skirt steak
BURRITO

Anyone who loves bold meaty flavours will be a big fan of these California-style burritos.

PREPARATION
15 minutes

COOKING TIME
6–8 minutes

max. max. max.

COOKING METHOD
Direct heat

RESTING TIME
3–5 minutes

1 Prepare the grill for a high direct heat (220–240°C/425–475°F).

2 Pat the steak dry, rub it all over with oil and scatter 1 teaspoon coarse sea salt evenly over both sides. Cover with baking parchment and leave to stand for about 10 minutes to allow it to come up to room temperature.

3 Meanwhile, start making the topping. Wash the tomatoes and pat them dry, then cut them in half, remove the stalk ends and finely dice. Peel and dice the onion. Cut the chilli in half, remove the seeds and finely dice the flesh. Wash the coriander, shake it dry and roughly chop the leaves and stalks. In a bowl, mix together the tomatoes, onions, chilli, coriander and the juice of ½ lime. Season with salt and pepper to taste.

4 Put the steak over a direct heat, close the lid and grill for 5–6 minutes, turning once, until the core temperature reaches 49–52°C (120–126°F). Take off the grill, transfer to a chopping board and leave to rest for 3–5 minutes.

5 Meanwhile, halve the avocados, remove the stones, scoop out the flesh with a spoon and cut it into wedges. Drizzle the remaining lime juice over the avocado wedges.

6 Place the tortillas on the grill, keep the lid open and toast for 1–2 minutes on one side, until grill marks form on the undersides.

7 Cut the meat across the grain into 5 mm (¼ inch) thick slices and arrange them on the tortillas. Season with salt. Top the tortillas with avocado slices, the marinated tomatoes and cheese and plenty of chipotle sauce. Fold in the sides, roll up the burritos from bottom to top and serve warm.

SERVES 4

1 skirt steak (about 600 g/1 lb 5 oz and 1.5–2 cm/about ¾ inch thick)

1–2 tablespoons oil for rubbing

coarse sea salt

freshly ground black pepper

TOPPING

2 tomatoes

1 onion

1 green jalapeño chilli

4 sprigs of fresh coriander

juice of 1 lime

2 ripe avocados

100 g (3½ oz) mild Cheddar cheese

100 g (3½ oz) mature Cheddar cheese

4 tortillas

Chipotle sauce (see page 58)

TIP: If your butcher doesn't sell skirt steak, try asking for flank or bavette steak. Luckily, these days more people appreciate the quality of this tasty cut of beef from the diaphragm.

Beef 'n' beer
BRISKET

The long and rather lean flat section of a full packer brisket should be sliced across the grain. However, the meat fibres run at a different angle in the pointed section, which is higher in fat, so you will need to slice it the other way.

SERVES 8–10

1 beef brisket
  (full packer, about
  4.5–5.5 kg/10–12 lb)

2–3 x Vanilla & pepper spice
  mix (see page 53)

2–3 x Beer & whisky mop
  sauce (see page 55)

EQUIPMENT

1 smoker box

1–2 handfuls of dry hickory
  wood chips for smoking

4–6 handfuls of hickory
  wood chips for smoking,
  *pre-soaked in water or
  non-alcoholic beer for at
  least 30 minutes*

1 roasting rack

1 heat shield

PREPARATION
25 minutes, plus at least
6 hours marinating (ideally
overnight)

COOKING TIME
12–14 hours

max.   off   max.

COOKING METHOD
Indirect heat

RESTING TIME
2–3 hours

1 To prepare the brisket, round off the corners of the meat and cut off some of the fatty layer, leaving about 1 cm (½ inch) of fat. Remove the thin silvery skin from the meat side. Remove any hard bits of fat or lumps of fat between the point and flat sections. Make the spice mix and mop sauce.

2 Scatter the spice mix over all sides of the brisket, cover and put in the refrigerator to marinate for at least 6 hours (ideally overnight), then take out and leave to stand for 30 minutes to come up to room temperature. Take out the grill racks. Fill the smoker box with the dry chips, place it on the flavorizer bars over a high direct heat (220–240°C/425–475°F), close the lid and burn for 6–8 minutes.

3 Replace the grill racks and place the smoker box on the rack. Prepare the grill for a very low indirect heat (110–125°C/225–260°F). Place the heat shield over the indirect heat and put the gridiron on it. Top up the smoker box with pre-soaked wood chips.

4 Place the brisket, skin side down, on the roasting rack over an indirect heat, close the lid and grill and smoke for 4–5 hours. Add the remaining pre-soaked wood chips during this time. After the initial grilling and smoking time is up, the brisket should be reddish-brown and have a lovely crust, and the core temperature at the thickest point should reach 65–70°C (149–158°F).

5 Take the meat off the grill, place it on two large pieces of butcher's paper or baking parchment, and brush generously with the mop sauce.

6 Wrap the brisket in the paper and roll it up so that it is completely enclosed. Put it back over an indirect heat, close the lid and continue cooking for 8–9 hours until the meat is so soft it gives way when you press it with a finger. The core temperature of the flat section should now be 93–96°C (199–205°F), while the point section should be 96–98°C (205–208°F). Take the brisket off the grill and leave in the paper to rest for 2–3 hours, ideally in a cool box or in a (switched-off) oven.

BRISKET

Burnt ends

SERVES 4: Prepare the grill for a very low to low indirect heat (115–125°C/240–260°F). Cut 800 g (1 lb 12 oz) smoked brisket into 4 cm (1½ inch) chunks. Put the brisket chunks in a ceramic dish and mix gently with 50 ml (2 fl oz) maple syrup, 200 ml (7 fl oz) strong beef stock, the Texas-style spice mix (see page 53) and 150 ml (¼ pint) Classic BBQ sauce (see page 57). Cover with butcher's paper or baking parchment, place over an indirect heat, close the lid and cook for 25–30 minutes.

With chips & garlic mayonnaise

SERVES 4: Prepare the grill for a medium to high direct heat (180–200°C/350–400°F). Attach a fine-meshed rotisserie basket to the rotisserie spit. Cut 800 g (1 lb 12 oz) washed but unpeeled floury or all-purpose potatoes (such as Desiree or Maris Piper) into batons 15 mm (about ¾ inch) thick. Place in a bowl and toss with 4 tablespoons oil. Use a slotted spoon to lift the potato batons out of the oil, drain them thoroughly and transfer to the rotisserie basket. Close the basket and fit it in the prepared barbecue. Start the basket rotating, close the BBQ lid and cook for 25–30 minutes. Meanwhile, wash 1 Romaine lettuce heart, pat dry and shred it. Tear 400 g (14 oz) smoked brisket chunks into small pieces.

Transfer the cooked chips to a big, pre-warmed metal bowl. Add the lettuce, torn brisket, 2 tablespoons coarsely grated Parmesan cheese and 2 tablespoons olive oil, season with sea salt flakes and freshly ground black pepper to taste and mix everything together well. Arrange on plates and top with the Basic mayonnaise with garlic (see page 58) or mix 250 g (9 oz) ready-made mayonnaise with 4 crushed garlic cloves. Add finely chopped flat-leaf parsley to taste.

With a mixed tomato salad

SERVES 4: Whisk 2 tablespoons balsamic vinegar, 1 tablespoon clear honey and 4 tablespoons olive oil together to make a vinaigrette and season to taste with fine sea salt and freshly ground black pepper. Peel and finely dice 1 red onion and stir it into the vinaigrette. Wash 400 g (14 oz) mixed tomatoes, pat them dry and cut into slices. Wash 80 g (2¾ oz) of rocket leaves and spin dry.

To serve, arrange the tomatoes on plates, add 400 g (14 oz) sliced smoked brisket and scatter the rocket over the top. Drizzle over plenty of vinaigrette and season with sea salt flakes and pepper to taste.

New York sandwich

SERVES 4: Prepare the grill for a medium to high direct heat (180–200°C/350–400°F). Meanwhile, finely slice 4 gherkins lengthways. Peel 1 red onion and slice it into thin rings. Cut 400 g (14 oz) smoked brisket into thin slices. Grate 100 g (3½ oz) mature Cheddar cheese. Spread 4 bread slices with 100 g (3½ oz) soft butter. Add a little Chipotle sauce (see page 58) and arrange half of the sliced gherkin and onions on top. Now add the brisket slices. Season the meat to taste with sea salt flakes and freshly ground black pepper, then top with the remaining gherkins and onion, grated cheese and remaining chipotle sauce. Add another bread slice on top and press down lightly.

Place the sandwiches on the grill rack over a direct heat, close the lid and grill for 5–6 minutes, turning halfway through. Cut the sandwiches in half and serve warm.

SIRLOIN STEAKS
with peppers & onions

Sirloin steaks come from the hindquarters of the animal. They are lean and have little marbling, but they do have an intense meaty flavour.

PREPARATION
10 minutes

COOKING TIME
15 minutes

COOKING METHOD
Direct heat

RESTING TIME
3–5 minutes

1 Pat the steaks dry, rub them all over with oil and scatter coarse sea salt evenly over both sides. Cover with baking parchment and leave to stand for about 15 minutes to come up to room temperature.

2 Prepare the grill for a medium to high direct heat (200–220°C/400–425°F). Put the GBS cast iron griddle over a direct heat, close the lid and preheat for 8–10 minutes.

3 Place the steaks over direct heat on the other side of the barbecue, close the lid and grill for 6–8 minutes, turning once, until you can clearly see the grill lines on the meat. At the end, the core temperature should be 49–52°C (120–126°F).

4 Meanwhile, pour the oil on the griddle and fry the onion until golden. Add the peppers and continue frying for 3–4 minutes. Add the paprika, sugar, vinegar, torn marjoram and salt and freshly ground black pepper to taste. Close the lid and cook for 2–3 minutes until the peppers and onions are cooked.

5 Use tongs to lift the grilled steaks on to a chopping board, season on both sides with pepper, then leave to rest for 3–5 minutes. Cut the meat into 1 cm (½ inch) thick slices across the grain and season the cut surfaces with sea salt flakes. Serve warm with the vegetables.

SERVES 4

4 sirloin steaks (about 300 g/10½ oz each and 3–4 cm/ 1¼–1½ inches thick)

1–2 tablespoons oil for rubbing

1 tablespoon coarse sea salt

freshly ground black pepper

sea salt flakes

PEPPERS & ONIONS

1 tablespoon oil

4 onions, *sliced*

2 red peppers, *sliced*

1 tablespoon sweet paprika

1 teaspoon brown sugar

2 tablespoons white balsamic vinegar

a few sprigs of marjoram, *leaves torn*

freshly ground sea salt

EQUIPMENT

1 GBS cast iron griddle or plancha

SIRLOIN STEAK

FLAVOUR UPGRADE

With apple & salted almonds

In a bowl, mix the juice of ½ lemon with 2 tablespoons brown sugar. Peel, core and finely dice 2 apples. Mix the diced apple with the lemon and sugar mixture, cover the bowl with baking parchment and leave the apple pieces to stand for about 20 minutes. Meanwhile, put a GBS cast iron griddle or plancha over a medium direct heat (180–200°C/350–400°F), close the lid and preheat for 15 minutes.

Roughly chop 4 tablespoons salted almonds. Roughly chop the leaves from 2 sprigs of flat-leaf parsley and 2 sprigs of mint. Put 1 tablespoon oil on the griddle, add the diced apple and its juice and caramelize for 5–6 minutes, while stirring. Remove from the grill. Mix the apple with the almonds and herbs, then season with sea salt and freshly ground black pepper. Spoon the mixture on to the grilled steaks and serve warm.

With plums & bacon

Wash 8 firm plums or damsons, pat them dry, cut them in half lengthways and remove the stones. Wash 4 sprigs of sage, shake them dry and tear off the leaves. Cut 8 thick bacon rashers in half. Stuff each plum half with sage and wrap in bacon. Put the plums in a dish, drizzle over 2 tablespoons olive oil and the juice of ½ lemon, and season to taste with sea salt and freshly ground black pepper.

Place the plums on the grate over a medium to high indirect heat (180–200°C/350–400°F), close the lid and grill for 6–8 minutes. Serve warm with the grilled steaks.

With green asparagus

Trim the ends of 20 green asparagus spears, then peel one-third of the way up each spear from the base. In a shallow baking dish, mix 2 tablespoons sesame oil, 2 tablespoons soy sauce and 1 tablespoon maple syrup together thoroughly, then turn the asparagus in the mixture. Cover the baking dish with baking parchment and leave the asparagus spears to marinate for 20 minutes. Take them out of the marinade and pat dry with kitchen paper.

Place the asparagus spears over a medium to high direct heat (180–200°C/350–400°F), arranging them so that they are perpendicular to the bars of the grate, close the lid and grill all over for 6–8 minutes. To serve, slice the asparagus into pieces at an angle and arrange on the barbecued steaks. Drizzle over the remaining marinade, scatter over 2 tablespoons of white and black toasted sesame seeds, season with sea salt and chilli powder to taste and serve warm.

With honey & sweetcorn pickle

Put 4 tablespoons clear honey in a fireproof pan and place it directly on the barbecue or on the side burner so that it warms up gently. Add 200 g (7 oz) sliced pickled baby corn and 4 tablespoons spring onions sliced into rings and cook for 3–4 minutes. Season to taste with the juice of ½ lemon, sea salt and freshly ground black pepper. Spoon the honey and sweetcorn pickle over the grilled steaks and serve warm.

DOUBLE-PLANKED PICANHA

Picanha, a Brazilian classic, is simply a cut of silverside rump, but with the layer of fat left on.

PREPARATION
25 minutes time

COOKING TIME
35–40 minutes

COOKING METHOD
Indirect heat

RESTING TIME
15 minutes

1 Prepare the grill for a medium to high direct heat (220–230°C/425–450°F). Grind the ingredients for the Herb seasoning roughly in a mortar.

2 Rub the picanha all over with oil and scatter over the seasoning. Cover with baking parchment and leave to stand for about 20 minutes to come up to room temperature. Meanwhile drain the smoking planks, put them over a direct heat and char for 12–15 minutes. Remove from the grill and leave to cool a little.

3 Prepare the grill for a low to medium indirect heat (140–160°C/275–325°F). Peel the onions and cut them into thin slices using a mandoline. Spread out half the onions on the charred side of one of the smoking planks. Place the picanha, fat side up, on the bed of onions, cover with the remaining onions and place the second plank on top, with the charred side facing down. Tie the two smoking planks together with the pre-soaked kitchen string.

4 Put the picanha sandwiched between the planks over an indirect heat, close the lid and cook for 35–40 minutes, turning occasionally, until the core temperature reaches 52–54°C (126–129°F). Take the cooked picanha off the grill and leave it between the planks to rest for 15 minutes.

5 To serve, untie the kitchen string, take off the upper plank and cut the meat into 1 cm (½ inch) thick slices. Season the cut surfaces with sea salt flakes to taste and serve the picanha warm, with the onions on the plank alongside.

SERVES 4–6

HERB SEASONING

1 tablespoon lemon pepper

1 tablespoon black peppercorns

1 tablespoon coriander seeds

1½ teaspoons dried herbes de Provence

1½ teaspoons coarse sea salt

1 tablespoon brown sugar

1 picanha (1.4–1.6 kg/ 3 lb 8 oz and about 6 cm/2½ inches thick), *ready to cook with its layer of fat*

oil for rubbing

2 red onions

sea salt flakes

EQUIPMENT

2 cedarwood smoking planks, *pre-soaked in water for at least 1 hour*

1 m (3 ft) kitchen string, *pre-soaked in water*

TIP: The fat layer of picanha makes it great for barbecuing but as ever, the quality of the meat determines whether it is wonderfully tender on the plate or not. We have had the best results with dry-aged meat.

BOURBON-GLAZED BEEF RIBS

A gas barbecue is a real plus, even for slow-cooked dishes like this one, as it's easy to maintain a low temperature over many hours.

PREPARATION
20 minutes, plus at least 6 hours marinating

COOKING TIME
8–10 hours

COOKING METHOD
Indirect heat

RESTING TIME
10–15 minutes

1 Remove the silvery skin from the beef ribs following the instructions on page 63. Rub the ribs all over with the spice mix, including the sides. Cover with baking parchment, put in the refrigerator and marinate for at least 6 hours. Before grilling, take out of the refrigerator and leave to stand for 30 minutes to come up to room temperature.

2 Take the grill racks out. Fill the smoker box with the dry chips, place it on the flavorizer bars over a high direct heat (220–240°C/425–475°F), close the lid and burn for 6–8 minutes. Place the drip tray on the flavorizer bars over an indirect heat and replace the grill racks. Place the smoker box on the grill rack and top it up with pre-soaked wood chips. Prepare the grill for a very low indirect heat (120–125°C/250–260°F).

3 Place the ribs on the rack over the drip tray and grill and smoke for 4–5 hours, topping up the wood chips until they are all used up. To make the mop sauce, mix all of the ingredients together until smooth.

4 Once the ribs have reached a core temperature of 56–60°C (133–140°F), take them off the grill, place them on two sheets of butcher's paper or baking parchment and brush generously with the mop sauce. Wrap the ribs in the paper and roll them up so that they are completely enclosed. Put the parcel over an indirect heat and continue grilling for 4–5 hours until the meat gives way when pressed with a finger.

5 About 10 minutes before the end of the grilling time, unwrap the ribs, place them over an indirect heat again and brush with the Bourbon glaze until it has all been used up.

6 The ribs are done once a wooden skewer pushes easily into the meat and the core temperature reaches 90–95°C (194–203°F).

7 Take the ribs off the grill and leave to rest for 10–15 minutes. Serve warm together with the onions left over from the Bourbon glaze.

SERVES 4

2–2.5 kg (4 lb 8 oz–5 lb 8 oz) beef ribs (short ribs)

2 x Basic spice mix (see page 52)

MOP SAUCE

70 ml (2½ fl oz) white balsamic vinegar

120 ml (4 fl oz) Bourbon whiskey

2 tablespoons maple syrup

Bourbon glaze (see page 55)

EQUIPMENT

1 smoker box

1–2 handfuls of dry hickory wood chips for smoking

3 handfuls of hickory wood chips for smoking, *pre-soaked in water for at least 30 minutes*

1 large aluminium drip tray

TIP: Glazed ribs are brushed with a glaze at the end of the cooking process to give them a lovely sheen. Dry ribs, by contrast, have the spice mix scattered over again after grilling, so they have a matt surface. If you have seasoned or marinated the ribs before cooking them, take care not to add too much.

BACON BOMB

You'll find it easiest to roll up the minced beef in the bacon lattice if you lay out the lattice on butcher's paper or baking parchment first.

PREPARATION
20 minutes

COOKING TIME
45–55 minutes

COOKING METHOD
Indirect heat

RESTING TIME
5 minutes

SERVES 4–6

800 g (1 lb 12 oz) minced beef (ideally 35–40% fat and freshly minced)*

Basic spice mix (see page 52)

100 g (3½ oz) mature Cheddar cheese

½ each green and yellow pepper

200 g (7 oz) bacon rashers (about 10 thick rashers)

150 ml (¼ pint) Classic BBQ sauce (see page 57)

1 Prepare the grill for a low to medium indirect heat (140–160°C/275–325°F). Knead the minced beef thoroughly with the spice mix and leave to stand for 10 minutes to come up to room temperature.

2 Meanwhile, cut the Cheddar into small dice. Trim and deseed the peppers and cut them into small dice, too. Add the diced cheese and peppers to the minced beef and mix in evenly. Shape the minced beef mixture into a large loaf about 25 cm (10 inches) long and 15 cm (6 inches) wide. It works best if you wet your hands with a little water first or wear disposable gloves.

3 To make the bacon lattice, lay out some bacon rashers on a surface side by side, to the width of the minced beef. At the bottom edge, lay 1 bacon rasher at right angles on top and weave it in and out of the other rashers, so that it goes alternately over and under them. Carry on doing this with the remaining bacon rashers until you have a pretty lattice effect. Place the minced beef on the bacon lattice and roll it up with the loose ends underneath.

4 Place the bacon bomb over an indirect heat, close the lid and cook for 45–55 minutes. Halfway through the cooking time, brush the bacon bomb with BBQ sauce and repeat every 10 minutes, until it is all used up. Once the bacon bomb reaches a core temperature of 65–68°C (149–154°F), take it off the grill.

5 Transfer the bacon bomb to a chopping board and leave to rest for 5 minutes. Cut it into 1 cm (½ inch) thick slices and serve.

* Ready-made minced beef usually has a fat content of no more than 20%, but this won't make the bacon bomb as lovely and succulent as it could be. To make home-minced beef with the right fat content, use either nicely marbled meat from the shoulder or neck or add some pork fat or untrimmed bacon.

TIP: If you're using very high quality meat, the core temperature of the bacon bomb can be 4–5°C (7–9°F) lower.

BACON BOMB

Chicken chilli bomb

Prepare the grill for a low to medium indirect heat (140–160°C/275–325°F). Mix 600 g (1 lb 5 oz) minced chicken (ideally corn-fed) evenly with 1 finely diced red onion, 2 finely chopped spring onions, 1 finely diced hot red pepper, 200 g (7 oz) mango cut into cubes and 1 teaspoon freshly ground sea salt. Lay 8 bacon rashers vertically side by side on a sheet of butcher's paper or baking parchment. Weave in a further 8 bacon rashers as described on page 141 to form a bacon lattice. Place the minced chicken towards the base of the bacon lattice and roll it up. Place the chicken chilli bomb over an indirect heat, close the lid and grill for 35–40 minutes until it reaches a core temperature of 74–76°C (165–169°F). Make 150 ml (¼ pint) Sweet chilli sauce (see page 57). Starting halfway through the grilling time, brush the bomb regularly with sauce until it is all used up. Transfer the bomb to a chopping board and leave to rest for 5 minutes. Cut it into 1 cm (½ inch) thick slices and serve warm with extra chilli sauce.

Macaroni cheese bomb

Prepare the grill for a medium to high direct heat (140–160°C/275–325°F). Cook 100 g (3½ oz) macaroni according to the packet instructions until al dente, then drain. Mix 1 kg (2 lb 4 oz) mixed minced meat (ideally 70% pork and 30% beef) with the Texas-style spice mix (see page 53). With damp hands or wearing disposable gloves, transfer the meat to butcher's paper or baking parchment and press out to a flat layer about 25 x 25 cm (10 x 10 inches). Scatter 100 g (3½ oz) grated Emmental cheese over the meat, then cover with the cooked pasta and another 100 g (3½ oz) grated Emmental. Scatter 4 tablespoons finely chopped flat-leaf parsley (including any soft stalks) over the top. Using the butcher's paper or baking parchment, roll up the meat from bottom to top and fold in the sides. Now lay out 8 bacon rashers side by side and slightly overlapping. Lay out another row of 8 rashers above the first row, again slightly overlapping, so that you can roll up the bacon bomb completely. Place the minced meat at the base of the bacon and roll it up. Put the bacon bomb over an indirect heat, close the lid and cook for 35–40 minutes. Make 150 ml (¼ pint) Classic BBQ sauce (see page 57). Starting halfway through the cooking time, brush the bomb regularly with the sauce until it is all used up. The bomb is cooked once the core temperature reaches 63–65°C (145–149°F). Take off the grill and leave to rest for 5 minutes. Cut it into 1 cm (½inch) thick slices and serve warm with more BBQ sauce.

Surf 'n' turf-style
with salmon & camembert

Prepare the grill for a low to medium indirect heat (140–160°C/275–325°F). Cut 600 g (1 lb 5 oz) salmon fillet (skin and bones removed) into cubes, then run them through a mincer on the coarsest setting. Mix the salmon with 2 finely diced shallots, 1 finely diced chilli, 1 spring onion sliced into rings, 100 g (3½ oz) diced Camembert cheese, 1 egg, 6 tablespoons panko breadcrumbs and 1 teaspoon fine sea salt. Divide the salmon mixture into four portions. Lay out 4 bacon rashers next to each other for each portion. Place the salmon portion at the base of the rashers and roll them up. Make 150 ml (¼ pint) Classic BBQ sauce (see page 57). Place the 4 bombs over an indirect heat, close the lid and grill for 12–15 minutes. From the very start, brush them regularly with the BBQ sauce until it is all used up. The bombs are cooked once the core temperature reaches 65–68°C (149¬154°F). Take off the grill, transfer to a chopping board and leave to rest for 5 minutes. Cut them into 1 cm (½ inch) thick slices and serve warm with more BBQ sauce if you like.

CARNE ASADA
with flank steak & potatoes

Flank steak, also called bavette, is a hearty, highly flavoursome cut from the abdomen.

PREPARATION
15 minutes

COOKING TIME
20–25 minutes

max.   max.   max.

COOKING METHOD
Direct heat

RESTING TIME
3–5 minutes

1 Prepare the grill for a medium to high direct heat (200–220°C/400–425°F).

2 Pat the steaks dry, rub all over with oil and scatter 1 teaspoon coarse sea salt evenly over both sides. Cover with baking parchment and leave to stand for about 15 minutes to come up to room temperature.

3 Wash the potatoes, pat them dry and cut up any large ones. Put them in a bowl, mix with 2 tablespoons oil and season with sea salt to taste. Place the potatoes on the GBS cast iron griddle over a direct heat and cook for 15 minutes, turning occasionally, until soft.

4 Meanwhile, wash the tomatoes, pat them dry, cut in half, remove the stalk ends and dice the tomatoes finely. Tear off the coriander leaves. Mix the diced tomato with the coriander, lime zest and juice, and season with pepper to taste. Set to one side.

5 Put the steaks over a direct heat, close the lid and grill for 6–8 minutes, turning once, until the core temperature reaches 52–54°C (126–129°F). Take off the grill, transfer to a chopping board and leave to rest for 3–5 minutes.

6 Remove the potatoes from the grill. Cut the flank steaks across the grain into 1 cm (½ inch) thick slices and season the cut surfaces with sea salt flakes to taste. Arrange the steak slices on top of the potatoes on the griddle. Top with the smashed avocado, marinated tomatoes and grated horseradish and serve warm.

SERVES 4

2 flank steaks (about 450 g/1 lb each and 1.5–2 cm/about ¾ inch thick)

1–2 tablespoons oil for rubbing

coarse sea salt

freshly ground black pepper

600 g (1 lb 5 oz) small potatoes (such as La Ratte or new potatoes)

2 tablespoons oil

2 tomatoes

8 sprigs of fresh coriander

zest and juice of ½ unwaxed lime

sea salt flakes

2 tablespoons freshly grated horseradish (or from a jar)

Smashed avocado (see page 59)

EQUIPMENT

1 GBS cast iron griddle or plancha

VEAL CHOPS
with stuffed mushrooms

Tender, almost fat-free veal on the bone becomes especially succulent and flavoursome on the barbecue.

PREPARATION
15 minutes

COOKING TIME
8–10 minutes

off   max.   max.

COOKING METHOD
Direct/indirect heat

RESTING TIME
2–3 minutes

1 Dab the chops dry and rub them all over with oil. Cover with baking parchment and leave to stand for about 10 minutes to come up to room temperature.

2 Clean the button mushrooms and remove the stalks. Cut out about 5 mm (¼ inch) of flesh from around the inside edge of the mushrooms and chop finely. In a bowl, season the whole mushrooms with sea salt and pepper to taste, and mix with the olive oil. Mix the chopped mushroom with the cream cheese, egg, breadcrumbs, parsley and half the Parmesan, then season with salt and pepper to taste. Stuff the mushrooms with the cream cheese mixture and scatter over the remaining Parmesan.

3 Prepare the grill for a high direct heat (220–240°C/425–475°F). Pat the smoking plank dry, place it over direct heat, close the lid and char for 2–3 minutes. As soon as it begins to crackle, turn the plank and char for a further 2–3 minutes, then remove from the grill.

4 Place the chops over direct heat, close the lid and grill for 4–6 minutes, turning once. Then place them over indirect heat, close the lid and continue cooking for 3–4 minutes until the core temperature (without touching the bones) reaches 52–54°C (126–129°F).

5 Prepare the grill for medium indirect heat (180–200°C/350–400°F). Lay the stuffed mushrooms on the plank, filling facing up, place the plank over a medium indirect heat, close the lid and cook for 8–10 minutes until they are soft and the filling is nicely golden.

6 Using tongs, transfer the cooked chops to a chopping board and scatter the spice mix over both sides. Leave to stand for 2–3 minutes. Remove the mushrooms from the grill.

7 Detach the meat from the bones and cut across the grain into 1 cm (½ inch) thick slices. Season the cut sides with sea salt flakes to taste and drizzle over olive oil. Serve warm, with the stuffed mushrooms alongside on the plank.

SERVES 4

4 veal tenderloin chops (about 250 g/9 oz each and 2–2.5 cm/¾–1 inch thick)

1–2 tablespoons oil for rubbing

Basic spice mix (see page 52)

sea salt flakes

olive oil for drizzling

STUFFED MUSHROOMS

12 large white mushrooms

sea salt and freshly ground black pepper

6 tablespoons olive oil

150 g (5½ oz) cream cheese

1 egg

4 tablespoons breadcrumbs

2 tablespoons finely chopped flat-leaf parsley

4 tablespoons grated Parmesan cheese

EQUIPMENT

1 cedarwood smoking plank, *pre-soaked in water for at least 1 hour*

VEAL CHOPS

TIP: You can tell top-quality veal by its dark pink to light reddish colour. Very pale or even white meat is a sign of the low-iron diet of 'milk-fed' calves and is therefore best avoided for animal welfare reasons.

Hangover chops

Halve and stone 1 peach. Brush the peach halves with olive oil, place them, cut sides down, over a medium direct heat (180–200°C/350–400°F), close the lid and grill for 3–4 minutes until grill marks form. Remove from the grill and cut into wedges.

Mix 200 g (7 oz) finely chopped mixed tomatoes with 1 finely diced red onion, the juice of ½ lemon, 1 tablespoon chopped rosemary and 2 tablespoons olive oil. Season the mixture with sea salt and chilli powder to taste. After the chops have rested, spoon the tomato topping and the peach wedges over the top and serve warm.

Philly-style chops

Trim, deseed and wash 1 red pepper and slice it finely. Peel 1 red onion and slice it finely.

After turning the chops, spread each one evenly with 100 g (3½ oz) cream cheese and add the pepper and onion slices and 1–2 slices of pancetta on top. Grill the chops as described on page 147 until they are cooked. Take off the grill and leave to rest. To serve, scatter a few marjoram leaves over the chops, drizzle with olive oil and season with sea salt flakes and freshly ground black pepper to taste.

Sweetcorn chops

To make the topping, mix 100 g (3½ oz) drained canned sweetcorn with 1 finely diced red onion, 1 sliced green jalapeño, 1 finely chopped spring onion, 1 handful of crushed nacho cheese-flavoured tortilla chips and 4 tablespoons grated Emmental cheese.

After turning the chops, spoon the topping on to the meat and grill the chops until done, as described on page 147. Take off the grill and leave to rest. To serve, scatter 1 tablespoon finely chopped flat-leaf parsley over the chops, drizzle over olive oil to taste and season with sea salt flakes and freshly ground black pepper.

VEAL TENDERLOIN STEAKS with lemon oil

Lemon and herbs make this tender, subtly flavoursome grilled veal a stand-out summer hit.

PREPARATION
10 minutes

COOKING TIME
15 minutes

COOKING METHOD
Direct/indirect heat

RESTING TIME
2–3 minutes

1 Prepare the grill for a medium to high direct heat (180–200°C/350–400°F). Mix the ingredients for the lemon oil together in a bowl.

2 Pat the steaks dry, rub them all over with oil and scatter coarse sea salt evenly over both sides. Cover with baking parchment and leave to stand for about 10 minutes to come up to room temperature.

3 Meanwhile, wash the aubergines, pat dry and cut diagonally into 2–3 cm (¾–1¼ inch) thick slices. Mix the slices with the olive oil and season with the sea salt and some black pepper. Cover with baking parchment and marinate for 15 minutes at room temperature.

4 Place the veal steaks over a direct heat, close the lid and grill for 4–6 minutes, turning once. Then place them over indirect heat, close the lid and continue cooking for 3–4 minutes, until the meat reaches a core temperature of 52–54°C (126–129°F).

5 Take the aubergine slices out of the marinade and pat them dry. Place them over a direct heat, close the lid and grill for 3–4 minutes, turning once. Then move to an indirect heat, close the lid and grill for 2–3 minutes until done. Season with pepper and remove from the grill.

6 Use tongs to lift the cooked steaks on to a chopping board and brush with half of the Lemon oil. Season with pepper and leave to rest for 2–3 minutes. Toss the remaining lemon oil with the aubergine.

7 Spread the mango sauce on plates. Cut the steaks in half, season the cut surfaces with sea salt flakes to taste and lay the steaks on the sauce. Cut the aubergine slices in half and arrange them alongside the steaks. Serve warm.

SERVES 4

LEMON OIL

2 tablespoons finely chopped flat-leaf parsley

2 tablespoons finely chopped thyme leaves

zest and juice of 1 unwaxed lemon

4 tablespoons olive oil

1 tablespoon clear honey

4 veal tenderloin chops (about 250 g/9 oz each and 2–3 cm/¾–1¼ inches thick)

1 tablespoon oil for rubbing

1 teaspoon coarse sea salt

freshly ground black pepper

sea salt flakes

AUBERGINES

2 large aubergines

50 ml (2 fl oz) olive oil

1 tablespoon sea salt

Sweet & sour mango sauce (see page 58)

VEAL SCHNITZEL
with grilled potato salad

PREPARATION
10 minutes

COOKING TIME
15 minutes

off   max.   max.

COOKING METHOD
Direct/indirect heat

RESTING TIME
2–3 minutes

1 Prepare the grill for a medium to high indirect and direct heat (200–220°C/400–425°F).

2 Wash the potatoes thoroughly and pat them dry. Place them over an indirect heat, close the lid and cook for 15–20 minutes, turning occasionally, until soft. About 10 minutes before the cooking time is up, put the unpeeled onions over an indirect heat. Now place the pointed peppers over a direct heat, close the lid and grill for 6–8 minutes, turning once.

3 Pat the veal schnitzels dry, rub them all over with oil and scatter salt evenly over both sides. Cover with baking parchment and leave to stand for about 10 minutes to come up to room temperature.

4 Remove the potatoes, onions and peppers from the grill and leave them to cool down a little. Cut the potatoes into rough chunks. Peel the onions and cut into quarters. Remove the skin from the peppers, cut them in half, remove the seeds and membranes, and cut into pieces. Put the GBS cast iron griddle over a direct heat, close the lid and preheat for 8–10 minutes.

5 Cut the lemon into 4 wedges. Place the schnitzels and lemon wedges over a direct heat, close the lid and grill for 2–3 minutes until the grill marks are clearly visible, turning them once. Take off the grill, transfer to a chopping board and leave to rest for 2–3 minutes.

6 Put the bacon lardons on the griddle pan and fry, stirring constantly, until crisp. Add the potatoes, quartered onions and pepper pieces to the pan and continue cooking for 3–4 minutes. Finely chop the spring onions and parsley. Remove the pan from the grill, tip the contents into a bowl and mix with the capers, vinegar and olive oil. Season to taste with sea salt and black pepper.

7 Arrange the schnitzels, lemon wedges and potato salad on plates. Scatter over the spring onions and parsley and serve warm.

SERVES 4

GRILLED POTATO SALAD

600 g (1 lb 5 oz) small potatoes (such as new potatoes or La Ratte)

2 onions

2 red pointed peppers

80 g (2¾ oz) bacon lardons

1 spring onion, *trimmed, washed and patted dry*

8 sprigs of flat-leaf parsley, *washed and shaken dry*

2 tablespoons capers

2 tablespoons white balsamic vinegar

4 tablespoons olive oil

8 veal topside escalopes (schnitzels) (100–120 g/3½–4 oz each and 1 cm/½ inch thick)

1–2 tablespoons oil for rubbing

sea salt

freshly ground black pepper

1 unwaxed lemon

EQUIPMENT

1 GBS cast iron griddle or plancha

VEAL SCHNITZEL

FLAVOUR UPGRADE

Ginger & lemongrass schnitzel
with rice noodles

Pat the veal schnitzels dry and make three cuts through each, 2–3 cm (¾–1¼ inches) apart. Coat the meat with 2 tablespoons teriyaki sauce and insert 1 stalk of lemongrass through the incisions in the middle of each schnitzel. Cover with baking parchment and marinate for 10 minutes at room temperature. Meanwhile, put a plancha over a medium to high direct heat (200–220°C/400–425°F), close the lid and preheat for 10 minutes. Cook 200 g (7 oz) broccoli florets briefly in salted water until firm to the bite. Trim and clean 80 g (2¾ oz) shiitake mushrooms. Trim and wash 1 red pointed pepper and slice it into rings. Cook 200 g (7 oz) rice noodles according to the packet instructions.

Put 2 tablespoons untoasted sesame oil on the preheated plancha. Put the schnitzels on the plancha, close the lid and cook for 2–3 minutes, turning once and seasoning with freshly ground black pepper. Add the vegetables and noodles to the plancha, mix with 4 tablespoons teriyaki sauce, close the lid and cook for about 5 minutes. Take the schnitzels off the grill, transfer to a chopping board and leave to rest for 2–3 minutes. Arrange the vegetables and noodles on plates, add the schnitzels on top, season with pepper and scatter over 2 tablespoons sesame seeds. Serve warm.

Garlic schnitzel with beans

Mix 4 finely chopped garlic cloves with 1–2 tablespoons oil. Pat the veal escalopes dry, season on both sides with sea salt and rub with the garlic oil. Cover with baking parchment and marinate for 10 minutes at room temperature. Meanwhile, trim and wash 300 g (10½ oz) green beans (such as French beans, fine green beans) and cook them briefly in salted water until firm to the bite. Peel 1 onion and cut it into thin wedges. Trim, deseed and wash 1 red pepper and cut it into strips. In a bowl, mix the beans, onion and pepper with 1 tablespoon oil.

Put a plancha over a medium to high direct heat (200–220°C/ 400–425°F), close the lid and preheat for 10 minutes. Put the schnitzels on the plancha, close the lid and cook for 2–3 minutes, turning once and seasoning with black pepper. Put the vegetables on the plancha and cook for about 5 minutes, turning once. Take the schnitzels off the grill, transfer to a chopping board and leave to rest for 2–3 minutes. Deglaze the vegetables in the plancha with 2 tablespoons soy sauce. Add a few sprigs of thyme and continue cooking for a few moments. Arrange the schnitzels and vegetables on plates, season with pepper and serve warm.

Ras el hanout & parsley schnitzel
with bulgur wheat

Pat the veal escalopes dry, rub both sides with 1–2 tablespoons oil, season with sea salt and freshly ground black pepper, then sprinkle with 2 tablespoons finely chopped parsley and 1 tablespoon ras el hanout. Cover with baking parchment and marinate for about 10 minutes at room temperature. Meanwhile, put a plancha over a medium to high direct heat (200–220°C/ 400–425°F), close the lid and preheat for 10 minutes. Cook 300 g (10½ oz) bulgur wheat according to the packet instructions. Fluff up the bulgur wheat with a fork, then mix with 1 diced red pepper, 1 diced mango, 2 roughly chopped spring onions, 2 tablespoons pomegranate seeds and 2 tablespoons pine nuts.

Pour 3 tablespoons sunflower oil on the preheated plancha. Put the schnitzels on the plancha, close the lid and cook for 2–3 minutes, turning once and seasoning with freshly ground black pepper. Add the bulgur mixture to the plancha, close the lid and cook for 5 minutes, turning once. Deglaze the plancha with 2–3 tablespoons ponzu sauce (citrus-flavoured soy sauce). Take the schnitzels off the grill, transfer to a chopping board and leave to rest for 2–3 minutes. Spoon the bulgur mixture on to plates, add the schnitzels on top, season with pepper and serve warm.

Breaded schnitzel with avocado, romaine lettuce & yogurt

Put a plancha over a medium direct heat (180–200°C/ 350–400°F), close the lid and preheat for about 15 minutes. Meanwhile, trim and wash 1 romaine lettuce, tear it into pieces and spin dry. Mix 4 tablespoons Basic mayonnaise (see page 58, or use ready-made mayonnaise) with 4 tablespoons medium Dijon mustard, then season this dijonnaise with sea salt and freshly ground black pepper to taste. Pat the veal escalopes dry and coat evenly with 2 tablespoons flour, tapping off any excess. Spread both sides with the dijonnaise then coat them in 150 g (5½ oz) panko breadcrumbs, pressing them on firmly.

Put 2 tablespoons oil on the preheated plancha. Place the breadcrumbed schnitzels on the plancha, close the lid and cook for 4–5 minutes, turning once. Take them off the grill, transfer to a sheet of kitchen paper and leave to rest for 3–4 minutes. Meanwhile, season 200 g (7 oz) yogurt with salt and pepper to taste, then spread it on plates. Slice 1 avocado and arrange on the plates with the lettuce and parsley. Place the schnitzels on top, grind over salt and pepper, drizzle ½ tablespoon olive oil over each plate and serve.

CHARCOAL VEAL TENDERLOIN
with peppers & sugarsnap peas

PREPARATION
15 minutes, plus overnight infusing of charcoal oil

COOKING TIME
12–14 minutes

COOKING METHOD
Direct/indirect heat

RESTING TIME
3–5 minutes

1 Trim, deseed and wash the peppers, pat them dry and cut into chunks. Trim and wash the sugarsnap peas, pat them dry and cut in half diagonally. Wash the Padrón peppers and pat dry. Rinse the herbs, shake them dry and tear into pieces. Chop half of them finely.

2 Prepare the grill for a medium to high direct and indirect heat (200–220°C/400–425°F). Put the GBS cast iron griddle over a direct heat, close the lid and preheat for 8–10 minutes.

3 Pat the veal medallions dry, rub them all over with oil and scatter sea salt evenly over both sides. Cover with baking parchment and leave to stand for about 15 minutes to come up to room temperature.

4 Place the medallions over a direct heat, close the lid and grill for 3–4 minutes, turning once, until the grill stripes are clearly visible. Then place over an indirect heat, close the lid and continue cooking for 5–6 minutes.

5 Meanwhile, heat 2 tablespoons olive oil on the preheated griddle over a direct heat, add all the vegetables and chopped herbs, close the lid and cook for 4–6 minutes, stirring occasionally. Season with the salt, honey and paprika, then remove the griddle from the grill.

6 Remove the cooked medallions from the grill, transfer them to a chopping board and leave to rest for 3–5 minutes. Season with pepper and add a few drops of charcoal oil. Arrange the vegetables on plates and scatter over the remaining herb leaves. Top with the medallions and serve warm.

HOMEMADE CHARCOAL OIL

To make the charcoal oil, ignite 1 piece of charcoal (50 g/1¾ oz) and leave it glowing in a fireproof pot for about 15 minutes. Deglaze the pot with 200 ml (7 fl oz) neutral-tasting oil. As soon as the charcoal has completely cooled, put a lid on the pot to make it airtight and leave the oil to infuse overnight. Pour the oil through a fine sieve and decant it into another vessel for storage, such as a spray bottle.

SERVES 4

VEGETABLES

1 red and 1 yellow pepper

200 g (7 oz) sugarsnap peas

200 g (7 oz) Padrón peppers

a few sprigs of mixed herbs (such as thyme, marjoram, oregano, curly parsley)

2 tablespoons olive oil

½ teaspoon fine sea salt

2 tablespoons clear honey

½ teaspoon sweet paprika

8 veal tenderloin medallions (120–150 g/4–5½ oz each and 3–4 cm/1¼–1½ inches thick)

1 tablespoon oil for rubbing

sea salt

freshly ground black pepper

a few drops of charcoal oil (see tip)

EQUIPMENT

1 GBS cast iron griddle or plancha

PORK
LAMB &
VENISON

FILLET OF PORK
on pineapple

Instead of a smoky flavour, this recipe has a Caribbean vibe. The pineapple slice gives the dish a fruity flavour and protects the meat from searing heat.

SERVES 4

Spice mix for beef
(see page 52)

600 g (1 lb 5 oz) pork fillet,
*excess fat and sinews
removed*

1 pineapple

1–2 tablespoons oil

Herb mix (see page 52)

3 tablespoons clear honey

zest and juice
of 1 unwaxed lemon

4 tablespoons olive oil

fine sea salt

freshly ground black
pepper

1 fennel bulb (about
400 g/14 oz)

PREPARATION
15–20 minutes,
plus 30 minutes
marinating

COOKING TIME
40–45 minutes

off   max.   max.

COOKING METHOD
Direct/indirect heat

RESTING TIME
6–8 minutes

1 Make the Spice mix for beef. Rub the pork fillet all over with two-thirds of the spice mix, then cover with baking parchment and put in the refrigerator to marinate for 15 minutes. Take the pork out of the refrigerator and leave to marinate for a further 15 minutes.

2 Prepare the grill for a high to very high direct heat (220–240°C/425–475°F). Cut the sides off the pineapple to leave a 3–4 cm (1¼–1½ inch) thick slice, then rub it all over with oil. (You can reserve the remaining pineapple for another use.) Make the herb mix.

3 Place the pineapple slice over a direct heat, close the lid and grill for 5–6 minutes until grill marks form. Turn it over, move it to the indirect heat zone, then turn the grill to low to medium heat (140–160°C/275–325°F). Scatter about 1 tablespoon of the Herb mix over the pineapple slice.

4 Place the pork fillet on top of the pineapple slice, close the lid and cook for 30–35 minutes over an indirect heat, turning the meat occasionally until its core temperature reaches 58–62°C (136–144°F).

5 Meanwhile, mix together the honey, lemon juice and zest and oil in a large bowl. Season the vinaigrette with salt and pepper to taste. Trim and wash the fennel bulb. Finely chop the fennel fronds. Using a mandoline, finely slice the bulb. Add the fennel slices and fronds to the vinaigrette in the bowl and mix well.

6 Remove the pork and pineapple from the grill. Leave the pork to rest for 6–8 minutes, then slice it. Cut away the skin and leaves of the pineapple and cut the fruit into pieces. Arrange the sliced pork and pineapple on plates and serve with the fennel salad.

FRUITY PORK & MELON SKEWERS

Sweet chunks of melon, mint leaves and a hint of orange give these grilled pork skewers a fabulous punchy flavour.

SERVES 4

600 g (1 lb 5 oz) pork fillet, *excess fat and sinews removed*

zest and juice of 1 unwaxed orange

1 teaspoon grated ginger

2–3 tablespoons soy sauce

1 teaspoon clear honey

½ teaspoon fine sea salt, plus extra for the skewers

freshly ground black pepper

2–3 tablespoons oil

¼ galia melon

½ cantaloupe melon

a few mint leaves

Sweet & sour mango sauce (see page 58; optional)

EQUIPMENT

4 double-pronged skewers

PREPARATION
15–20 minutes, plus
30 minutes marinating

 COOKING TIME
8–10 minutes

 max. max. max.
COOKING METHOD
Direct heat

 RESTING TIME
3–5 minutes

1 Cut the pork fillet into 2–3 cm (¾–1¼ inch) slices. To make the marinade, put the zest and juice of the orange in a small bowl and mix in the grated ginger, soy sauce and honey, then add ½ teaspoon sea salt and season with black pepper to taste. Place the meat and marinade in a large bowl, cover, and transfer to the refrigerator to marinate for 30 minutes.

2 Cut the skin from the melon, scoop out the seeds with a spoon and cut the flesh into chunks 2 cm (about ¾ inch) wide and 5 cm (2 inches) long. Prepare the grill for a medium to high direct heat (200–220°C/400–425°F). Take the pork out of the marinade (reserving the marinade) and gently pat it dry. Thread the pork and melon pieces alternately on to the skewers.

3 Brush the skewers all over with the oil and season with salt. Put the skewers over direct heat, close the lid and grill for 8–10 minutes, turning once, until the core temperature of the meat reaches 58–62°C (136–144°F). After turning, brush with the remaining marinade and season with pepper. Take off the grill and leave to rest for 3–5 minutes. Scatter with the torn mint leaves and serve warm, with Sweet & sour mango sauce, if you like.

TIP: When grilling poultry, fish or lean meat skewers, make sure the chunks of fruit and vegetable have roughly the same texture and firmness so all the ingredients cook at the same rate.

Classic
PULLED PORK

Beef brisket, pulled pork and spare ribs are the holy trinity of BBQ meats. They demand top-quality meat, a great spice mix and plenty of time.

SERVES 6–8

1–2 x Basic spice mix (see page 52)

1 boneless pork neck (1.5–1.8 kg/3 lb 5 oz– 4 lb; ideally dry-aged), *well trimmed*

2–3 tablespoons oil

1–2 × Beer & whisky mop sauce (see page 55)

300 ml (½ pint) Classic BBQ sauce (see page 57)

EQUIPMENT

1 smoker box

1 handful of dry hickory wood chips for smoking

2–3 handfuls of hickory wood chips for smoking, *soaked for at least 30 minutes*

1 spare rib rack and grilling basket

1 large aluminium drip tray

PREPARATION
30–35 minutes, plus
at least 6 hours marinating
(ideally overnight)

 COOKING TIME
10–11 hours

 **COOKING METHOD**
Indirect heat

 RESTING TIME
1–2 hours

1 Make the Basic spice mix. Rub the pork neck all over with oil and scatter over the spice mix in an even coating. Cover with baking parchment and put in the refrigerator to marinate for at least 6 hours (or ideally overnight). Before cooking, take it out of the refrigerator and leave to stand for 30 minutes to come up to room temperature. Take the grill racks out. Fill the smoker box with the dry chips, place it on the flavorizer bars over a high direct heat (220–240°C/425–475°F), close the lid and burn for 6–8 minutes.

2 Fill the drip tray with 500 ml (18 fl oz) water and place it on the flavorizer bars. Replace the grill racks and place the smoker box on top. Prepare the grill for a very low to low indirect heat (125–135°C/260–275°F). Place the marinated pork neck in the grilling basket over the drip tray, close the lid and smoke for 4–5 hours. Top up the smoker box with pre-soaked chips during this time. Make the Beer & whisky mop sauce.

3 The meat should now be nice and crispy on the outside and have a reddish-brown colour, with a core temperature of 48–56°C (118–133°F). Continue grilling for 3–4 hours, brushing the meat repeatedly with the Beer & whisky mop sauce until it is all used up and the core temperature is 78–86°C/172–187°F). Remove the pork from the grill and place it on a double layer of butcher's paper or baking parchment. Fold the sides of the paper over the meat, then roll the meat up tightly in the paper.

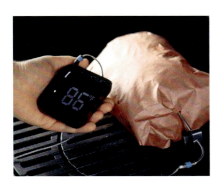

4 With the lid closed, continue cooking for 2–3 hours, until the paper disintegrates when you touch it (ideally, the core temperature should now be 92–95°C/198–203°F).

5 Remove the wrapped meat from the grill and leave it to rest for 1–2 hours, ideally in a cool box. Meanwhile, make the Classic BBQ sauce.

6 Unwrap the pulled pork. Tip any roasting juices in the paper into the BBQ sauce. Use two forks or a special meat shredding claw to pull the pork apart into shreds. Serve with the BBQ sauce.

PULLED PORK

Pulled pork salad

SERVES 4: Wash and dry 200 g (7 oz) mixed salad leaves (such as frisée, iceberg lettuce or wild herbs) and slice 2 avocados. Mix 100 g (3½ oz) sweetcorn and kidney beans (from a can) with 1 finely chopped tomato and 1 cored, deseeded and finely diced red pepper. Mix 100 g (3½ oz) soured cream with 100 g (3½ oz) yogurt, the juice of 1 lemon and 4 tablespoons olive oil until smooth, then season the dressing to taste with salt and freshly ground black pepper. Mix the salad leaves, avocado slices, sweetcorn and kidney bean mixture with 400 g (14 oz) shredded pulled pork and 3–4 tablespoons olive oil. Season with salt and pepper. Arrange on plates, drizzle over the dressing and finish with a few fresh coriander leaves.

Pulled pork bowls

SERVES 4: In a small pan, mix 400 g (14 oz) pulled pulled pork with 100 ml (3½ fl oz) Classic BBQ Sauce (see page 57), then heat it up and keep warm. Wash 1 sweet potato (400 g/14 oz) thoroughly, then, without peeling, slice finely using a mandoline. Peel 2 red onions and slice them finely in the same way, then dice 1 red apple. Put 2–3 tablespoons oil in a frying pan, add the sweet potato slices and sauté for 6–8 minutes. Add the sliced onions and diced apple and continue cooking for 3–4 minutes. Season with salt, freshly ground black pepper and ½ teaspoon sweet paprika. Arrange the pulled pork and sweet potato mixture in bowls, add 2–3 tablespoons shredded iceberg lettuce, 2 tablespoons soured cream and 2 tablespoons Parmesan shavings, then top with 2 tablespoons chopped spring onions.

Pulled pork burgers

SERVES 4: In a small pan, mix 600 g (1 lb 5 oz) pulled pork with 140 ml (5 fl oz) Classic BBQ sauce (see page 57), then heat it up and keep warm. Mix 200 g (7 oz) finely shredded white cabbage with 100 g (3½ oz) shredded carrot, 50 g (1¾ oz) mayonnaise, 50 g (1¾ oz) yogurt and 1 tablespoon finely chopped flat-leaf parsley. Add 1 tablespoon white balsamic vinegar, then season with salt and freshly ground black pepper to taste. Peel 1 red onion and slice it into fine rings. Slice open 4 burger buns, brush the cut surfaces with 1 tablespoon melted butter and toast on a open grill. Arrange the meat on the bottom halves of the buns and layer up with the coleslaw and onion rings. Top with 1 tablespoon BBQ sauce if you like, then replace the tops of the buns.

MOINK BALLS

The name of this BBQ classic comes from 'moo' (for the beef) and 'oink' (for the pork, or in this case, the bacon).

SERVES 4–6

1 kg (2 lb 4 oz) minced
   beef (ideally freshly
   minced)

1 teaspoon coarse sea salt

1 tablespoon sweet
   paprika

1 tablespoon clear honey

freshly ground
   black pepper

1–2 tablespoons olive oil

32 bacon rashers
   (for 16 moink balls)

Classic BBQ sauce
   (see page 57)

EQUIPMENT

1 smoker box

1 handful fruitwood chips
   for smoking (such as
   applewood)

2 handfuls fruitwood
   chips for smoking
   (such as applewood),
   *soaked for at least
   30 minutes*

PREPARATION
20 minutes

COOKING TIME
30–40 minutes

COOKING METHOD
Indirect heat

RESTING TIME
3–5 minutes

1 In a large bowl, mix the minced beef thoroughly with the salt, paprika and honey, and season well with pepper.

2 Rub your hands with a little of the oil or some water and shape the minced beef into 16 balls, each about 3–4 cm (1¼–1½ inches) across.

3 Lay the bacon rashers out in twos, each pair forming a cross. Place a meatball in the centre of each cross and roll the rashers up so that the meatballs are completely wrapped in the bacon.

4 Take the grill racks out. Fill the smoker box with the dry chips, place it on the flavorizer bars over a high direct heat (220–240°C/425–475°F), close the lid and burn for 6–8 minutes. Remove the box, replace the grill racks and place the smoker box over indirect heat. Prepare the grill for a very low to low indirect heat (125–135°C/260–275°F). Place the moink balls on the grill rack over indirect heat.

5 Close the lid and grill and smoke for 20–25 minutes, topping up the soaked wood chips every now and then. Meanwhile, make the Classic BBQ sauce.

6 Cook for a further 10 minutes, brushing the moink balls frequently with 150 ml (¼ pint) Classic BBQ sauce, until it is all used up. Serve the moink balls on a bed of salad (see below), with the remaining BBQ sauce alongside.

CREAMY ICEBERG SALAD

Divide 300 g (10 oz) shredded iceberg lettuce among 4–6 plates and top with 50 g (1¾ oz) Parmesan shavings. Mix 50 g (1¾ oz) soured cream with 1 teaspoon mustard, 3–4 tablespoons milk, 100 g (3½ oz) yogurt, the juice of 1 orange and 4 tablespoons olive oil until smooth, then season with salt and pepper. Drizzle the dressing over the salad.

MOINK BALLS

FLAVOUR UPGRADE

TIP: Moink balls make great BBQ finger food. Simply shape the minced beef and pork mixture into 26–28 smaller balls (30–40 g/1–1½ ounces each), wrap each in a single bacon rasher and hold the bacon in place with a pre-soaked cocktail stick.

El Fuego balls

To make spicy balls, mix 1 kg (2 lb 4 oz) minced beef with the Pepper & chilli spice mix on page 52. Shape this mixture into 16 meatballs as described on page 169. Wrap the meatballs in bacon, then grill and smoke them using the same method as previously described. During the last 10 minutes of cooking time, brush the meatballs with 150 ml (¼ pint) Sweet chilli sauce (see page 57).

Crunchy corn balls

Mix 1 kg (2 lb 4 oz) minced beef with 100 g (3½ oz) canned sweetcorn (drained), ½ teaspoon sea salt, 1 tablespoon curry powder and 2–3 tablespoons teriyaki sauce. Shape this mixture into 16 meatballs as described on page 169, wrap them in bacon, then grill and smoke. During the last 10 minutes of cooking, brush the meatballs with 150 ml (¼ pint) Sweet & sour mango sauce (see page 58), until the sauce is all used up. Coat the meatballs with 1–2 handfuls of finely crushed cornflakes before serving.

Cheese balls

Mix 800 g (1 lb 12 oz) minced beef with 100 g (3½ oz) diced Cheddar, 50 g (1¾ oz) grated Emmental, 1 teaspoon sea salt, 1 tablespoon paprika and 2 tablespoons maple syrup. Season the mixture with black pepper to taste. Roll into balls and wrap in bacon as described on page 169, then grill and smoke using the same method. During the last 10 minutes of cooking, brush with 150 ml (¼ pint) Classic BBQ sauce (see page 57).

Smoked spit-roasted
ROLLED PORK

SERVES 6–8

1 boneless pork shoulder
(2.5–3 kg/5 lb–6 lb
8 oz) or pork neck, *well
trimmed*

Tomato & chilli spice
paste (see page 56)

1 teaspoon coarse sea salt

2 × Vanilla & pepper spice
mix (see page 53)

EQUIPMENT

1 smoker box

1 handful of dry hickory
wood chips for
smoking

2–3 handfuls of hickory
wood chips for
smoking, *soaked for at
least 30 minutes*

kitchen string, soaked in
water

1 large aluminium drip
tray

1 rotisserie

 **PREPARATION**
20 minutes, plus at least 1 hour marinating

 **COOKING TIME**
4 hours–4 hours 30 minutes

 COOKING METHOD
Indirect heat

 RESTING TIME
1 hour 30 minutes

1 Start by butterflying the pork: place the meat on a chopping board with what would have been the skin side down and use a sharp knife to make a cut down the middle of the meat, without cutting all the way through. Cut into the meat horizontally from this cut on both sides, almost to the edges, and open it out.

2 Make the Tomato & chilli spice paste. Season the pork with salt and spread the spice paste over it, leaving 2–3 cm (about 1 inch) around the edges so that the paste doesn't run off during grilling. Roll up the meat. Make the Vanilla & pepper spice mix.

3 Tie up the rolled pork with kitchen string. Knot the string tightly at one end of the pork roll and lay the string along the entire length of the meat, then make loops at 1–2 cm (½–¾ inch) intervals all the way to the end. Pull the string tight by running it back along the length, and knot it at the starting end.

4 Rub the Vanilla & pepper spice mix into the pork, cover with baking parchment and put in the refrigerator to marinate for at least 1 hour. Before grilling, take the pork out of the refrigerator and leave to stand for 20–30 minutes to allow it to come up to room temperature.

5 Take the grill racks out. Fill the smoker box with the dry chips, place it on the flavorizer bars over a high direct heat (220–240°C/425–475°F), close the lid and burn for 6–8 minutes. Meanwhile, thread the rolled pork on to the rotisserie and fix it in place with the prongs.

6 Fill the drip tray with 500 ml (18 fl oz) water and place it on the flavorizer bars in the indirect heat zone. Replace the grill racks, put the smoker box on top and top up with soaked wood chips. Prepare the grill for a low indirect heat (130–150°C/265–300°F). Insert the rotisserie into the grill, close the lid and smoke for 4–4 hours 30 minutes over the drip tray, topping up the smoker box with soaked chips every so often. At the end, the core temperature of the meat should be 72–76°C (162–169°F).

7 Take the pork off the spit, wrap it in two sheets of butcher's paper (or in baking parchment and then in kitchen foil) and place it in a cool box to rest for 1 hour. Remove the string and slice.

PORK NECK STEAKS

These steaks come from the front part of the pork loin – a highly marbled and extremely tender cut of meat. They are particularly good for grilling.

Tip: As far as we're concerned, neck steaks grill better than any other cut – in other words, we're big fans. But please be sure to buy good-quality and sustainably produced meat. And why not marinate the steaks yourself or make your own topping for them?

PREPARATION
15–20 minutes

COOKING TIME
10–30 minutes

COOKING METHOD
Direct heat

ⓐ With curry sauce & honey-infused plums

SERVES 4

4 tablespoons honey, 1 onion, *finely diced,* 50 g (2 oz) salami, *diced,* 3 red or yellow plums, *cut into wedges,* fine sea salt, freshly ground black pepper, 4 pork neck steaks (200–250 g/7–9 oz each and 2 cm/ ¾ inch thick), 1 tablespoon olive oil, ½ teaspoon curry powder, 4 tablespoons spring onions, *chopped*

To make the topping, heat the honey in a pan, add the onion and salami, and sweat over a medium heat until the onion is soft and translucent. Add the plums and continue cooking for 2–3 minutes, then season with salt and pepper. Keep the topping warm.

Rub the neck steaks all over with oil and season with sea salt to taste. Place the steaks over a high direct heat (200–220°C/400–425°F), close the lid and grill for 10–12 minutes, turning once and seasoning with pepper and the curry powder. At the end, the core temperature should be 56–58°C (133–136°F). Remove from the grill. Spoon the warm plum topping on to the steaks and scatter with the spring onions.

ⓑ With grilled onions

SERVES 4

4–5 onions, *unpeeled,* 4 pork neck steaks (200–250 g/7–9 oz each and 2 cm/¾ inch thick), 1 tablespoon oil, fine sea salt, freshly ground black pepper, 1½ teaspoons each of chopped rosemary and thyme, juice of ½ lemon, 1 tablespoon honey

To make the topping, place the unpeeled onions over a medium to high indirect heat (180–200°C/ 350–400°F), close the lid and cook for 20 minutes, turning occasionally. Take them off the grill and, with the skin on, leave to sweat for about 10 minutes.

Rub the neck steaks all over with oil and season with sea salt to taste. Place the steaks over a high direct heat (200–220°C/400–425°F), close the lid and grill for 10–12 minutes, turning once and seasoning with black pepper. At the end, the core temperature should be 56–58°C (133–136°F).

Peel the grilled onions and cut them into wedges. In a bowl, mix them with the rosemary, thyme, lemon juice and honey. Take the steaks off the grill, top them with the onion mixture and serve warm.

ⓒ With roasted peppers

SERVES 4

2–3 tablespoons olive oil, 1 onion, *sliced,* 1 red and 1 yellow pepper, *cored, deseeded and sliced,* 1 tablespoon honey, juice of 1 orange, 50 g (1¾ oz) tomato ketchup, 4 pork neck steaks (200–250 g/7–9 oz each and 2 cm/¾ inch thick), 1 tablespoon oil, fine sea salt, freshly ground black pepper, ½ teaspoon sweet paprika

To make the topping, heat the olive oil in a pan and sweat the onion briefly. Add the red and yellow peppers and continue cooking for 3–4 minutes. Add the honey, orange juice and tomato ketchup and reduce for several minutes, stirring constantly, until thick. Keep the topping warm until you're ready to serve the pork.

Rub the neck steaks all over with oil and season with sea salt to taste. Place the steaks over a high direct heat (200–220°C/400–425°F), close the lid and grill for 10–12 minutes, turning once and seasoning with black pepper and paprika. At the end, the core temperature should be 56–58°C (133–136°F). Take the steaks off the grill, spoon the topping over them and serve warm.

READY-MARINATED MEAT

Watch out for meat that is sold in ready-made liquid marinades. These might appear to promise quick and delicious grilling, but often the marinade is just there to keep the meat tender and on the shelf for as long as possible. Such marinades also tend to burn very quickly, so they end up tasting bitter and leave little of the meaty flavour to enjoy.

CLASSIC SPARE RIBS

Alongside beef brisket and pulled pork, ribs make up the holy trinity of barbecued meats. All three are very special indeed. Preparing them takes some effort and requires patience, but you're off to a real head start if you have a gas barbecue!

PREPARATION
15–20 minutes, plus at least 1 hour marinating

COOKING TIME
8–9 hours

COOKING METHOD
Indirect heat

RESTING TIME
1 hour

SERVES 4–6

- 2–2.5 kg (4 lb 8 oz–5 lb 8 oz) spare ribs
- 2 × Texas-style spice mix (see page 53)

MOP SAUCE

- 100 ml (3½ fl oz) orange juice
- 5 teaspoons white balsamic vinegar
- 1 tablespoon brown sugar
- 1 tablespoon Worcestershire sauce

- Classic BBQ sauce (see page 57)

EQUIPMENT

- 1 handful of dried fruitwood chips for smoking (such as applewood)
- 1–2 handfuls of fruitwood chips for smoking (such as applewood), *soaked for at least 30 minutes*
- 1 spare rib rack
- 1 large aluminium drip tray

1 Remove the silvery skin from the bony side of the ribs (see page 63).

2 Rub the ribs all over with the Texas-style spice mix, including the edges and sides. Cover with baking parchment and put in the refrigerator for at least 1 hour to marinate.

3 Prepare the grill for a high direct heat (220–240°C/425–475°F). Take the grill racks out. Fill the smoker box with the dry chips, place it on the flavorizer bars over a direct heat, close the lid and burn for 6–8 minutes. As soon as smoke begins to form, fill the drip tray with 500 ml (18 fl oz) water and place it on the flavorizer bars in the indirect heat zone.

4 Replace the grill racks and place the smoker box on the rack in the indirect zone. Put a handful of soaked chips in the box and set the temperature for a very low indirect heat (115°–125°C/240–260°F). Put the ribs on the rib rack, put it over the drip tray, close the lid and smoke for 2–2 hours 30 minutes. During this period, gradually top up the box with the remaining smoked chips.

5 To make the mop sauce, whisk the orange juice, vinegar, sugar and Worcestershire sauce together until the sugar has completely dissolved. After smoking, continue grilling for 2 hours over indirect heat, brushing regularly with the sauce until it is all used up.

6 Then take the ribs off the grill and wrap them tightly in two sheets of butcher's paper so that they are completely enclosed. Place them over indirect heat and continue grilling for 3 hours 30 minutes– 4 hours.

7 Carefully unwrap the ribs and mix any roasting juices in the paper with the BBQ sauce. Brush the ribs thoroughly all over with the sauce, put them back in the rack over an indirect heat, and continue grilling for 30–45 minutes, brushing frequently with the BBQ sauce until it is all used up. At the end, the ribs should have a core temperature of 84–92°C (183–198°F).

8 Remove the ribs from the grill and leave to rest for 1 hour, ideally in a cool box to keep them warm.

SOUVLAKI SKEWERS
with tzatziki

This classic Greek dish is great on its own, with side dishes or simply stuffed into a toasted pitta, takeaway style.

PREPARATION
15–20 minutes, plus 4 hours marinating

COOKING TIME
12–15 minutes

COOKING METHOD
Direct heat

RESTING TIME
3–5 minutes

1 Cut the pork neck into quarters lengthways, and then into 1 cm (½ inch) thick pieces.

2 To make the marinade, peel and halve the onion and cut it into wedges. Wash the parsley and oregano, shake dry and roughly chop the leaves and stalks. Put the onion and herbs in a bowl and mix with the vinegar, zest and juice of the citrus fruits, sea salt and crushed pepper. Mix the meat with the marinade, cover and put in the refrigerator to marinate for 4 hours.

3 Meanwhile, to make the tzatziki, peel the cucumber, cut it in half lengthways and scrape out the seeds with a teaspoon. Grate the halved cucumber roughly, mix with ¼ teaspoon sea salt and leave to stand for 10 minutes. Transfer to a clean tea towel and thoroughly wring out the moisture. Wash the parsley, shake it dry and finely chop the leaves and stalks. Peel and finely chop the garlic. Mix all of the tzatziki ingredients together and season with salt and pepper to taste.

4 Prepare the grill for a medium to high direct heat (200–220°C/400–425°F).

5 Take the meat and onion wedges out of the marinade, pat them dry and thread on to skewers up to the halfway point, without leaving any gaps. Place over direct heat, close the lid and grill for 12–15 minutes, turning once. Take the meat off the grill and leave to rest for 3–5 minutes before serving.

6 Spoon the tzatziki on to plates, place 1–2 skewers on each and serve warm. Toasted pitta and potatoes go well with this dish (see below).

SERVES 6–8

600 g (1 lb 5 oz) boneless pork neck, *well trimmed*

MARINADE

1 onion

4–6 sprigs of flat-leaf parsley

4–6 sprigs of oregano

40 ml (1½ fl oz) cider vinegar

zest and juice of 1 unwaxed lemon

zest and juice of 1 unwaxed orange

1 teaspoon coarse sea salt

½ teaspoon crushed black peppercorns

TZATZIKI

½ cucumber

½ bunch of flat-leaf parsley

1–2 garlic cloves

250 g (8 oz) Greek yogurt

zest and juice of ½ unwaxed orange

2–3 tablespoons olive oil

fine sea salt

freshly ground black pepper

EQUIPMENT

12–16 wooden or bamboo skewers, *soaked for at least 30 minutes*

GREEK SIDE DISHES

In Greece, souvlaki is traditionally served with toasted pittas and oven-baked potato slices, but you could cook some potatoes on the plancha to serve alongside the meat. To do this, simply peel 400 g (14 oz) waxy potatoes, cut them into 5 mm (¼ inch) thick slices and toss with 2–3 tablespoons oil. Season with salt to taste and cook on the preheated plancha over a medium to high direct heat (180–200°C/350–400°F) for 12–15 minutes, turning occasionally, under soft. To serve, season with freshly ground black pepper and drizzle with 2–3 tablespoons olive oil.

Herb-crusted
LAMB SHOULDER

The thick salt crust keeps
the lamb succulent,
while the herbs impart a
delicious savoury flavour.

SERVES 4–6

1–2 × Herb mix (see
page 52)

1 lamb shoulder on the
bone (1.5–1.7 kg/
3 lb 5 oz–3 lb 12 oz)

150 ml (¼ pint) egg
whites

75 ml (2½ fl oz) water

150 g (5½ oz) flour

2.5 kg (5 lb 8 oz) coarse
sea salt

100 g (3½ oz) fresh herbs
(such as rosemary, bay
leaves, thyme, sage)

EQUIPMENT

1 large ceramic BBQ dish
with plenty of space for
the lamb

1 sheet of baking
parchment, *pre-soaked*

PREPARATION
20 minutes, plus
at least 3 hours
marinating

COOKING TIME
1 hour 30 minutes–2 hours

max.   off   max.

COOKING METHOD
Indirect heat

RESTING TIME
25–30 minutes

1 Make the Herb mix. Remove any excess fat from the underside of the lamb shoulder. Rub the lamb all over with the spice mix, cover with baking parchment and put in the refrigerator to marinate for at least 3 hours.

2 Mix the egg whites with the measured water. In a large bowl, mix the flour and coarse sea salt together. Pour in the egg white and water mixture and stir together for a few minutes. Prepare the grill for a low to medium indirect heat (140–160°C/275–325°F).

3 Line the ceramic dish with the pre-soaked baking parchment and spread one-third of the salt on it. Place half the herbs on top and lay the lamb on the herbs. Put the remaining herbs on top of the lamb, then completely cover the meat with the remaining salt.

4 Place the lamb in the dish over an indirect heat, close the lid and cook for 1 hour 30 minutes–2 hours until the core temperature reaches 55–58°C (131–136°F). Take off the grill and leave in the salt crust to rest for 25–30 minutes.

5 To break open the salt crust, take a bread knife and cut carefully around the sides of the lamb. Take off the salt 'lid', lift out the lamb shoulder and slice the meat. Serve warm.

Tip: To make a salt crust, you generally need 1–2 egg whites per kilogram of salt. This recipe calls for 150 ml (¼ pint) egg whites, which is roughly 5 medium egg whites.

LAMB CHOPS
with green beans

You should only ever grill lamb chops for a short time, so that they stay pink and tender on the inside.

PREPARATION
20 minutes

COOKING TIME
6–8 minutes

COOKING METHOD
Direct heat

RESTING TIME
3–5 minutes

1 Prepare the grill for a medium to high direct heat (180–200°C/350–400°F) and place the GBS cast iron griddle on it to preheat for 6–8 minutes.

2 Rub the lamb chops all over with the olive oil and season with sea salt.

3 To make the green bean medley, peel and finely dice the onion. Wash the courgettes, pat dry and cut in half lengthways. Trim, halve, deseed and wash the pointed peppers and pat them dry. Wash the tomatoes, pat them dry and cut in half. Wash the thyme, shake it dry, then strip off the leaves and chop them finely.

4 Put the chops over direct heat, close the lid and grill for 6–8 minutes, turning once and seasoning with pepper. At the end, the core temperature should be 52–54°C (126–129°F). Take off the grill and leave to rest for 3–5 minutes.

5 Heat the oil in the preheated griddle, add the bacon lardons and fry for 2–3 minutes until golden. Add the onion, courgettes, peppers, tomatoes and pre-cooked beans and continue cooking for 3–4 minutes. Season the vegetables with salt and pepper and add the thyme. Remove the pan from the grill. Remove any wilted parsley sprigs, wash the parsley, shake dry and chop the leaves roughly.

6 To serve, spoon the vegetables on to plates and arrange 2–3 chops on top. Scatter the parsley over the chops and serve warm.

SERVES 4

12 lamb chops (100–120 g/3½–4¼ oz each)

1–2 tablespoons olive oil

fine sea salt

freshly ground black pepper

GREEN BEAN MEDLEY

1 onion

4 baby courgettes

8 baby pointed red peppers

100 g (3½ oz) cherry tomatoes

4 sprigs of thyme

50 g (1¾ oz) bacon lardons

1–2 tablespoons olive oil

250 g (8 oz) green beans, *pre-cooked*

3–4 sprigs of parsley

EQUIPMENT

1 GBS cast iron griddle

RACK OF LAMB
in hay

The hay wrapping imparts a lot of flavour into the meat, so it's best to use good-quality organic hay with plenty of wild flowers.

PREPARATION
25 minutes

COOKING TIME
40–45 minutes

COOKING METHOD
Direct/indirect heat

RESTING TIME
6–8 minutes

1 Prepare the grill for a medium to high indirect and direct heat (140–160°C/ 275–325°F).

2 Make the Herb mix, then stir in the dried parsley. Rub both racks of lamb all over with the oil and scatter over the Herb mix. Cut the head of garlic in half horizontally and separate the unpeeled halved cloves.

3 Moisten the hay with a few drops of water and lay half of it in the ceramic dish. Scatter the garlic cloves over the hay and place the lamb racks on top. Arrange the rest of the hay on top of the lamb racks, put the dish over an indirect heat, close the lid and cook for 40–45 minutes. At the end, the core temperature should be 52–54°C (126–129°F).

4 Meanwhile, fill a large bowl with 2 litres (3½ pints) cold water. Pour the juice from the 2 lemons into the water. Wearing disposable gloves, scrub the black salsify roots under cold running water, then trim the ends, cut in half and peel them. Place the peeled salsify roots in the lemon water until you're ready to use them, so that they don't go brown.

5 About 12–15 minutes before the end of the cooking time for the lamb racks, take the black salsify roots out of the lemon water and pat them dry. Wrap each with 1–2 bacon rashers and grill over a direct heat, turning occasionally, until the roots are soft and the bacon is crispy.

6 Remove the dish containing the lamb from the grill and leave the lamb racks to rest for 6–8 minutes. Take them out of the hay, cut into chops and season the cut surfaces with sea salt flakes and pepper to taste. Take the black salsify roots off the grill, cut them in half diagonally and serve warm with the chops.

SERVES 4

RACK OF LAMB

Herb mix (see page 52)

2–3 tablespoons dried parsley

2 lamb racks (600–800 g/1 lb 5 oz–1 lb 12 oz each), *silvery skin removed*

2 tablespoons olive oil

1 garlic bulb

sea salt flakes

freshly ground black pepper

BLACK SALSIFY

juice of 2 lemons

500 g (1 lb 2 oz) black salsify roots

12–16 bacon rashers

EQUIPMENT

3–4 handfuls of organic hay with wild flowers

1 ceramic BBQ dish

TIP: Meat grilled in hay smells and tastes incredible. Give it a try! The hay surrounding the lamb racks and the herbs give them a wonderfully refined flavour reminiscent of top-flight alpine cuisine.

VENISON
on cinnamon skewers

Long cinnamon sticks serve as skewers in this recipe. They pass on their exquisite flavour to the meat, and they look great, too!

PREPARATION
20 minutes

COOKING TIME
8–10 minutes

COOKING METHOD
Direct heat

RESTING TIME
5–8 minutes

1 Prepare the grill for a medium to high direct heat (200–220°C/400–425°F).

2 Cut the saddle of venison in half lengthways, then cut the halves into 4 equal medallions about 3 cm (1¼ inches) thick. Rub the medallions all over with oil and season with coarse sea salt to taste. Thread a medallion on to each cinnamon stick.

3 Wash and halve the cranberries. In a small pan, mix the honey with the measured water and vanilla seeds. Bring the mixture to the boil on the side burner or directly on the grill, then add the cranberries and simmer for 1–2 minutes. Remove from the grill and set aside.

4 To make the salad, wash, quarter and core the apples. Trim and wash the celery and cut the sticks in half. Rub the apples and celery with the oil, scatter over a little salt, then place them over a direct heat on the grill, close the lid and grill for 8–10 minutes, turning occasionally.

Remove from the grill, transfer to a bowl, cover with clingfilm and leave to rest for 5–8 minutes. Then cut into 1 cm (½ inch) pieces and mix in a bowl with the honey and orange juice.

5 Put the skewers over direct heat, close the lid and grill for 6–8 minutes, turning once, until the core temperature of the medallions reaches 55–57°C (131–135°F). Take off the grill and leave to rest for 3–5 minutes.

6 To serve, lay 2 skewers on each plate and top with the cranberries. Serve the salad alongside and up the flavour with a little Espresso & pepper spice mix, if you like.

SERVES 4

1 boneless saddle of venison (600–800 g/ 1 lb 5 oz–1 lb 12 oz), *without fat or sinews*

1–2 tablespoons oil

fine sea salt

freshly ground black pepper

CRANBERRIES

80 g (2¾ oz) fresh cranberries

25 g (1 oz) clear honey

50 ml (2 fl oz) water

seeds from ½ vanilla pod

APPLE & CELERY SALAD

2 red apples

2 celery sticks

1 tablespoon oil

2 tablespoons clear honey

juice of ½ orange

Espresso & pepper spice mix (see page 52), to serve (optional)

EQUIPMENT

8 cinnamon sticks (15–18 cm/6–7 inches long)

PICKLED CRANBERRIES

Fresh cranberries are bursting with flavour and packed with minerals and vitamin C, so these little red superfoods are an especially prized ingredient in autumn and winter. Unfortunately, they have a very bitter taste. To overcome it, it's a good idea to pickle them. We usually make a pickling broth from 400 ml (14 fl oz) water, 200 g (7 oz) clear honey, 2 dried lime leaves, 2–3 green cardamom pods, 2 cloves, 1 vanilla pod and a few grated tonka beans. Place everything in a pan and bring to the boil, then add 250 g (9 oz) halved cranberries and boil for 1–2 minutes. Allow to cool and store in airtight jars in the refrigerator.

VENISON CIABATTA
with port-braised onions

SERVES 4

1–2 tablespoons Espresso & pepper spice mix (see page 52)

4 venison fillets (60–80 g/2¼–2¾ oz each)

5–6 tablespoons melted butter

ONIONS

3 red onions

1–2 tablespoons clear honey

¼ teaspoon fine sea salt

juice of ½ lemon

50 ml (2 fl oz) white port

1 x Pickled cranberries (see page 187)

100 g (3½ oz) Basic mayonnaise (see page 58)

1 ciabatta loaf (ideally freshly baked)

sea salt flakes, to serve

freshly ground black pepper, to serve

EQUIPMENT

1 GBS cast iron griddle

 **PREPARATION**
15 minutes, plus
10 minutes marinating

 COOKING TIME
15 minutes

 max. max. max. **COOKING METHOD**
Direct heat

 RESTING TIME
2–3 minutes

1 Prepare the grill for a high direct heat (200–220°C/400–425°F). Make the Espesso & pepper spice mix. Put the griddle over a direct heat, close the lid and preheat for 6–8 minutes. Place the venison fillets on a chopping board, silvery skin facing down, and remove the skin with a sharp knife.

2 Brush the fillets with 1–2 tablespoons melted butter on both sides, then scatter over 1–2 tablespoons spice mix. Cover with baking parchment and leave at room temperature to marinate for about 10 minutes.

3 Meanwhile, peel and halve the onions and slice them thinly.

4 Put the honey in the griddle, add the onions, close the lid and cook for 4–5 minutes. Season with salt, deglaze with the lemon juice and pour in the port. Close the lid and braise the onions until the liquid has completely evaporated. Remove the griddle from the grill.

5 Mix half of the pickled cranberries with the mayonnaise in a small bowl.

6 Cut the ciabatta into 4 pieces and split them open. Brush the cut surfaces with the remaining melted butter, place over direct heat, close the lid and toast for 1–2 minutes, keeping an eye on them. At the same time, place the fillets over direct heat and grill for 3–4 minutes, turning once. At the end, the core temperature should be 56–58°C (133–136°F). Take the meat off the grill and leave the fillets to rest for 2–3 minutes.

7 Spread the cranberry mayonnaise over the bottom halves of the ciabatta. Spoon half of the onions on top. Cut the fillets diagonally into 1 cm (½ inch) thick slices and season the cut surfaces with sea salt flakes and pepper to taste. Place the venison slices on top of the onions, then top with the remaining onions and the drained cranberries.

POULTRY

Cornflake-crusted
CHICKEN

The cornflake crust and hot plancha make this chicken crispy on the outside and tender and succulent on the inside.

PREPARATION
15 minutes, plus
10–15 minutes
marinating

COOKING TIME
6–8 minutes

max.   max.   max.

COOKING METHOD
Direct heat

RESTING TIME
3–5 minutes

1 Prepare the grill for a medium to high direct heat (180–220°C/350–425°F). Preheat the plancha with the lid closed for 12–15 minutes.

2 Remove any sinews from the inner fillets. In a bowl, mix the orange zest and juice with the soy sauce, then season thoroughly with pepper. Lay the chicken fillets in the mixture, cover and leave to marinate in the refrigerator for about 10 minutes.

3 Meanwhile, make the coleslaw. Trim the cabbage and remove the stalk. Wash the cabbage, pat it dry and slice into very fine strips using a knife or a mandoline. Peel the carrots and slice into thin strips using a knife or a mandoline. Peel and finely dice the onion. In a large bowl, mix the vinegar with the honey, mustard, mayonnaise and buttermilk and season generously with sea salt and pepper. Add the cabbage and carrot strips and work the mixture through with your hands for a few minutes, until it softens a little. Cover and leave to infuse for about 10 minutes. Tear the parsley leaves from their stalks and chop them roughly.

4 Take the chicken fillets out of the marinade and pat them dry. Put the flour in a bowl and beat the eggs in a separate bowl. Crumble the cornflakes until you have a fine crumb and put them in a shallow-sided dish. Coat the fillets in the flour first, then dip them in the beaten egg and finally roll them in the cornflakes. Thread the cornflake-coated chicken fillets lengthwise on to the skewers.

5 Carefully coat the hot plancha with the oil, then add the chicken skewers and grill for 6–8 minutes with the lid closed, turning them once or twice, until the core temperature reaches 78–80°C (172–176°F). Take the skewers off the grill and leave to rest for 3–5 minutes.

6 Put the coleslaw in a dish and scatter over the chopped parsley. Serve the chicken skewers alongside the coleslaw and season with sea salt.

TIP: The coleslaw tastes best made with homemade mayonnaise (Basic mayonnaise, see page 58) and left to marinate overnight in the refrigerator before serving.

SERVES 4

CHICKEN BREAST FILLETS

8–12 chicken inner fillets

zest and juice of ½ unwaxed orange

4 tablespoons soy sauce

freshly ground black pepper

4 tablespoons flour

2 eggs

2 handfuls cornflakes

3–4 tablespoons oil

COLESLAW

½ white cabbage (about 800 g/1 lb 12 oz)

1 carrot

1 small onion

2 tablespoons white balsamic vinegar

4 tablespoons clear honey

1 teaspoon mustard

100 g (3½ oz) mayonnaise (see tip)

50 ml (2 fl oz) buttermilk

fine sea salt

25 g (1 oz) flat-leaf parsley

ACCESSORIES

1 plancha or cast iron griddle plate

8–12 bamboo or wooden skewers, soaked for at least 30 minutes.

SPATCHCOCK CHICKEN

This dish is sometimes nicknamed 'roadkill chicken', as the butterflying and flattening method makes it look as though it's been run over.

SERVES 4

CHICKEN

2 corn-fed chickens (about 1 kg/2 lb 4 oz each)

2 × Five-spice mix (see page 53)

1–2 dried chillies (optional)

2–3 tablespoons olive oil

HERB OIL

1 garlic clove

2 sprigs of rosemary, *washed and dried*

2 sprigs of thyme, *washed and dried*

75 g (3 oz) mixed soft herbs (such as tarragon, parsley, chives, chervil, salad burnet, cress), *washed and dried*

zest and juice of 1 unwaxed lemon

1 teaspoon sea salt

75 ml (3 fl oz) olive oil

freshly ground black pepper

 **PREPARATION**
15 minutes, plus
25–30 minutes
marinating

 COOKING TIME
40–45 minutes

 COOKING METHOD
Direct heat

 RESTING TIME
5–8 minutes

1 Place one of the chickens on a chopping board, breast side down. Using scissors, cut along one side of the backbone, from back to front.

2 Now cut along the other side of the backbone in the same way. Remove and discard the spine.

3 Turn the chicken over, pull it open and, using both hands, press down firmly to flatten it. Do the same with the other chicken.

4 Grind the dried chilli(es), if using, into the Five-spice mix. Brush both sides of the chicken with the oil, scatter over the spice mix, cover, put in the refrigerator and leave to marinate for 20 minutes. Prepare the grill for a medium to high direct heat (180–200°C/350–400°F). Meanwhile, make the herb oil. Peel the garlic clove, chop it finely and put it in a bowl. Strip the rosemary and thyme leaves from their stalks, chop them finely and add them to the garlic. Chop the soft herbs and stalks finely, add them to the bowl, mix with the lemon zest and juice, sea salt and olive oil, and season with pepper to taste.

5 Take the chickens out of the refrigerator and leave to stand for about 10 minutes to come up to room temperature. Place them over the direct heat on the grill rack, skin side down, press down lightly, close the lid and grill for 25–30 minutes. Turn the chickens, brush them with the herb-flavoured oil and grill for about 15 minutes, until their core temperature (measured at the thickest part of the thigh) reaches 78–80°C (172–176°F). Take them off the grill and leave to rest for 5–8 minutes before serving.

TIP: To prevent the chickens curling up while on the grill, you could weight them down with a cast iron casserole or frying pan so that they stay flat on the grill.

CHICKEN DRUMSTICKS

Drumsticks are the lower part of the chicken leg. They are small and quick to cook and easy to hold, making them the ideal finger food when catering for lots of guests.

TIP: Whatever flavourings you go for (and it will be a difficult choice!) the key things are to season the meat well before grilling and to factor in enough time for it to marinate in the refrigerator.

PREPARATION
15 minutes, plus
25–30 minutes
marinating

COOKING TIME
20–25 minutes

max. off max.

COOKING METHOD
Indirect heat

RESTING TIME
3–5 minutes

ⓐ BBQ drumsticks

To make these drumsticks, you'll need the BBQ spice mix for poultry (see page 53). Mix 1 kg (2 lb 4 oz) chicken drumsticks with 2–3 tablespoons olive oil, scatter over the spice mix evenly, cover and put in the refrigerator to marinate for 20 minutes. Prepare the grill for a medium to high indirect heat (180–200°C/350–400°F). Before grilling, take the chicken drumsticks out of the refrigerator and leave to stand for 5–10 minutes to come up to room temperature. Put them over an indirect heat, close the lid and cook for 20–25 minutes. Brush with 2–3 tablespoons of honey to serve.

ⓑ Lemon drumsticks

To make these drumsticks, you'll need the Lemon marinade with parsley (see page 54). Mix 1 kg (2 lb 4 oz) chicken drumsticks with the marinade, cover and put them in the refrigerator to marinate for 20 minutes. Prepare the grill for an indirect medium to high heat (180–200°C/350–400°F). Wipe the marinade off the drumsticks (reserving the marinade), then leave to stand for 5–10 minutes to come up to room temperature. Put them over an indirect heat, close the lid and cook for 20–25 minutes. About 5 minutes before the end of the cooking time, brush them with the remaining marinade until it is all used up.

ⓒ Chicken chilli drumsticks

To make these drumsticks, you'll need the Sweet chilli sauce (see page 57). Mix 1 kg (2 lb 4 oz) chicken drumsticks with 2–3 tablespoons of olive oil, season evenly with ½ teaspoon of fine sea salt, then cover and put in the refrigerator to marinate for 20 minutes. Prepare the grill for a medium to high indirect heat (180–200°C/ 350–400°F). Before grilling, take the drumsticks out of the refrigerator and leave to stand for 5–10 minutes to come up to room temperature. Put them over an indirect heat, close the lid and cook for 20–25 minutes. About 10 minutes before the end of the cooking time, brush them with the sauce and serve the remaining sauce alongside the drumsticks.

ⓓ Texan-style smoky drumsticks

To make these drumsticks, you'll need the Texas-style spice mix (see page 53). Mix 1 kg (2 lb 4 oz) chicken drumsticks with 2–3 tablespoons of olive oil, scatter over the spice mix evenly, cover and put in the refrigerator to marinate for 20 minutes. Prepare the grill for an indirect medium to high heat (180–200°C/350–400°F) and smoking. Before cooking, take the chicken drumsticks out of the refrigerator and leave to stand for 5–10 minutes to come up to room temperature. Put 1–2 handfuls of dry hickory chips into the smoker box and set them alight. As soon as thick smoke starts to form, place the drumsticks on the grill over an indirect heat, close the lid and smoke for 20–25 minutes. Brush the drumsticks with 2–3 tablespoons of honey to serve.

1 To shorten the grilling time by 5–8 minutes, score the inner side of the drumstick through to the bone.

2 Make the marinade or spice mix, place the drumsticks in the marinade or scatter the seasonings over them, then cover and put in the refrigerator to marinate. Take them out and let them come up to room temperature shortly before putting them on the barbecue.

3 Wipe off wet marinades before cooking so they don't burn. About 5–10 minutes before the end of the cooking time, brush the drumsticks with the remaining marinade until it is all used up. At the end, the core temperature of the drumsticks should be 76–78°C (169–172°F). Take off the grill and leave to rest for 3–5 minutes.

SMOKY CHICKEN WINGS

Here this classic dish from the city of Buffalo in New York state is given the BBQ treatment for a subtle sweetness and wonderfully smoky flavour.

SERVES 4

1 kg (2 lb 4 oz) chicken wings

BBQ spice mix for poultry (see page 53)

juice of 2 lemons

50 ml (2 fl oz) maple syrup

ACCESSORIES

1 smoker box

1–2 handfuls of dry applewood chips for smoking

1–2 handfuls of applewood chips for smoking, *soaked for at least 30 minutes*

1 large aluminium drip tray

 **PREPARATION**
15 minutes, plus
25–30 minutes
marinating

 COOKING TIME
20–25 minutes

 off   max.   max.
COOKING METHOD
Indirect heat

 RESTING TIME
3–5 minutes

1 Cut the chicken wings in half through the joint and place them in a bowl.

2 Make the spice mix and place in a bowl with the lemon juice and maple syrup to make a marinade.

3 Pour the marinade over the prepared chicken wings, mix thoroughly, cover and put in the refrigerator to marinate for about 20 minutes. Meanwhile, prepare the grill for a high direct heat (220–240°C/ 425–475°C).

4 Remove the grill racks and place the drip tray on the flavorizer bars over an indirect heat. Replace the grill racks. Put the dry chips in the smoker box over a high direct heat, close the lid and leave them to burn for 6–8 minutes.

5 Take the chicken out of the refrigerator 5–10 minutes before grilling. As soon as smoke starts to form, prepare the grill for a low to medium indirect heat (140–160°C/275–325°C). Put the smoker box in the indirect zone and top up with soaked wood chips.

6 Place the chicken wings over the drip tray, close the lid and smoke for 25–30 minutes. About 5–10 minutes before the end of the cooking time, brush them with the remaining marinade. At the end, the core temperature should be 76–78°C (169–172°F). Take off the grill and leave to rest for 3–5 minutes.

SWEET POTATO MASH ON THE SIDE

Put 600 g (1 lb 5 oz) diced sweet potatoes, 2 tablespoons butter and 150 g (5½ oz) cream in a pan, cover and cook over a medium heat for 15–20 minutes until tender, then mash roughly. Season the mash with 1–2 tablespoons of the spice mix you used for the wings (see pages 200–201). Mix 1 finely diced red onion with 1 tablespoon chopped rosemary, 1 tablespoon honey and the juice of ½ lime and scatter this mixture over the mash.

CHICKEN WINGS

With onion & rosemary

In a blender, blitz 1 peeled onion and 1 peeled garlic clove to a purée, then mix with the juice of ½ lime, ½ teaspoon salt, 1 tablespoon honey and 2 tablespoons roughly chopped rosemary. Prepare 1 kg (2 lb 4 oz) chicken wings as described on page 199 and mix with the marinade. Cover and put in the refrigerator to marinate for about 20 minutes. About 5–10 minutes before cooking, take the chicken wings out of the refrigerator and leave them to come up to room temperature. Wipe off any excess marinade and place the chicken wings over an indirect heat to grill as described on page 199, without smoking. About 5–10 minutes before the end of the cooking time, brush the wings with the remaining marinade.

With teriyaki sauce & sesame seeds

Mix 2 tablespoons light sesame oil or olive oil together with 150 ml (¼ pint) teriyaki sauce, the juice of ½ lemon and 2–3 tablespoons sesame seeds. Prepare 1 kg (2 lb 4 oz) chicken wings as described on page 199 and mix with the marinade. Cover and put in the refrigerator to marinate for about 20 minutes. About 5–10 minutes before you're ready to grill, take the chicken wings out of the refrigerator and leave them to come up to room temperature. Wipe off any excess marinade and place the chicken wings over an indirect heat to cook as described on page 199, without smoking. About 5–10 minutes before the end of the cooking time, brush the wings with the remaining marinade.

With curried mango

In a blender, blitz the flesh of ½ mango to a purée, then mix in the juice of ½ lime and ½ quantity of the Curry spice mix (see page 52). Prepare 1 kg (2 lb 4 oz) chicken wings as described on page 199 and mix with the marinade. Cover and put in the refrigerator to marinate for about 20 minutes. About 5–10 minutes before cooking, take the chicken wings out of the refrigerator and leave them to come up to room temperature. Wipe off any excess marinade and place the chicken wings over an indirect heat to cook as described on page 199, without smoking. About 5–10 minutes before the end of the cooking time, scatter the remaining spice mix over the chicken wings.

CLASSIC CHICKEN LEGS

TIP: If you've ever grilled chicken legs before, you'll know that paprika and other spices can burn before the skin gets properly crispy. To prevent this, always wait until 5–10 minutes before the end of the grilling time to brush the legs with a seasoned glaze – that way it won't burn and the chicken will taste even better.

PREPARATION
15 minutes

COOKING TIME
35–40 minutes

COOKING METHOD
Direct/indirect heat

RESTING TIME
3–5 minutes

ⓐ Paprika chicken legs

SERVES 4

4 chicken legs (about 250 g/9 oz each), 2 tablespoons oil, coarse sea salt, freshly ground black pepper

GLAZE

1 roasted red pepper from a jar, 1 teaspoon chopped thyme, 1 tablespoon sweet paprika, 1 tablespoon clear honey, 1 tablespoon tomato ketchup

Score each of the chicken legs 6–8 times, cutting 5 mm (¼ inch) into the flesh. Rub with the oil all over and season with coarse sea salt. Before grilling, leave them to stand for 10–15 minutes to come up to room temperature. Meanwhile, prepare the grill for a medium to high direct heat (180–220°C/350–425°F). Dice the pepper and mix with the thyme, paprika, honey and ketchup to make the glaze.

Put the chicken legs over a direct heat, close the lid and grill for 6–8 minutes on each side. Then move them to an indirect medium heat (160–180°C/325–350°F), close the lid and grill for 20–25 minutes until done – their core temperature should be 76–78°C (169–172°F). About 10 minutes before the end of the grilling time, brush them with the glaze until it is all used up and season with pepper. Take the chicken legs off the grill and leave to rest for 3–5 minutes before serving.

ⓑ Bourbon-glazed chicken legs

SERVES 4

4 chicken legs (about 250 g/9 oz each), 2 tablespoons oil, coarse sea salt

GLAZE

50 ml (2 fl oz) Bourbon, 50 ml (2 fl oz) craft beer, 2 tablespoons maple syrup, juice of 1 lemon, freshly ground black pepper

Score each of the chicken legs 6–8 times, cutting 5 mm (¼ inch) into the flesh. Rub with the oil all over and season with coarse sea salt. Before grilling, leave them to stand for 10–15 minutes to come up to room temperature. Meanwhile, prepare the grill for a medium to high direct heat (180–220°C/350–425°F). To make the glaze, mix the Bourbon, beer, maple syrup and lemon juice together and season with pepper.

Put the chicken legs over a direct heat, close the lid and grill for 6–8 minutes on each side. Then move them to an indirect medium heat (160–180°C/325–350°F), close the lid and grill for 20–25 minutes until done – their core temperature should be 76–78°C (169–172°F). About 10 minutes before the end of the grilling time, brush them with the glaze until it is all used up. Take the chicken legs off the grill and leave to rest for 3–5 minutes before serving.

ⓒ Chicken legs with lime & honey

SERVES 4

4 chicken legs (about 250 g/9 oz each), 2 tablespoons oil, coarse sea salt, 1 unwaxed lime

GLAZE

zest and juice of 2 unwaxed limes, 1 teaspoon grated ginger, 3 tablespoons brown sugar, 50 ml (2 fl oz) ginger ale, freshly ground black pepper

Score each of the chicken legs 6–8 times, cutting 5 mm (¼ inch) into the flesh. Rub with the oil all over and season with coarse sea salt. Before grilling, leave them to stand for 10–15 minutes to come up to room temperature. Meanwhile, prepare the grill for a medium to high direct heat (180–220°C/350–425°F). Wash the lime in hot water, rub it dry and cut into thin slices. To make the glaze, mix the zest and juice of the 2 limes thoroughly with the ginger, sugar and ginger ale, then season with pepper.

Put the chicken legs over a direct heat, close the lid and grill for 6–8 minutes on each side. Then move them to an indirect medium heat (160–180°C/325–350°F), close the lid and grill for 20–25 minutes until done – their core temperature should be 76–78°C (169–172°F). About 10 minutes before the end of the grilling time, brush them with the glaze until it is all used up. Take the chicken legs off the grill and leave to rest for 3–5 minutes before serving.

TIP: Scoring the flesh on the upper side of the leg as described can reduce the grilling time by 5-10 minutes.

Crispy **DUCK BREASTS**

It's best to go easy on the spices here, so that they don't overpower the flavours of the duck meat. With their crispy skin, these duck breasts are a feast for all the senses.

SERVES 4

4 duck breasts
   (250–300 g /9–10½ oz
   each)

100 g (3½ oz) coarse sea
   salt

2–3 tablespoons olive oil

sea salt flakes

freshly ground
   black pepper

ACCESSORIES

1 plancha or cast iron
   griddle

PREPARATION
15 minutes, plus
20 minutes standing

COOKING TIME
12–15 minutes

max. max. max.

COOKING METHOD
Direct heat

RESTING TIME
3–5 minutes

1 Remove any tendons or sinews from the meat side of the duck breasts. Turn the breasts over and use a sharp knife to score the fatty layer in a diagonal or criss-cross pattern, but without cutting into the meat itself.

2 In a large bowl, press the duck breasts into the sea salt one at a time, then put them in the refrigerator to stand for 20 minutes. Leave the duck uncovered to allow the salt to draw any excess water out of the fat and prevent the duck breasts sweating while they cook.

3 Prepare the grill for a medium to high direct heat (180–220°C/350–425°F). Preheat the plancha with the lid closed for 12–15 minutes. Wipe any excess salt off the duck breasts, using a little water if necessary, then pat them dry thoroughly. Rub them all over with the oil.

4 Place the duck breasts on the pre-heated plancha, skin side down. Press down on them with a barbecue slice for a few seconds so that they are lying flat against the plancha and the fatty side will cook evenly. Then close the lid and cook for 12–15 minutes, turning the duck breasts once, until their core temperature reaches 52–54°C (126–129°F). Take off the grill and leave to rest for 3–5 minutes.

5 Slice the duck breasts and season the cut surfaces with sea salt flakes and pepper to taste.

RED CABBAGE & FIG SALAD

This salad goes perfectly with the duck breasts. Trim and shred 300 g (10½ oz) red cabbage and ½ iceberg lettuce. Cut 3 figs into quarters, then into slices. Pick 6 sprigs of chervil and ½ bunch of watercress and discard any wilted leaves. To make the dressing, mix 2 teaspoons mustard with 2 teaspoons soured cream, 3 tablespoons white balsamic vinegar, 2–3 tablespoons water, 1 tablespoon honey and 2–3 tablespoons olive oil, then season with sea salt and freshly ground black pepper to taste. Mix the dressing with the cabbage, lettuce and figs, and finish with the fresh herbs.

FRUITY TURKEY SKEWERS

The mild flavour of turkey makes it ideal for combining with all sorts of ingredients such as onions, peppers and mango. Why not try a few different combinations?

SERVES 4–6

1 turkey breast (about 1 kg/2 lb 4 oz), *excess fat and sinews removed*

2–3 tablespoons olive oil

Curry spice mix (see page 52)

PEPPERS & ONIONS

1 red pepper

1 yellow pepper

2 red onions

2–3 tablespoons olive oil

WATERMELON

½ seedless watermelon (about 800 g/1 lb 12 oz)

2–3 tablespoons olive oil

AUBERGINE & PINEAPPLE

1 small pineapple

1 small aubergine

2–3 tablespoons olive oil

MANGO & AVOCADO

1 mango

1 avocado

2–3 tablespoons oil

ACCESSORIES

4–6 double-pronged skewers

PREPARATION
15 minutes

COOKING TIME
8–12 minutes

COOKING METHOD
Direct heat

RESTING TIME
3–5 minutes

ⓐ Peppers & onions

Prepare the turkey breast as described in Step 1. Season the meat, bring it up to room temperature and prepare the barbecue. Trim, quarter and deseed the two peppers and cut them into 3 cm (1¼ inch) pieces. Peel the onions and cut into wedges. Thread the vegetables on the skewers, alternating with the turkey pieces, then brush all over with the oil. Grill the skewers as described in Step 3, then leave to rest before serving.

ⓑ Watermelon

Prepare the turkey breast as described in Step 1. Season the meat, bring it up to room temperature and prepare the barbecue. Peel the watermelon and cut the flesh into 2–3 cm (¾–1¼ inch) chunks. Thread the watermelon chunks on the skewers, alternating with the turkey pieces, then brush all over with the oil. Grill the skewers as described in Step 3, then leave to rest before serving.

ⓒ Aubergine & pineapple

Prepare the turkey breast as described in Step 1. Season the meat, bring it up to room temperature and prepare the barbecue. Peel and quarter the pineapple, remove the core and cut the flesh into 3 cm (1¼ inch) chunks. Trim the aubergine, cut it into quarters lengthways, and then into 1 cm (½ inch) slices. Thread the fruit and vegetables on the skewers, alternating with the turkey pieces, then brush all over with the oil. Grill the skewers as described in Step 3, then leave to rest before serving.

ⓓ Mango & avocado

Prepare the turkey breast as described in Step 1. Season the meat, bring it up to room temperature and prepare the barbecue. Peel the mango and cut the flesh into 3 cm (1¼ inch) chunks. Halve the avocado, remove the stone and spoon out the flesh. Cut it into 3 cm (1¼ inch) chunks. Thread the mango and avocado on the skewers, alternating with the turkey pieces, then brush all over with the oil. Grill the skewers as described in Step 3, then leave to rest before serving.

1 Cut the turkey breast into 3 cm (1¼ inch) chunks and mix with 2–3 tablespoons olive oil and the spice mix until evenly coated. Cover and leave to stand for about 10 minutes to come up to room temperature. Prepare the grill for a medium to high direct heat (200–220°C/400–425°F).

2 Trim and peel the fruit or vegetables as necessary, then cut into 3 cm (1¼ inch) chunks. Thread the meat, fruit and vegetable chunks on to the skewers, then brush all over with the oil.

3 Put the skewers over a direct heat, close the lid and grill for 8–12 minutes, turning once, until the core temperature of the meat is 76–78°C (169–172°F). Take off the grill and leave to rest for 3–5 minutes.

TIP: When grilling poultry, fish or lean meat skewers, make sure that the chunks of fruit or veg have roughly the same texture and firmness as the meat or fish, so all of the ingredients cook evenly.

CORN-FED CHICKEN BREAST with asparagus

Grilling corn-fed chicken with its skin on and bones in really brings out its delicious flavour.

SERVES 4

CORN-FED CHICKEN

4 corn-fed chicken breasts, skin on with bones (about 250 g/ 9 oz each)

2–3 tablespoons olive oil

1 teaspoon coarse sea salt

freshly ground black pepper

ASPARAGUS

500 g (1 lb 2 oz) green asparagus

2–3 tablespoons olive oil

coarse sea salt

SESAME SAUCE

250 g (9 oz) drained canned chickpeas

3 tablespoons soured cream

1 tablespoon tahini (sesame paste)

juice of ½ lemon

2 tablespoons sesame seeds

3–4 tablespoons olive oil

4 tablespoons finely chopped flat-leaf parsley

PREPARATION
20 minutes

COOKING TIME
15–20 minutes

off   max.   max.

COOKING METHOD
Direct/indirect heat

RESTING TIME
3–5 minutes

1 Prepare the grill for a medium to high direct heat (180–220°C/350–425°F). Rub the chicken breasts all over with the oil, then season with sea salt and black pepper to taste. Cover the meat and leave to stand for about 10 minutes to come up to room temperature.

2 Meanwhile, peel the lower parts of the asparagus spears. Trim the woody ends by 2–3 cm (¾–1¼ inches).

3 Drizzle the asparagus with the oil and season with salt and pepper.

4 Use a food processor to blend the ingredients for the sesame sauce to a thick paste, then season with sea salt and pepper to taste.

5 Place the chicken over a direct heat on the grill rack, skin side down, close the lid and grill for 6–8 minutes, turning once. Transfer to an indirect heat and grill for 9–12 minutes until done and the core temperature reaches 72–76°C (162–169°F). Take off the grill and leave to rest for 3–5 minutes. Place the asparagus over a direct heat, close the lid and grill for 6–8 minutes, turning occasionally.

6 To serve, spread the sesame sauce on the plates and arrange the asparagus on top. Cut the chicken breasts in half, place them on top of the asparagus and season the cut sides with salt and pepper.

TIP: A chicken breast that comes with its skin and bones is known as a chicken supreme.

CORN-FED CHICKEN BREAST

With feta & petits pois

Prepare, grill and rest the corn-fed chicken breasts as described on page 209. To make the topping, mix 125 g (4½ oz) diced feta with 50 g (1¾ oz) defrosted petits pois, 2–3 tablespoons white balsamic vinegar and 2 tablespoons olive oil. Season with salt and freshly ground black pepper. Spoon over the grilled chicken breasts and scatter over a few lemon balm leaves.

With pineapple & wasabi nuts

Prepare, grill and rest the corn-fed chicken breasts as described on page 209. To make the topping, mix 300 g (10½ oz) finely diced pineapple with 2 tablespoons clear honey, juice of 1 lemon and ½ teaspoon finely chopped ginger, then season with salt and chilli powder to taste. Drizzle over the grilled chicken breasts and scatter over 1 tablespoon chopped wasabi nuts and a few fresh coriander leaves.

With tomatoes, mozzarella & rocket

Prepare, grill and rest the corn-fed chicken breasts as described on page 209. To make the topping, mix 2 finely diced tomatoes with 1 diced ball of buffalo mozzarella, 2–3 tablespoons olive oil, the juice of ½ lemon and a handful of rocket, then season with salt and freshly ground black pepper to taste. Spoon the topping on to or alongside the grilled chicken breasts and scatter over 2–3 tablespoons Parmesan shavings and 2 tablespoons toasted pine nuts.

FISH & SEAFOOD

MANGO SALMON CUTLETS
with cucumber & edamame

SERVES 4

SALMON CUTLETS

½ ripe mango

4 tablespoons ponzu (citrus-seasoned soy sauce)

juice of ½ lemon

1 red chilli

2 spring onions

4 salmon cutlets with skin (200–250 g/7–9 oz each and 2.5–3 cm/ 1–1¼ inches thick)

2–3 tablespoons olive oil

coarse sea salt

SALAD

2–3 baby cucumbers

1 red chilli

100 g (3½ oz) frozen edamame beans, *defrosted*

juice of ½ lemon

2 tablespoons honey

4 tablespoons olive oil

fine sea salt

freshly ground black pepper

small bunch of Thai basil

 **PREPARATION** 15 minutes, plus at least 30 minutes marinating

 COOKING TIME 10–12 minutes

 COOKING METHOD Direct heat

 RESTING TIME 3–5 minutes

1 Peel the mango, cut the flesh from the stone and blend to a purée using a hand-held blender. Mix in a bowl with the ponzu and lemon juice. Wash the chilli, pat dry and dice finely. Trim and wash the spring onions, cut in half lengthways and slice finely. Mix all of the ingredients together in the bowl.

2 Spread the marinade over the salmon cutlets, cover and put in the refrigerator to marinate for at least 30 minutes. Meanwhile, wash the baby cucumbers for the salad, pat them dry and slice thinly lengthways. Then wash, pat dry, deseed and finely dice the chilli. Mix the chilli and cucumbers with the edamame beans in a bowl. Whisk the lemon juice, honey, olive oil and a pinch of salt to make a dressing, pour into the bowl and toss everything together. Leave the salad to stand at room temperature.

3 Prepare the grill for a medium direct heat (160–180°C/325–350°F). Remove the salmon from the refrigerator, scrape off the excess marinade (reserving it for later) and pat the cutlets dry. Brush the cutlets with the oil and season with sea salt to taste.

4 Put the cutlets over a direct heat, close the lid and grill for 10–12 minutes, turning once halfway through.

5 Spread the marinade over the salmon cutlets and continue cooking until the core temperature reaches 58–65°C (136–149°F). Remove from the grill and leave to rest for 3–5 minutes.

6 Season the salad with salt and pepper and spoon on to plates. Remove the skin from the salmon and grill the skin for a few minutes more until crispy, then cut into pieces. Remove the bones from the cutlets, shred the flesh into bite-sized pieces and arrange on top of the salad with the crispy skin. Season with salt and top with Thai basil leaves.

FISH & CHIPS
with salmon

A perennial British favourite with a twist – firm, hearty salmon and crispy chips are cooked on a plancha and topped with onions and herbs.

SERVES 4

800 g (1 lb 12 oz) large floury potatoes

sea salt

hot paprika

600 g (1 lb 5 oz) salmon fillet (preferably from the middle of a Norwegian Atlantic salmon), *skin and bones removed*

flour for coating

6–8 tablespoons oil

BATTER

50 g (1¾ oz) cornflour

150 g (5 oz) plain flour

2 eggs

½ teaspoon salt

150 ml (¼ pint) pale ale

TO SERVE

1 red onion

1 handful of flat-leaf parsley

4 tablespoons champagne or tarragon vinegar

EQUIPMENT

1 plancha

1 wooden skewer

PREPARATION
10 minutes

COOKING TIME
20–25 minutes

max. max. max.

COOKING METHOD
Direct heat

1 Prepare the grill for a medium to high direct heat (200–220°C/400–425°F). Place the plancha on the grill and preheat for 12–15 minutes. Scrub the potatoes thoroughly and cut them into finger-sized chips. Place in water until ready to use.

2 Cut the salmon fillet into 3 cm (1¼ inch) chunks, season with a little salt and toss in flour to coat.

3 To make the batter, place the cornflour, plain flour, eggs and salt in a bowl, add the beer and whisk everything into a smooth mixture.

4 Remove the chips from the water and pat dry thoroughly. Drizzle half the oil on the preheated plancha and arrange the chips on it in a single layer. With the lid closed, cook for 15 minutes, turning occasionally, until tender. Season the chips with a little salt and paprika near the end of the cooking time. Meanwhile, for the topping, peel and finely chop the onion. Rinse and shake dry the parsley, then finely chop that too.

5 Push the chips to the back of the plancha. Drizzle the front of the plancha with the remaining oil. One by one, coat the chunks of salmon with the batter using the wooden skewer to dip them, then place them on the plancha. Cook for 6–8 minutes with the lid closed, turning them once.

6 Divide the fish and chips between the plates and season with a little extra sea salt and paprika. Top with the diced onion and parsley and serve the vinegar on the side.

FISH & CHIPS

FLAVOUR UPGRADE

Pollack loin & sweet potato

Prepare the grill as described on page 217 and preheat the plancha. Mix 800 g (1 lb 12 oz) sweet potato chips with 1–2 tablespoons soy sauce. Place the chips in a large resealable plastic bag, add 3–4 tablespoons cornflour, seal the bag and shake vigorously. Remove the chips from the bag, shaking off any excess cornflour. Drizzle 4 tablespoons oil on the plancha, arrange the sweet potato chips in a single layer, close the lid and cook for 12–15 minutes, turning occasionally. Cut 600 g (1 lb 5 oz) pollack loin into 3 cm (1¼ inch) chunks, season with sea salt and coat with 3–4 tablespoons cornflour. Push the chips to the back of the plancha. Drizzle 3–4 tablespoons oil on the free surface, place the fish pieces on it, close the lid and cook for 6–8 minutes, turning once. To serve, top the fish and chips with the pulp of 2 passion fruit and 4 tablespoons of chopped spring onions. Season with sea salt and hot paprika to taste.

Pike perch & beetroot

Prepare the grill as described on page 217 and preheat the plancha. Meanwhile, cut 800 g (1 lb 12 oz) peeled beetroot into finger-sized chips and mix with 2 tablespoons of Worcestershire sauce. Place the beetroot chips in a large resealable plastic bag, add 3–4 tablespoons of cornflour, seal the bag and shake vigorously. Remove the chips from the bag and shake off any excess cornflour. Drizzle 3–4 tablespoons oil on the preheated plancha, then arrange the beetroot chips on it in a single layer, close the lid and cook for 12–15 minutes, turning occasionally. Cut 600 g (1 lb 5 oz) skinless pike perch fillet into 2–3 cm (¾–1¼ inch) chunks. Season the fish chunks with salt, coat them in 4–5 tablespoons of flour, dip them in 2 beaten eggs and then roll them in a handful of panko breadcrumbs. Push the beetroot to the back of the plancha. Drizzle 3–4 tablespoons oil on the free surface, place the fish pieces on top, close the lid and cook for 6–8 minutes, turning once. To serve, top the fish and chips with 2 tablespoons chopped chives, the juice of ½ lemon and 2 tablespoons freshly grated horseradish (or from a jar). Season with salt and ground black pepper.

Arctic char & root vegetables

Prepare the grill as described on page 217 and preheat the plancha. Meanwhile, peel 800 g (1 lb 12 oz) parsnips or carrots and cut them lengthways into finger-sized chips. Season with ½ teaspoon sea salt and toss with 3–4 tablespoons oil. Spread the root vegetables out on the plancha in a single layer, close the lid and cook for 12–15 minutes, turning occasionally. Cut 600 g (1 lb 5 oz) skinless char fillet into 2–3 cm (¾–1¼ inch) chunks. Season the chunks of fish with salt, toss them with 4–5 tablespoons flour, dip them in 2 beaten eggs and then roll them in a handful of breadcrumbs to coat. Push the root vegetables to the back of the plancha. Drizzle 3–4 tablespoons oil on the free surface, place the fish pieces on top, close the lid and cook for 6–8 minutes, turning once. To serve, scatter 2 tablespoons finely chopped flat-leaf parsley over the fish and chips, drizzle over the juice of ½ orange and season to taste with sea salt and ground black pepper.

Grilled
SALMON STEAK

Salmon is perfect for grilling, because its high fat content makes the flesh stay juicy, even if the temperature on the grill is hot.

SERVES 4

SALMON STEAKS

4 skin-on boneless salmon steaks (about 250 g/9 oz each)

Fish & seafood seasoning mix (see page 53)

2 tablespoons oil

SAUCE

1 handful dill sprigs, *rinsed and shaken dry*

4 tablespoons wild honey

2 tablespoons fine Dijon mustard

2 tablespoons coarse Dijon mustard

juice of ½ lime

sea salt flakes, to serve (optional)

PREPARATION
5 minutes, plus
10–12 minutes marinating

COOKING TIME
10–12 minutes

COOKING METHOD
Direct heat

RESTING TIME
3–5 minutes

1 Prepare the grill for a medium direct heat (170–180°C/340–350°F). Scatter the seasoning mix over the salmon steaks on the flesh side, cover and marinate for 10–12 minutes at room temperature. Brush the skin of the steaks with oil.

2 Place the steaks on the grill over direct heat, skin side down, and grill for 5–6 minutes.

3 Brush the flesh of the salmon with a little oil, turn the steaks over, close the lid and continue grilling for 5–6 minutes until the core temperature reaches 58–64°C (136–147°F). Remove the steaks from the grill and leave them to rest for 2–3 minutes. Meanwhile, finely chop the dill for the sauce. Mix the honey with both the mustards and the lime juice until smooth, then stir in the dill. To serve, top the salmon steaks with the sauce and season with sea salt flakes as desired.

TIP: Have you ever stumbled across the terms 'wild salmon' and 'wild water salmon' while shopping? They do not mean the same thing! Wild salmon lives in the wild and is also caught there, whereas wild water salmon comes from a fish farm where the fish are kept in running water.

SALMON STEAK

FLAVOUR UPGRADE

With horseradish & diced potato

Rub the salmon steaks with 1–2 tablespoons oil and season the flesh side with sea salt. Then grill as described on page 221.

For the topping, put 250 g (9 oz) peeled and diced waxy potatoes in a frying pan with 2–3 tablespoons oil over a medium heat and fry for 8–10 minutes until crispy. Drain on kitchen paper and season with salt and freshly ground black pepper. Cut 4 radishes into thin slices with a mandoline. Mix 150 g (5½ oz) soured cream with 2 tablespoons finely chopped flat-leaf parsley and 1 teaspoon wholegrain mustard and season with salt and pepper. Top the salmon with the soured cream mixture and add the diced potato, radish slices and 1 teaspoon of finely chopped parsley. Top with 2 tablespoons of freshly grated horseradish (or from a jar).

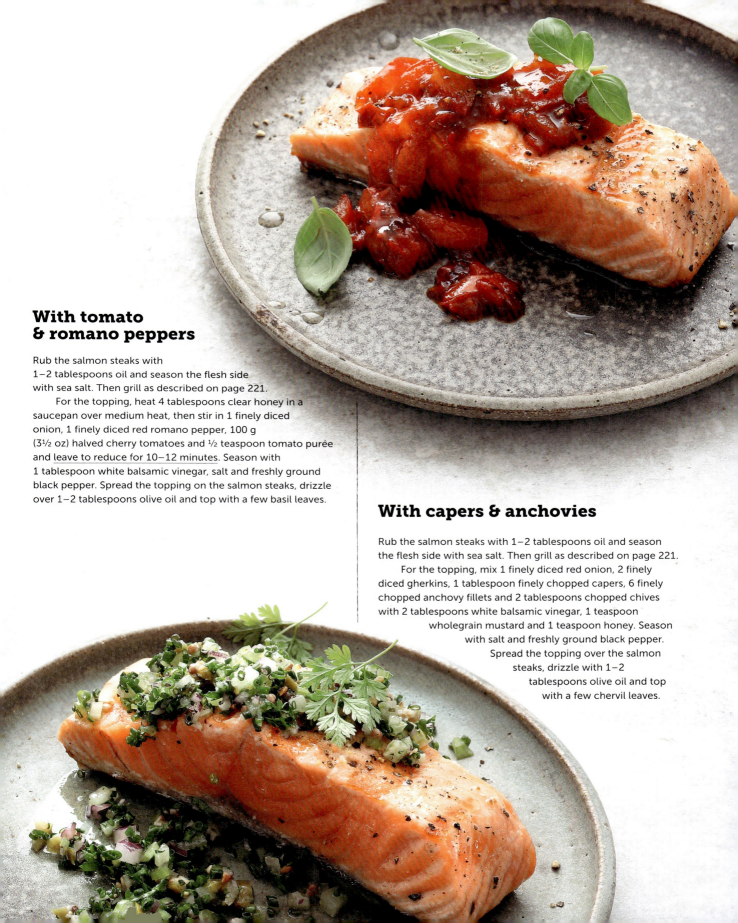

With tomato
& romano peppers

Rub the salmon steaks with
1–2 tablespoons oil and season the flesh side
with sea salt. Then grill as described on page 221.

For the topping, heat 4 tablespoons clear honey in a
saucepan over medium heat, then stir in 1 finely diced
onion, 1 finely diced red romano pepper, 100 g
(3½ oz) halved cherry tomatoes and ½ teaspoon tomato purée
and leave to reduce for 10–12 minutes. Season with
1 tablespoon white balsamic vinegar, salt and freshly ground
black pepper. Spread the topping on the salmon steaks, drizzle
over 1–2 tablespoons olive oil and top with a few basil leaves.

With capers & anchovies

Rub the salmon steaks with 1–2 tablespoons oil and season
the flesh side with sea salt. Then grill as described on page 221.

For the topping, mix 1 finely diced red onion, 2 finely
diced gherkins, 1 tablespoon finely chopped capers, 6 finely
chopped anchovy fillets and 2 tablespoons chopped chives
with 2 tablespoons white balsamic vinegar, 1 teaspoon
wholegrain mustard and 1 teaspoon honey. Season
with salt and freshly ground black pepper.
Spread the topping over the salmon
steaks, drizzle with 1–2
tablespoons olive oil and top
with a few chervil leaves.

COD LOIN
with Serrano ham & fennel

SERVES 4

COD

2 cod loins (250–300 g/
9–10½ oz each)

2 tablespoons Basic
mayonnaise
(see page 58)

2 tablespoons Dijon
mustard

sea salt and freshly
ground black pepper

40 g (1½ oz) mixed herbs
(such as flat-leaf
parsley, chives, chervil),
plus extra to serve

10 slices Serrano ham

FENNEL SALAD

1–2 fennel bulbs (about
400 g/14 oz)

8 radishes

3 tablespoons clear honey

juice and zest of
½ unwaxed lemon

3–4 tablespoons olive oil

EQUIPMENT

kitchen string,
pre-soaked in water

PREPARATION
20 minutes

COOKING TIME
8–10 minutes

max.   max.   max.

COOKING METHOD
Direct heat

RESTING TIME
3–5 minutes

1 Prepare the grill for a medium to high direct heat (180–200°C/350–400°F). Mix the mayonnaise and mustard in a bowl and season with salt and pepper.

2 Sort through the herbs, discarding any wilted leaves, then rinse, shake dry and chop finely. Set aside one-third of the herbs.

3 Coat the cod loins with some of the mayonnaise and roll in the remaining two-thirds of the herbs. Lay out 5 slices of Serrano ham on a work surface, slightly overlapping, then place one cod loin at one end and roll it up in the ham. Repeat with the remaining ham and cod loin. Tie in place using the kitchen string.

4 Put the loins over a direct heat, close the lid and grill for 8–10 minutes, turning once, until their core temperature reaches 58–60°C (136–140°F). Remove from the grill and rest for 3–5 minutes.

5 Clean the fennel, halve it and cut into thin slices. Place in a bowl and mix with the honey, the zest and juice of the lemon and the oil. Season with salt and pepper. Slice the radishes thinly and top the fennel salad with the radishes and reserved herbs.

6 Spread the remaining mayonnaise on the plates. Remove the string from the loins, cut the loins into medallions and arrange them on the mayonnaise. Serve with the fennel salad and garnish with extra herb leaves.

SEA BREAM
à la bordelaise

Royal bream and other types of sea bream are popular fish: with their firm, aromatic flesh, they are perfect for grilling whole, stuffing or cooking as fillets.

SERVES 4

1 royal sea bream
(1–1.2 kg/2 lb 4 oz–2 lb 10 oz), *gutted and scaled*

1–2 tablespoons olive oil

Fish & seafood seasoning mix (see page 53)

BORDELAISE CRUMB

½ onion, *finely diced*

3 tablespoons finely chopped flat-leaf parsley

50 g (1¾ oz) breadcrumbs or panko breadcrumbs

40 g (1½ oz) grated Parmesan

1 egg

zest of 1 unwaxed lemon

50 g (1¾ oz) butter, softened

EQUIPMENT

1 cedarwood smoking plank, *soaked for at least 1 hour*

 **PREPARATION**
15 minutes, plus
10–15 minutes
marinating

 COOKING TIME
10–12 minutes

 COOKING METHOD
Direct/indirect heat

 RESTING TIME
3–5 minutes.

1 Prepare the grill for a high to very high direct heat (240–260°C/475–500°F). Remove the fins from the bream and cut off the head using a V-cut, coming in from either side.

2 Use a sharp knife to remove the top fillet by slicing horizontally above the central bone. Turn the fish over and remove the other fillet in the same way.

3 Carefully run your knife under any belly cavity bones lying on the surface of the fillets to remove them, then use tweezers to pull out any other bones in the fish.

4 Prepare the Fish & seafood seasoning mix. Rub the fillets with the oil and scatter over 1 tablespoon of the seasoning mix. Cover with baking parchment and put in the refrigerator to marinate for 10–15 minutes. For the topping, mix the ingredients together in a bowl and season with ½ teaspoon seasoning mix.

5 Place the cedarwood smoking plank over a direct heat, close the lid and char for 4–6 minutes on each side. Allow to cool a little. Prepare the grill for a medium to high indirect heat (180–200°C/350–400°F). Place the fillets with the skin side down on the plank and spread the topping on the fish.

6 Put the fillets on the plank over an indirect heat, close the lid and cook for 10–12 minutes until the core temperature reaches 58–64°C (136–147°F). Remove from the grill and leave to rest on the plank for 3–5 minutes before serving.

ROYAL SEA BREAM
in a salt crust

The salt crust ensures the fish cooks in its own juices and doesn't dry out. Just be careful not to damage the skin of the fish while preparing it.

SERVES 4

1 royal sea bream (1.4–1.6 kg/3 lb–3 lb 8 oz) or 2 royal sea bream (800 g/1 lb 12 oz each), *gutted and scaled*

1 handful of rocket

5 kumquats

2–3 tablespoons dried rose petals (or sprigs of rosemary, thyme and bay leaves)

SALT CRUST

4 egg whites

1.5–1.8 kg (3 lb 5 oz–4 lb) coarse sea salt

EQUIPMENT

1 sheet of baking parchment, *pre-soaked*

1 plancha

PREPARATION
15 minutes

COOKING TIME
35–40 minutes

max. off max.

COOKING METHOD
Indirect heat

RESTING TIME
10 minutes

1 Prepare the grill for a medium to high indirect heat (200–220°C/ 400–425°F). Cut the fins off the fish and rinse the cavity under cold running water then pat dry.

2 For the salt crust, whisk the egg whites with 4 teaspoons water in a small bowl. Place the salt in a large bowl and thoroughly mix in the egg whites.

3 Line the plancha with the pre-soaked baking parchment and spread one-third of the salt on it. Sort through the rocket, discarding any wilted leaves, then wash it and shake dry. Slice the kumquats.

4 Place the sea bream on the bed of salt and fill the cavity with the rocket. Scatter the kumquats and rose petals over the fish and cover the fish completely with the remaining salt.

5 Put the plancha over an indirect heat, close the lid and cook for 35–40 minutes, until the core temperature reaches 60–64°C (140–147°F). Remove the plancha from the grill and leave to rest for 10 minutes. To serve, tap the salt crust all over to break it, carefully remove it, then peel off the skin of the fish.

TIP: If you are expecting a number of guests and want to prepare several sea breams, you could place an additional sheet of baking parchment over the fish before covering them with the salt crust, making it quicker and easier to remove the salt after cooking.

FISH IN A PARCEL

FLAVOUR UPGRADE

Brown trout in newspaper

Prepare the grill for medium indirect heat (180°C/350°F). Season a scaled and gutted brown trout (1 kg/2 lb 4 oz) inside and out with sea salt and freshly ground black pepper. Rinse 2 unwaxed lemons in hot water, rub dry and cut into slices. Sort through 100 g (3½ oz) fresh herbes de Provence (rosemary, thyme and bay leaves), then rinse and shake dry. Place 2 sheets of newspaper on top of each other and spread one-third of the lemon slices and herbs on it. Place the trout on top, fill the cavity with another third of the lemon slices and herbs and then place the remainder on top of the fish. Fold the paper in at the sides and roll up the fish in the paper. Place the fish parcel over indirect heat on the grate, close the lid and grill for about 25 minutes, turning occasionally, until the core temperature reaches 60–64°C (140–147°F). Remove from the grill and leave to rest for 5 minutes before serving.

Wood-wrapped pollock

Prepare the grill for a medium to high direct heat (200°C/400°F). Season 4 pollock loins (about 200 g/7oz each) with sea salt and freshly ground black pepper. Mix 150 g (5½ oz) root vegetables, cut into matchsticks, with 1 teaspoon diced ginger and 1 teaspoon finely chopped red chilli. Stir in 3 tablespoons fish sauce, 1 tablespoon clear honey and 1 tablespoon chopped coriander leaves. Divide half the vegetables between four BBQ wood wraps that have been pre-soaked for at least 30 minutes. Place a pollock loin on each and top the loins with the remaining vegetables. Roll up the wraps and tie up with kitchen string pre-soaked in water. Put the loins over a direct heat, close the lid and grill for 8–10 minutes, turning once, until the core temperature reaches 62–65°C (144–149°F).

Banana leaf salmon

Prepare the grill for a medium to high direct heat (200°C/400°F). Meanwhile, prepare the Basic spice mix (see page 52). Put 2 banana leaves (from the chiller cabinet at Asian supermarkets) over a direct heat and grill for a few seconds, turning once, to make the leaves softer and more flexible. Cut the banana leaves to make 4 pieces 30 cm (12 inches) wide. Place 2 slices of tomato and 2 slices of lemon in the middle of each piece of leaf. Scatter the spice mix over 4 skinless salmon fillets (about 200 g/7 oz each) and place them on top. Scatter with 4 tablespoons sliced mangetout and 2 small sliced romano peppers and drizzle over 1 tablespoon olive oil. Top each with 1 sprig of thyme then fold the long sides of the banana leaves over the fillets and then tuck the short sides underneath. Put the parcels over a direct heat, close the lid and grill for 8–10 minutes, turning once, until their core temperature reaches 58–64°C (136–147°F).

Sashimi **TUNA** with lemon vinaigrette

Tuna of the highest quality, briefly grilled on both sides – this is a quick, top-class dish!

PREPARATION
20 minutes, plus 10–15 minutes marinating

COOKING TIME
6–8 minutes

COOKING METHOD
Direct heat

RESTING TIME
3–5 minutes

1 Prepare the grill for a high to very high direct heat (240–260°C/ 475–500°F).

2 For the vinaigrette, blanch the lemons in boiling water for a few seconds, then take them out and leave to cool. Zest 1 of the lemons, then halve it and squeeze out the juice. Cut the second lemon into thin slices using a sharp knife or a mandoline.

3 Place the lemon juice and the measured water in a small fireproof pan with the honey and lime leaves. Add the zest and lemon slices, bring to the boil, then remove the pan from the heat and leave the vinaigrette to stand for about 10 minutes.

4 In the meantime, rub the tuna steaks all over with oil and, with the lid open, grill over a direct heat for 6–8 minutes, turning once, until the core temperature reaches 42–46°C (108–115°F). Remove the tuna from the grill, brush with the soy sauce, scatter the seasoning mix evenly over it and leave to rest for 3–5 minutes.

5 Strain the vinaigrette through a sieve and transfer the lemon slices and zest to a plate. Season the vinaigrette with salt and pepper and stir in the olive oil. Sort through the rocket, discarding any wilted leaves, then wash it and shake dry. In a bowl, toss the rocket with the vinaigrette, zest and lemon slices.

6 Place the tuna on plates and cut into slices as desired. Arrange the rocket salad next to the tuna and drizzle over any remaining vinaigrette from the bowl.

SERVES 4

4 tuna steaks (about 200 g/7 oz each and 3 cm/1¼ inches thick)

1– 2 tablespoons oil

2 tablespoons soy sauce

Fish & seafood seasoning mix (see page 53)

100 g (3½ oz) rocket

VINAIGRETTE

2 unwaxed lemons

50 ml (2 fl oz water)

50 g (1¾ oz) clear honey

2 dried lime leaves

sea salt and freshly ground black pepper

4–6 tablespoons olive oil

EQUIPMENT

1 small fireproof pan

TIP: Did you know that sashimi not only refers to a specific cut, but also to the second highest-quality level of fish such as tuna or salmon? The highest level is called super sashimi.

Sashimi TUNA

With lemongrass & pickled pumpkin

Prepare the Asian-inspired marinade (see page 54). Rub the tuna steaks on both sides with two-thirds of the marinade and put in the refrigerator to marinate for at least 30 minutes. Meanwhile, cut ¼ small pumpkin lengthways into very fine slices. Mix 50 g (1¾ oz) clear honey with 50 ml (2 fl oz) white balsamic vinegar and 4 tablespoons olive oil in a saucepan and bring to the boil. Remove the pan from the heat, add the pumpkin slices and leave to stand for 12–15 minutes. Sort through 125 g (4½ oz) lamb's lettuce, discarding any wilted leaves, then wash it and shake dry.

Take the tuna steaks out of the marinade, reserving the marinade in the bowl, then place the bowl of marinade next to the grill. Grill the steaks as described in Step 4 on page 233 and, after turning, coat them with the remaining marinade and finish grilling. Remove from the grill and leave to rest for 3–5 minutes. Remove the pumpkin from the liquid and mix in a bowl with the lamb's lettuce. Drizzle over the liquid from the saucepan and the remaining third of the marinade. Arrange the tuna steaks on plates, scatter with coriander leaves and serve with the pumpkin salad.

With cucumber & carrot pickles

Prepare the Basic spice mix (see page 52). Peel 2 carrots, wash ½ cucumber and rub dry. Then cut the carrots and cucumber into very fine strips. Mix 50 g (1¾ oz) clear honey with 50 ml (2 fl oz) white balsamic vinegar and 4 tablespoons olive oil in a saucepan and bring to the boil. Remove from the heat, add the carrot and cucumber strips and leave to stand for 12–15 minutes. Roughly chop some dill sprigs, wash ¼ head of frisée lettuce and shake dry. Rub oil all over the tuna steaks and grill as described in Step 4 on page 233. Remove from the grill, scatter over the seasoning mix and leave to rest for 3–5 minutes. Mix the carrot and cucumber strips and their liquid with the dill and frisée. Cut the tuna into slices and serve with the vegetable pickles and salad.

With romaine salad & sweet & sour grilled onions

Prepare the grill for medium to high indirect heat (200°C/400°F). Meanwhile, prepare the Texan-style spice mix (see page 53). Put 3 red onions, with skin on, over an indirect heat, close the lid and grill for about 20 minutes. Remove from the grill and leave to rest for 10 minutes. Mix 2 tablespoons white balsamic vinegar with 1 tablespoon clear honey and 4 tablespoons olive oil. Peel the cooled onions, cut into wedges and mix with the sweet and sour dressing. Wash 2 romaine lettuce hearts and shake dry. Mix 1 teaspoon mustard with 100 g (3½ oz) yogurt, 1 tablespoon mayonnaise and 4 tablespoons olive oil and season the yogurt dressing with sea salt and freshly ground black pepper. Prepare the grill for a high to very high direct heat (240–260°C/475–500°F).

Rub oil all over the tuna steaks and grill as described in Step 4 on page 233. Remove from the grill, scatter over the seasoning mix and leave to rest for 3–5 minutes. Mix the romaine lettuce with the yogurt dressing. Slice the tuna steaks and arrange on plates with the salad and grilled onions.

PRAWN KEBABS
with watermelon gazpacho

For an extra burst of flavour, add 100 ml (3½ fl oz) of plum wine to the gazpacho.

SERVES 4

4 raw XXL giant shell-on prawns (heads removed and deveined) or 8–12 large tiger prawns (size 8/12)

MARINADE

1 small garlic clove

1 walnut-sized piece of ginger

1 red chilli

½ teaspoon red curry paste

juice of ½ unwaxed lemon

1 tablespoon ponzu (citrus seasoned soy sauce)

4 tablespoons light sesame oil or olive oil

GAZPACHO

1 small watermelon (about 1 kg/2 lb 4 oz)

1 walnut-sized piece of ginger

1 red chilli

1 tablespoon brown sugar

juice of ½ lemon

sea salt

3–4 tablespoons olive oil

a few sprigs of coriander

EQUIPMENT

4 wooden skewers (25 cm/10 inches long), *pre-soaked for at least 30 minutes*

PREPARATION
15 minutes, plus
15 minutes marinating

COOKING TIME
6–8 minutes

max. max. max.

COOKING METHOD
Direct heat

1 To make the marinade, peel and finely chop the garlic and ginger. Halve the chilli lengthways, remove the seeds, wash and finely dice. Mix the ingredients with the curry paste, lemon juice, ponzu and oil in a large bowl. Prepare the grill for a medium to high direct heat (200–220°C/400–425°F).

2 Lift the shells of the prawns away from the flesh slightly and spread some marinade under them. Place the prawns in the remaining marinade, cover and put in the refrigerator to marinate for about 15 minutes.

3 While the prawns marinate, cut a thin slice off the base of the watermelon so it stands up, without damaging the flesh. Then cut a 3–4 cm (1¼–1½ inch) thick lid off the top of the melon. Use a spoon to scoop out the flesh from the melon lid and cut it into 1 cm (½ inch) cubes, then completely hollow out the melon. Cut one-third of the flesh into cubes and purée the rest using a hand-held blender. Peel and finely chop the ginger. Cut the chilli in half lengthways, remove the seeds and finely dice. Mix the puréed watermelon with the ginger, chilli, sugar, lemon juice and olive oil. Season to taste with salt. Finely chop the coriander leaves and add to the melon cubes.

4 Remove the excess marinade from the prawns and thread them on the pre-soaked skewers.

5 Place the prawns over a direct heat, close the lid and grill for 6–8 minutes, turning once.

6 Fill the hollowed-out watermelon with the gazpacho, add the melon cubes and coriander leaves and garnish with coriander sprigs. Serve the hot prawn skewers with the cold gazpacho.

TIP: If the gazpacho is too sweet, add a little extra lemon juice. If you don't like fresh coriander, try using chervil, cress or flat-leaf parsley instead.

PRAWNS

TIP: You can use different spice mixtures to refine the taste of the prawns. The prawns are delicious with the Curry spice mix (see page 52), BBQ spice mix for poultry (see page 53) or Texas-style spice mix (see page 53) – but take care not to salt the prawns too much before grilling if you have used a spice mix.

ⓐ With papaya & raspberry vinaigrette

Prepare the grill for a medium to high direct heat (200–220°C/400–425°F). Peel 8–12 large tiger prawns, season with sea salt and mix with 1–2 tablespoons light sesame oil or olive oil. Set aside. Peel ½ papaya and slice it into wedges. Cut 50 g (1¾ oz) cleaned mangetout diagonally in half and blanch briefly. Sort through 250 g (9 oz) raspberries and discard any spoilt fruit. For the vinaigrette, mix 2 tablespoons clear honey, 2 tablespoons raspberry vinegar, 1 tablespoon sesame seeds and 3–4 tablespoons light sesame oil or olive oil in a large bowl, then season with sea salt and freshly ground black pepper. Mix in the papaya wedges, mangetout and raspberries.

Place the prawns over a direct heat, close the lid and grill for 5–6 minutes, turning once. Mix the warm prawns with the papaya salad, arrange in bowls and top with the zest of an unwaxed lemon.

ⓑ With Pattaya mango & spring onion

Prepare the grill for a medium to high direct heat (200–220°C/400–425°F). Peel 8–12 large tiger prawns, season with sea salt and mix with 1–2 tablespoons olive oil. Set aside. Peel 1 mango (preferably the Thai variety Nam Dok Mai), then chop the flesh into chunks. Trim and wash 2 spring onions, pat dry, then slice diagonally into rings. For the vinaigrette, mix 4 tablespoons clear honey with the pulp of 1–2 passion fruit, 1 teaspoon grated ginger, 1 teaspoon finely diced red chilli and 6 tablespoons olive oil in a bowl. Season with sea salt and chilli powder. Mix the mango and spring onions with the vinaigrette and arrange in bowls.

Place the prawns over a direct heat, close the lid and grill for 5–6 minutes, turning once. Remove from the grill and serve on the mango mixture.

ⓒ With French beans

Prepare the grill for a medium to high direct heat (200–220°C/400–425°F). Peel 8–12 large tiger prawns, season with sea salt and mix with 1–2 tablespoons olive oil. Set aside. In a bowl, mix 1 tablespoon finely diced sun-dried tomatoes and 1 tablespoon finely diced olives with ½ finely diced green pepper, ½ finely diced red pepper, 1 finely diced red onion and 8 cm (3¼ inches) of cucumber, finely diced. Whisk 4 tablespoons olive oil with 2 tablespoons balsamic vinegar, 2 tablespoons clear honey and 1 teaspoon wholegrain mustard and season to taste with sea salt and freshly ground black pepper. Mix with the ingredients in the bowl. Add 300 g (10½ oz) blanched French beans, toss together and arrange in bowls.

Place the prawns over a direct heat, close the lid and grill for 5–6 minutes, turning once. Remove from the grill and serve in the bowls.

ⓓ With coconut & lemon grass

Prepare the grill for a medium to high direct heat (200–220°CF/400–425°CF). Preheat a cast iron griddle pan. Score 8–12 large shell-on tiger prawns down their backs, about half way through the flesh. Slice 1 red onion, 100 g (3½ oz) cleaned mangetout and 1 trimmed pointed pepper. Finely chop 1 clove of garlic and 1 walnut-sized piece of ginger. Slice 1 chilli and cook 200 g (7 oz) rice noodles according to the packet instructions.

Cut 2 lemon grass stalks in half diagonally and place with 4 tablespoons groundnut oil in the preheated griddle pan. Add the prawns and sauté for 3–4 minutes. Add the remaining ingredients except for the noodles, stir and deglaze with 4 tablespoons fish sauce, 150 ml (¼ pint) chicken stock and 200 ml (7 fl oz) coconut milk. Close the lid and allow the mixture to simmer for 4–5 minutes. Arrange the noodles in bowls, add the prawns with the stock and vegetables and top with lemon balm leaves.

OCTOPUS WITH CHORIZO from the plancha

Prepared this way, octopus is wonderfully tender and aromatic.

SERVES 4

1 octopus (700–800 g/ 1 lb 9 oz–1 lb 12 oz), *cleaned and prepared*

1 cured chorizo (about 200 g/7 oz)

2 onions

2 garlic cloves

1 unwaxed lemon

3–4 tablespoons olive oil

sea salt

freshly ground black pepper

STOCK

2 onions

about 500 g (1 lb 2 oz) mixed stock vegetables (carrots, leeks, celery)

large bunch of parsley

40 g (1½ oz) fresh herbes de Provence (rosemary, thyme and bay leaves)

25 g (1 oz) sea salt

3 litres (5¼ pints) water

EQUIPMENT

1 Dutch oven or cast-iron casserole

1 plancha

PREPARATION
20 minutes

COOKING TIME
1 hour 10 minutes–1 hour 15 minutes

max.   max.   max.

COOKING METHOD
Direct heat

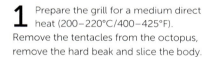

1 Prepare the grill for a medium direct heat (200–220°C/400–425°F). Remove the tentacles from the octopus, remove the hard beak and slice the body.

2 Peel and slice the onions for the stock. Peel the stock vegetables and cut them into large chunks. Roughly chop the parsley. Put all the stock ingredients, reserving a little of the parsley for serving, into the casserole. Place the pot over a direct heat, close the lid and bring to the boil. Add the octopus, close the lid and cook for about 45 minutes until tender (the cooking time may vary, depending on the size of the octopus).

3 Meanwhile, remove the skin from the chorizo and cut it into cubes. Peel the onions and slice them thinly. Peel and roughly chop the garlic cloves. Cut the lemon in half. Preheat the plancha for 12–15 minutes. Remove the cooked octopus from the stock and drain. Drizzle the olive oil on the preheated plancha, add the octopus with the chorizo, onions and garlic, close the lid and cook for 12–15 minutes, turning occasionally. Place the lemon halves on the grate with the cut sides down over a direct heat and grill for 4–5 minutes. Just before the end of the cooking time, squeeze the lemons over the octopus. To serve, season everything with sea salt and pepper and top with the chopped parsley.

SAY GOODBYE TO RUBBERY OCTOPUS

Some people avoid cooking octopus because its flesh can become tough and rubbery, but this method works every time. I recently rediscovered it myself. One evening, I prepared octopus this way for some friends and they were literally over the moon after eating it. Apparently they had rarely eaten such wonderfully tender and aromatic octopus. Now you can do the same!

VEGETABLES, FRUIT & SIDES

HASSELBACK POTATOES

This method of preparation is ingenious – slicing into the potatoes increases their surface area, allowing the seasoning ingredients to impart their flavours particularly well.

SERVES 4

4–6 medium potatoes (about 800 g/1 lb 12 oz)

3–4 tablespoons olive oil, plus extra for drizzling

sea salt and freshly ground black pepper

40 g (1½ oz) mixed herbs (such as chives, flat-leaf parsley, chervil, cress)

50 g (2 oz) Parmesan cheese

TIP: For Hasselback potatoes, floury potato varieties such as King Edward or Maris Piper are best.

PREPARATION
10 minutes

COOKING TIME
35–40 minutes

max. off max.

COOKING METHOD
Indirect heat

1 Prepare the grill for a medium to high indirect heat (180–220°C/ 350–425°F). Scrub the potatoes and pat them dry. Make a series of evenly spaced cuts down into the potatoes, making sure not to cut all the way through. Space the cuts about 5 mm (¼ inch) apart.

2 Coat the potatoes all over with the olive oil and season well with salt and freshly ground black pepper.

3 Place the potatoes on the grill over an indirect heat, close the lid and cook for 30 minutes.

4 In the meantime, sort through the herbs, discarding any wilted leaves, then rinse, shake dry and chop finely. Finely grate the Parmesan. About 10 minutes before the end of the cooking time, scatter the herbs and Parmesan over the potatoes.

5 With the lid closed, continue cooking for 5–10 minutes, then remove the potatoes from the grill and drizzle with extra olive oil to taste.

CUTTING THE POTATOES

To avoid accidentally slicing all the way through the potatoes, place a chopstick or wooden spoon on either side of the potato as you slice into it, to stop the knife from going any further down.

HASSELBACK POTATOES

With halloumi & balsamic onions

Prepare and cook the potatoes as described on page 245. For the topping, roughly grate 100 g (3½ oz) halloumi and 100 g (3½ oz) green courgettes. Season with 4 tablespoons olive oil, 1 tablespoon chopped thyme leaves, sea salt and freshly ground black pepper. For the balsamic onions, bring 4 tablespoons white balsamic vinegar, 4 tablespoons clear honey and 1 sliced red onion to the boil in a fireproof pan, then remove the pan from the heat and leave the onions to infuse for about 10 minutes. Scatter the grated halloumi and courgettes over the top of the potatoes 5–10 minutes before the end of their cooking time, followed by the onions.

With pebre

Prepare and cook the potatoes as described on page 245. To make the topping, mix 40 g (1½ oz) finely chopped parsley, 1 finely diced tomato, 2 tablespoons finely chopped capers and 1 finely diced shallot with 4 tablespoons olive oil and the juice of ½ lime. Season to taste with sea salt and chilli powder. Remove the cooked potatoes from the barbecue, top with the pebre and serve warm.

With pico de gallo

Prepare and cook the potatoes as described on page 245. To make the topping, mix 20 g (¾ oz) finely chopped coriander leaves, ½ finely diced avocado, 2 tablespoons sliced olive, 1 finely diced onion and 1 finely diced tomato with 4 tablespoons olive oil and the juice of ½ lime. Season with sea salt and chilli powder. Remove the cooked potatoes from the grill, top with the salsa and serve warm.

With crème fraîche & caviar

Prepare and cook the potatoes as described on page 245. Remove the cooked potatoes from the barbecue and top each one with 1 tablespoon crème fraîche, 2–3 tablespoons finely chopped parsley and 40 g (1½ oz) trout caviar.

STUFFED AUBERGINES

The combination of aubergine, feta and redcurrants with a large dose of barbecue flavour makes for a real taste explosion. You have to try it for yourself!

SERVES 4

3 aubergines
(about 250 g/9 oz each)

2 tablespoons coarse
sea salt

50 ml (2 fl oz) olive oil

STUFFING

1 garlic clove

150 g (5½ oz) feta cheese

15 g (½ oz) flat-leaf
parsley

50 g (1¾ oz) redcurrants

50 g (1¾ oz) cottage
cheese

freshly ground
black pepper

3–4 tablespoons olive oil

EQUIPMENT

1 plancha or cast iron
griddle

TIP: If you have a used smoking plank to hand, you can finish cooking the aubergines on it and then serve them on the plank. This will make it easier to get the stuffed aubergines from the grill to the table.

PREPARATION
15 minutes, plus
15 minutes marinating

COOKING TIME
20–25 minutes

COOKING METHOD
Direct/indirect heat

RESTING TIME
10 minutes

1 Cut the aubergines in half lengthways and then cut a diamond pattern into the flesh, leaving about 1 cm (½ inch) around the edge. Prepare the grill for a medium to high indirect heat (180–200°C/350–400°F). Place the plancha over a direct heat, close the lid and preheat for 8–10 minutes.

2 Rub coarse sea salt over the cut surfaces of the aubergines and place them cut side down on a baking tray. Cover with clingfilm and leave to stand for about 15 minutes at room temperature. Then wipe off any excess salt with kitchen paper and brush the cut surfaces with half the olive oil.

3 Drizzle the remaining olive oil on the plancha and add the aubergine halves, cut side down. Close the lid and cook for 5–8 minutes until golden brown. Turn the aubergines and cook for a further 4–5 minutes. Remove the aubergines from the grill and let cool slightly, then cover with clingfilm and leave to rest for about 10 minutes.

4 For the topping, peel and finely chop the garlic. Cut the feta into 1 cm (½ inch) cubes. Rinse the parsley, shake dry and chop finely. Sort through the redcurrants, discarding any that are mushy. Mix all the prepared ingredients in a bowl with the cottage cheese.

5 Scoop out the flesh of 2 of the aubergine halves with a spoon and place in the bowl, discarding the skins. Carefully remove the flesh from the other 4 halves, leaving about 1 cm (½ inch) of flesh around the edges, and place in the bowl. Thoroughly mix the ingredients in the bowl and season with pepper to taste.

6 Stuff the filling into the 4 aubergine halves and place them on the grate over an indirect heat. Close the lid and cook for 12–15 minutes until the filling is heated through. Remove from the grill, drizzle with olive oil and serve warm.

ROOT VEG
with salsa verde

The hearty flavours of root vegetables blend well with the smoky aroma. With its acidity and fresh herbs, the salsa provides an exciting contrast. Make sure the vegetables are all about the same size.

PREPARATION
15 minutes, plus
20 minutes marinating

COOKING TIME
8–10 minutes

COOKING METHOD
Direct heat

RESTING TIME
6–8 minutes

1 Prepare the grill for a medium to high direct heat (180–200°C/ 350–400°F).

2 Trim, peel and halve or quarter the root vegetables as needed, depending on their size. Mix the oil with the orange juice in a large dish. Add the root vegetables, mix to coat evenly and scatter over the spice mix.

3 Cover the dish with clingfilm and leave to marinate for about 20 minutes at room temperature.

4 In the meantime, for the salsa verde, sort through the herbs, discarding any wilted leaves, then rinse, shake dry and roughly chop. Set a few leaves aside for a garnish. In a food processor, finely blend the herbs together with the remaining salsa ingredients, then season with salt and pepper to taste.

5 Remove the root vegetables from the marinade, place them on the grate over a direct heat, close the lid and cook for 8–10 minutes, turning from time to time, until al dente. After cooking, return the veg to the dish, cover with clingfilm and leave to sweat for 6–8 minutes.

6 Top the cooked root vegetables with the salsa verde, garnish with the reserved herb leaves and serve warm. Season with salt and pepper to taste.

SERVES 4

ROOT VEGETABLES

800 g (1 lb 12 oz) mixed root vegetables (such as rainbow carrots, parsnips and/or Hamburg parsley root)

2 tablespoons oil

juice of ½ orange

2 tablespoons Potato & vegetable spice mix (see page 53)

SALSA VERDE

75 g (2¾ oz) mixed herbs (such as parsley, mint, basil)

1 garlic clove

1 tablespoon sun-dried tomatoes

1 tablespoon capers

1 teaspoon mustard

1 teaspoon white balsamic vinegar

50 ml (2 fl oz) olive oil

sea salt and freshly ground black pepper

SPICY CORN
on the cob

Grilled corn on the cob is delicious served with salt and butter but this spicy version raises the bar. Always use the freshest corn cobs; they absorb the flavour of the spices as they cook.

SERVES 4

4–6 fresh corn cobs

juice of ½ lime

sea salt

50 ml (2 fl oz) melted butter

1–2 tablespoons Texas-style spice mix (see page 53)

SPICY STOCK

3 litres (5¼ pints) water

6 tablespoons brown sugar

2 tablespoons sea salt

1 cinnamon stick

2 star anise

1 tablespoon black peppercorns

EQUIPMENT

1 Dutch oven or cast iron casserole

PREPARATION
5 minutes

COOKING TIME
40–45 minutes

max.   max.   max.

COOKING METHOD
Direct heat

1 Remove the husks and silks from the corn cobs.

2 Remove the grate of the GBS system if necessary to use the casserole. Prepare the grill for a high direct heat (220–240°C/425–475°F).

3 To make the spicy stock, pour the measured water into the casserole, then add the sugar, salt and spices. Cover with the lid and bring the stock to the boil over a direct heat.

4 Place the corncobs in the spicy stock, cover with the pot lid, close the grill lid and cook for 25–30 minutes until soft. Because the corncobs will float and may not cook evenly, you can cover them with a sheet of baking parchment and weigh them down with tablespoons.

5 Take the cooked corncobs out of the spicy stock with tongs, drain briefly and set aside on a baking tray or large plate. Wearing BBQ gloves, remove the casserole and replace the GBS grate, close the lid and preheat for 6–8 minutes.

6 Drizzle lime juice over the corncobs and season with sea salt. Place on the grate, close the lid and cook over a direct heat for 4–5 minutes, turning occasionally and brushing with melted butter. Remove from the grill, scatter over the spice mix and serve warm.

CORN ON THE COB

Tomato & chilli

Prepare and cook the corncobs as described on page 253, then prepare the grill for a high indirect heat (220–240°C/425–475°F). Place the drained corncobs over an indirect heat, spread each one with 1–2 tablespoons tomato ketchup, top with 3 halved cherry tomatoes, close the lid and cook for 5 minutes. Remove from the grill and scatter over ¼ teaspoon dried chilli flakes. Top with finely chopped parsley.

Bacon & cheese

Prepare and cook the corncobs as described on page 253, then prepare the grill for a high indirect heat (220–240°C/425–475°F). Wrap each of the drained corncobs in 4 bacon rashers then place over indirect heat, scatter over 1 tablespoon finely diced red onion, some crushed tortilla chips and 1 tablespoon grated Cheddar. Close the lid and cook for 5 minutes.

Soured cream

Prepare and cook the corncobs as described on page 253, then prepare the grill for a high indirect heat (220–240°C/ 425–475°F). Place the corncobs over an indirect heat, spread each with 1 tablespoon soured cream and 1 tablespoon chopped peanuts, close the lid and cook for 5 minutes. To serve, scatter a few lemon balm leaves over the corncobs.

BBQ corn on the cob

Prepare and cook the corncobs as described on page 253, then prepare the grill for a high indirect heat (220–240°C/ 425–475°F). Place the corncobs over an indirect heat, spread each cob with 1 tablespoon Classic BBQ sauce (see page 57) and 1 teaspoon chopped garlic, then top with 3–4 thin red onion slices, close the lid and cook for 5 minutes.

CAULIFLOWER QUICHE with courgette

To make sure that this hearty cauliflower, courgette and Parmesan quiche doesn't stick, grease the pan generously.

SERVES 6–8

800 g (1 lb 12 oz) cauliflower

4 eggs

150 g (5½ oz) Parmesan cheese, grated

½ teaspoon ras el hanout

sea salt and freshly ground black pepper

1 tablespoon butter, softened

3–4 tablespoons breadcrumbs

1 small green courgette (about 150 g/5½ oz)

1 small yellow courgette (about 150 g/5½ oz)

40 g (1½ oz) mixed herbs (such as parsley, chives, chervil, basil)

4–6 tablespoons olive oil

EQUIPMENT

1 cast iron GBS pan

TIP: To create a low-carb version, simply leave out the breadcrumbs and line the pan with baking parchment instead.

PREPARATION
15 minutes

COOKING TIME
40–45 minutes

max. off max.
COOKING METHOD
Indirect heat

RESTING TIME
5–8 minutes

1 Prepare the grill for a medium indirect heat (160–180°C/ 325–350°F). Rinse and pat dry the cauliflower, cut it into large chunks and blitz in a food processor until it has the consistency of couscous. Place the cauliflower crumbs in a bowl, mix with the eggs and Parmesan and season with ras el hanout and salt and pepper to taste.

2 Grease the cast iron GBS pan with butter up to the rim and scatter the breadcrumbs evenly over the base and sides of the pan.

3 Add the cauliflower mixture to the pan and spread out evenly.

4 Wash and trim the courgettes, pat them dry and cut into 5mm (¼ inch) thick slices. Spread the courgette slices evenly over the cauliflower base and season to taste with salt and pepper.

5 Remove the GBS grate and insert the cast iron GBS pan over a direct heat. Close the lid and cook for 40–45 minutes until the quiche is lightly browned. In the meantime, sort through the herbs, discarding any wilted leaves, then rinse, shake dry and chop finely.

6 Shortly before the end of the cooking time, scatter the herbs over the quiche and drizzle with the olive oil. Remove the pan from the grill and leave it to cool for 5–8 minutes. Cut into slices and serve warm with a salad of cherry tomatoes and wild herbs.

SMASHED POTATOES

You need floury potatoes for this dish — smashed potatoes are particularly good when you use varieties such as Maris Piper or King Edward.

PREPARATION
5 minutes

COOKING TIME
40–45 minutes

COOKING METHOD
Indirect heat

RESTING TIME
5–8 minutes

1 Prepare the grill for a medium to high indirect heat (180–200°C/ 350–400°F).

2 Wash and dry the potatoes. Place them on the grate over an indirect heat, close the lid and cook for 40–45 minutes until soft.

3 Sort through the herbs, discarding any wilted leaves, then rinse, shake dry and chop finely. Dice the tomatoes and slice the olives into fine rings.

4 Mix the soured cream with the mustard and two-thirds of the herbs and season to taste with salt and pepper.

5 Remove the cooked potatoes from the grill and leave them to rest for 5–8 minutes. Place on a large serving dish and crush the potatoes with a potato masher or the base of a pan. Season with salt and pepper.

6 To serve, spoon the soured cream, tomatoes and olives over the potatoes and scatter over the remaining herbs. Top with 2–3 tablespoons tomato or olive oil to taste.

SERVES 4

6 medium floury potatoes (about 800 g/1 lb 12 oz)

40 g (1½ oz) mixed herbs (such as parsley, chives, tarragon, cress)

50 g (1¾ oz) sun-dried tomatoes (preferably preserved in oil)

50 g (1¾ oz) mixed olives, *pitted*

200 g (7 oz) soured cream

4 teaspoons mustard

sea salt and freshly ground black pepper

oil from the jar of sun-dried tomatoes, or olive oil, to finish

SUN-DRIED TOMATOES IN OIL

I prefer to use sun-dried tomatoes preserved in oil. They are highly fragrant and soft, and the oil can be used to finish the potatoes or as the base for mayonnaises and dressings. You can also easily preserve sun-dried tomatoes in oil yourself: Simply bring 150 ml (¼ pint) water to the boil, add 50 g (1¾ oz) sun-dried tomatoes and simmer over a low heat for about 15 minutes. Then drain thoroughly and place the tomatoes in a jar with 75 ml (2½ fl oz) oil, a few sprigs of rosemary and thyme and 1 peeled and pressed garlic clove. These will be the perfect preserved tomatoes for your next barbecue.

VEGGIE BURGER PATTIES

These patties are made from vegetables, nuts and seeds, with the right mix of spices. But just like their meaty counterparts, they should be nice and thick.

TIP: It's important to make sure that the patties aren't too thin! They should be at least 2–3 cm (¾–1¼ inches) thick with a diameter of 8–10 cm (3¼–4 inches). To give the patties a more professional finish, you can shape them with a pastry ring or a burger press, both of which should be greased with oil before use.

PREPARATION
15 minutes

COOKING TIME
20–25 minutes

COOKING METHOD
Direct heat

ⓐ Green choice patties

FOR 2–3 PATTIES

To make the patties, blanch 75 g (2¾ oz) baby spinach in boiling water for a few seconds, plunge the wilted spinach into a bowl of iced water to cool, then squeeze the spinach thoroughly to remove any excess water. Mix the spinach with 200 g (7 oz) coarsely grated courgette, 100 g (3½ oz) chopped avocado, 75 g (2¾ oz) ground pumpkin seeds, 75 g (2¾ oz) breadcrumbs and 25 g (1 oz) sesame seeds. Season to taste with sea salt and freshly ground black pepper. Shape into patties of equal size and place them on a preheated, lightly oiled plancha over a medium direct heat (150–160°C/300–325°F), close the lid and for cook for 20–25 minutes, turning halfway through.

ⓑ Farmer's gold patties

FOR 2–3 PATTIES

To make the patties, mix 200 g (7 oz) coarsely grated sweet potatoes with 200 g (7 oz) coarsely grated floury potatoes, 1 teaspoon fine mustard and 2 tablespoons flour and season well with sea salt, black pepper and grated nutmeg. Shape into patties of equal size and place them on a preheated, lightly oiled plancha over a medium direct heat (150–160°C/300–325°F), close the lid and cook for 20–25 minutes, turning halfway through.

ⓒ Purple patties

FOR 2–3 PATTIES

To make the patties, mix 250 g (9 oz) grated beetroot with 75 g (2¾ oz) grated Hamburg parsley root or parsnips, 100 g (3½ oz) ground sunflower seeds and 1 tablespoon wholegrain mustard. Season generously with sea salt and black pepper. Shape into patties of equal size and place them on a preheated, lightly oiled plancha over a medium direct heat (150–160°C/300–325°F), close the lid and cook for 20–25 minutes, turning halfway through.

ⓓ Spicy bean patties

FOR 2–3 PATTIES

To make the patties, put 250 g (9 oz) drained canned cannellini beans, 75 g (2¾ oz) sliced leeks, 100 g (3½ oz) ground almonds and 25 g (1 oz) cress in a food processor and blitz until medium-coarse. Season with 1 tablespoon chilli sauce, sea salt, chilli powder and the juice of ½ lemon. Shape into patties of equal size and place them on a preheated, lightly oiled plancha over a medium direct heat (150–160°C/300–325°F), close the lid and cook foror 20–25 minutes, turning halfway through.

ⓔ Delicious nacho patties

FOR 2–3 PATTIES

To make the patties, put 75 g (2¾ oz) tortilla chips, 25 g (1 oz) grated Cheddar cheese, 100 g (3½ oz) white bread cubes, 50 g (1¾ oz) peanuts, 75 g (2¾ oz) breadcrumbs, 1 egg, 75 ml (2½ fl oz) BBQ sauce and 4 tablespoons groundnut oil in a food processor and blitz to a fine purée. Season the mixture well with sea salt and black pepper. Shape into patties of equal size and place them on a preheated, lightly oiled plancha over a medium direct heat (150–160°C/300–325°F), close the lid and cook for 20–25 minutes, turning halfway through.

TIP: These spicy, succulent patties are very easy to make and just show if you choose a vegetarian or vegan option, you are not sacrificing taste. Serve these at your next barbecue and your guests are sure to get a taste for veggies!

MARINATED TOFU

Make sure the tofu is of good quality: it should be fresh and firm, but not too solid, so that it can absorb the spicy and smoky flavours well.

1 Mix 175 ml (6 fl oz) teriyaki sauce with 2–3 tablespoons light sesame or olive oil and the juice of ½ lemon. Evenly coat 300 g (10½ oz) firm tofu with the marinade. Cover and leave to marinate for about 20 minutes at room temperature. Prepare the grill for a medium to high direct and indirect heat (180–200°C/350–400°F).

2 Remove the tofu from the marinade, pat dry and rub all over with a thin layer of oil. Scatter 1-2 tablespoons Basic spice mix (see page 52) evenly over the tofu to coat on all sides.

3 Put the tofu over a direct heat, close the lid and cook for 4–6 minutes, turning once. Then move to the indirect heat area, close the lid and cook for 4–6 minutes. Remove from the grill.

PREPARATION
15 minutes, plus
10–20 minutes
marinating

COOKING TIME
20–25 minutes

off   max.   max.
COOKING METHOD
Direct/indirect heat

ⓐ **Smoked tofu** with grilled aubergine

SERVES 4

Prepare the grill for a medium direct and indirect heat (160–180°C/ 325–350°F). Mix 1 tablespoon clear honey with the juice of ½ lemon. Rub 300 g (10½ oz) smoked tofu on all sides with the honey and lemon mixture. Season the tofu to taste with sea salt and freshly ground black pepper. Place the tofu over a direct heat, close the lid and cook for 15–20 minutes. At the same time, cook 2 unpeeled red onions over an indirect heat on the grill, turning the tofu and onions halfway through.

Meanwhile, cut 1 aubergine diagonally into finger-thick slices. Season the slices generously with sea salt and leave to stand for 5–10 minutes to allow the salt to draw out the moisture. Halve or quarter 6–8 capers, depending on their size. Halve an avocado, remove the stone, use a tablespoon to remove the flesh and cut into slices. Wash a romaine lettuce and tear it into bite-sized pieces. Pat dry the salted aubergine slices and rub both sides with 2½ tablespoons olive oil and the juice of ½ lemon. Put over a direct heat and cook for 4–6 minutes, turning once, until the slices are soft and golden brown. Remove from the barbecue.

Remove the cooked tofu and onions from the barbecue. Cut the tofu into thin slices. Peel the onions and cut them into wedges. Cut the cooked aubergine slices in quarters. Put the tofu, onions and aubergines in a bowl, then mix in the capers, avocado, lettuce and 2–3 tablespoons soy sauce. Season to taste with salt and pepper. Arrange the mixture on salad plates and scatter over 2–3 tablespoons chopped peanuts and basil leaves . Finish with a few drops of olive oil.

ⓑ **BBQ tofu bowl**

SERVES 4

Prepare 300 g (10½ oz) firm tofu as described in Steps 1–3, marinate and cook on the grill. Set aside the remaining marinade.

Preheat a cast iron GBS pan or a fireproof pot over a direct heat for 8–10 minutes. Cut 2 cleaned pak choi into quarters, brush them with 2 tablespoons light sesame or olive oil, put over a direct heat and cook for 4–6 minutes, turning once. Add 2 tablespoons sesame oil or olive oil to the griddle pan, then add 1 diced onion, 150 g (5½ oz) sliced shiitake mushrooms, 1 red pepper, cut into strips, and 2 sliced spring onions and cook for 4–6 minutes. Dice the cooked tofu and add to the pan. Add the pak choi, deglaze with 300 ml (10 fl oz) vegetable stock and season with the reserved marinade. Bring to the boil with the grill lid closed. Then arrange in four bowls, scatter over 2 tablespoons white and black sesame seeds and serve garnished with a few leaves of coriander or flat-leaf parsley.

ⓒ **BBQ tofu** with beans & rocket

SERVES 4

Prepare 300 g (10½ oz) firm tofu as described in Steps 1–3, marinate and cook on the grill.

Drain a can of cannellini or other white beans and rinse under running cold water (250 g /9 oz drained weight). To make a vinaigrette, mix a finely diced red onion with 1 tablespoon mustard, 1 tablespoon honey, 3 tablespoons white balsamic vinegar and 4 tablespoons olive oil. Season with salt and freshly ground black pepper. Mix the vinaigrette with the beans. Sort through 100 g (3½ oz) wild herbs and some chervil sprigs, discarding any wilted leaves, then rinse, shake dry and pick or strip the herbs off their stalks. Mix the beans with 75 g (2¾ oz) rocket and the herbs and arrange on plates. Cut the warm tofu diagonally into slices, arrange next to the salad and serve.

WATERMELON STEAKS
with sweet potato fries

PREPARATION
20 minutes, plus
10–15 minutes marinating

COOKING TIME
about 20 minutes

COOKING METHOD
Direct heat

1 Prepare the grill for a high to very high direct heat (240–260°C/ 475–500°F).

2 Remove the watermelon flesh from the rind and cut into 3 cm (1¼ inch) thick slices. Rub the slices with the oil, scatter over the spice mix, cover and leave to marinate for 10–15 minutes at room temperature.

3 In the meantime, peel the sweet potatoes and cut them into batons the size of a finger. Mix the eggs and soy sauce together in a bowl. Coat the sweet potato batons first in flour, then in the egg mixture and finally in the breadcrumbs.

4 Put the watermelon steaks over a direct heat, close the lid and grill for 8–10 minutes, turning once. Remove from the grill, drizzle with olive oil and keep warm.

5 Prepare the grill for a medium to high direct heat (180–200°C/350–400°F), put the plancha on it and preheat for 6–8 minutes. Drizzle half the oil on the plancha and place the sweet potato batons on it in a single layer, then close the lid and cook for 8–10 minutes, turning occasionally and drizzling with the remaining oil half way through.

6 Cut the melon steaks into slices. Salt the sweet potato fries to taste and serve with the watermelon steaks.

SERVES 4

WATERMELON STEAKS

1–1.4 kg (2 lb 4 oz–3 lb) seedless watermelon

3–4 tablespoons olive oil

2–3 tablespoons Basic spice mix (see page 52)

SWEET POTATO FRIES

2 large sweet potatoes (about 700 g/1 lb 9 oz)

2 eggs

2 tablespoons soy sauce

50 g (1¾ oz) flour

150 g (5½ oz) panko breadcrumbs

50 ml (2 fl oz) oil

fine sea salt

EQUIPMENT

1 plancha or cast iron griddle

BUTTERHEAD SALAD

This salad is the perfect accompaniment to the watermelon steaks and fries. Wash a butterhead lettuce, cut the leaves into bite-sized pieces and spin dry. To make the dressing, mix together 1 tablespoon mayonnaise, 1 teaspoon mustard, 150 g (5½ oz) soured cream, 2 tablespoons white balsamic vinegar, 50 ml (2 fl oz) cold vegetable stock and 4 tablespoons olive oil. Season with salt and pepper and finish with 1 teaspoon clear honey. Toss with the leaves and serve garnished with parsley.

PINEAPPLE STEAKS
with Caesar salad

Grilled pineapple is always a treat. For best results, choose a ripe, sweet fruit as it will contain a lot of fructose, which caramelizes on the barbecue.

SERVES 4

PINEAPPLE STEAKS

1–1.4 kg (2 lb 4 oz–3 lb) pineapple

3–4 tablespoons oil

5–6 tablespoons brown sugar

½ teaspoon coarse sea salt

4 tablespoons clear honey

SALAD

2–3 romaine lettuce hearts

1 garlic clove

2 egg yolks

juice and zest of ¼ unwaxed lemon

1 teaspoon Worcestershire sauce

1 teaspoon smooth mustard

25 ml (1 fl oz) water

100 ml (3½ fl oz) olive oil

50 g (1¾ oz) Parmesan cheese

sea salt and freshly ground black pepper

PREPARATION
20 minutes, plus
10–15 minutes
marinating

COOKING TIME
8–10 minutes

max. max. max.

COOKING METHOD
Direct heat

RESTING TIME
5–8 minutes

1 Prepare the grill for a high to very high direct heat (240–260°C/ 475–500°F). Cut the unpeeled pineapple lengthway into 2–3 cm (¾–1¼ inch) thick slices. Completely remove the skin from the two outer slices.

2 Lay the slices on a baking tray, rub both sides with oil, scatter over the sugar and season with sea salt.

3 Cover the baking tray with clingfilm and leave the pineapple slices to marinate for 10–15 minutes.

4 In the meantime, wash and spin dry the salad leaves, tear into bite-sized pieces and place in a salad bowl. To make the dressing, peel the garlic and chop it finely. In a small bowl, mix the garlic with the egg yolks, lemon zest and juice, Worcestershire sauce, mustard and water, then whisk in the oil, first drop by drop, then in a steady stream. Season the dressing with sea salt and pepper and grate the Parmesan on the salad.

5 Put the pineapple steaks over a direct heat, close the lid and cook for 8–10 minutes, turning once, until they are nicely browned on both sides. After turning, brush them with the honey. Remove from the barbecue, allow to cool a little, then cover with clingfilm and leave to rest for 5–8 minutes before serving.

6 To serve, trim the pineapple steaks, removing the skin and leaves, and cut into slices. Mix the salad with the dressing and serve the pineapple alongside.

TIP: A ripe pineapple smells fruity and has a golden-brown surface. You should be able to pull out one of the leaves in the middle of the pineapple.

CELERIAC STEAK SANDWICH

Hearty, fruity and succulent – this mouthwatering grilled celeriac, fig and mango sandwich is a must-try.

PREPARATION
20 minutes, plus
10–15 minutes
marinating

COOKING TIME
15–20 minutes

COOKING METHOD
Direct heat

RESTING TIME
8–10 minutes

1 Prepare the grill for a medium to high direct heat (180–200°C/350–400°F).

2 Wash and peel the celeriac and cut into 2–3 cm (¾–1¼ inch) thick slices. Rub the slices with olive oil and scatter the seasoning mix evenly over them. Cover and marinate for 10–15 minutes at room temperature.

3 Meanwhile, peel the mango and place the flesh in a blender. Blitz with the mustard, lemon juice, honey and olive oil to make a chunky sauce.

4 Put the celeriac steaks over a direct heat, close the lid and cook for 10–12 minutes, turning once. Remove from the grill and leave them to sweat for 8–10 minutes.

5 To make the sandwiches, cut the crusts off the slices of bread. Brush the slices on one side with olive oil. Wash the figs, pat dry and cut into 5 mm (¼ inch) thick slices. Wash and spin dry the lettuce leaves.

6 Cut the celeriac diagonally into 5mm (¼ inch) thick slices. Spread the oiled side of 1 slice of bread with mango sauce, then top with a lettuce leaf, a slice of fig and a slice of celeriac. Repeat with a further slice of bread spread with mango sauce, a lettuce leaf, fig and celeriac. Top with a lettuce leaf and finish the sandwich with a slice of bread spread with mango sauce, sauce side down. Build three more sandwiches in the same way, then put them over a direct heat, close the lid and cook for 4–6 minutes, turning once. Remove from grill and serve.

SERVES 4

CELERIAC STEAKS

800 g (1 lb 12 oz) celeriac

3–4 tablespoons olive oil

2–3 tablespoons Basic spice mix (see page 52)

SAUCE

1 mango

1 tablespoon mustard

juice of ½ lemon

1 tablespoon clear honey

4–6 tablespoons olive oil

TO SERVE

12 slices bread

6 tablespoons olive oil

4 figs

12 lettuce leaves (such as oakleaf, butterhead or romaine)

CAULIFLOWER STEAKS with couscous

The cauliflower should be large and firm, so you can cut it into steaks of a reasonable size.

SERVES 4

CAULIFLOWER STEAKS

1 cauliflower (about 800 g/1 lb 12 oz)

4–6 tablespoons olive oil

2 tablespoons ras el hanout

sea salt and freshly ground black pepper

COUSCOUS

1½ peppers (red, yellow or green)

1 red onion

6 sprigs of flat-leaf parsley

150 g (5½ oz) couscous, *cooked according to packet instructions*

cayenne pepper

juice of ½ lemon

4–6 tablespoons olive oil

Sweet chilli sauce (see page 57)

PREPARATION
20 minutes, plus
10–15 minutes
marinating

COOKING TIME
10–12 minutes

max. max. max.

COOKING METHOD
Direct heat

RESTING TIME
10 minutes

1 Prepare the grill for a medium to high direct heat (180–200°C/350–400°F). Clean the cauliflower and remove the outer leaves.

2 Cut the cauliflower into 3 cm (1¼ inch) thick slices. Finely chop any florets too small to be cut into steaks and set aside for the couscous.

3 Place the cauliflower steaks on a baking tray, then rub them with the oil and season evenly with the ras el hanout, sea salt and ground pepper.

4 Cover the baking tray with clingfilm and leave the cauliflower to marinate for 15 minutes at room temperature.

5 In the meantime, wash the peppers, pat dry and finely dice. Peel and finely dice the onion and finely chop the parsley, setting some aside for garnish. Mix the cooked couscous with the chopped cauliflower florets, peppers, onion and parsley. Season with sea salt and cayenne pepper to taste. Drizzle over the lemon juice and olive oil and toss to mix.

6 Put the cauliflower steaks over a direct heat, close the lid and cook for 10–12 minutes, turning once, until they are nicely browned. Remove from the grill, cover with clingfilm and leave to sweat for 8–10 minutes. To serve, arrange the cauliflower steaks on plates with the couscous and scatter with the reserved parsley. Serve with Sweet chilli sauce.

MUSHROOM SALAD

Mushrooms develop an incredibly intense flavour when cooked on the barbecue, as well as developing a good crunch. Both cultivated and wild mushrooms are ideal in this recipe.

PREPARATION
20 minutes, plus 10–15 minutes marinating

COOKING TIME
20–25 minutes

COOKING METHOD
Direct heat

RESTING TIME
15 minutes

SERVES 4

400 g (14 oz) large chestnut mushrooms

4 tablespoons hoisin sauce

juice of 1 lime

8 tablespoons olive oil

sea salt and freshly ground black pepper

2 red peppers

1 bunch of spring onions

50 g (1¾ oz) rocket

2 tablespoons clear honey

1 Prepare the grill for a medium to high direct heat (180–200°C/ 350–400°F).

2 Clean the mushrooms and remove the stalks. Mix the hoisin sauce with half the lime juice and half the olive oil in a large bowl. Season with sea salt and pepper to taste. Add the mushrooms, mix thoroughly, cover and leave to marinate for 10–15 minutes at room temperature.

3 Meanwhile, brush the peppers all over with 1 tablespoon oil, place on the grate over a direct heat, close the lid and cook 6–8 minutes, turning several times until the skin is charred and blistered. Then place in a bowl, cover with clingfilm and leave the peppers to sweat for 6–8 minutes.

4 Trim the spring onions, rub with 1 tablespoon oil and season with salt and pepper. Put over a direct heat, close the lid and cook for 6–8 minutes, turning

occasionally. Remove from the grill, leave to cool slightly, then cut into 2 cm (¾ inch) pieces. Peel the skin off the peppers, cut them into quarters, remove the stalk, seeds and ribs and cut the flesh into 2 cm (¾ inch) pieces. Put the vegetables in a serving bowl.

5 Now place the marinated mushrooms gill-side down over a direct heat on the grate, close the lid and cook for 8–10 minutes, turning after half the cooking time. Meanwhile, rinse and spin dry the rocket. Remove the cooked mushrooms from the barbecue, leave to cool slightly, then cut into slices and add to the vegetables in the bowl. Mix the mushrooms and vegetables with the remaining lime juice, honey and 2 tablespoons olive oil. Stir in the rocket and season the salad with salt and pepper.

CLEANING MUSHROOMS

Always clean mushrooms with a pastry brush, a mushroom or vegetable brush or kitchen paper. Most mushrooms that are available to buy (such as button mushrooms, chestnut mushrooms, king oyster and oyster mushrooms) are cultivated with a high water content. If you wash them, they soak up additional water, literally diluting the taste. In contrast, wild mushrooms (such as black chanterelles, golden chanterelles, morels) can be briefly rinsed in water to remove any dirt. However, they should then be dried very thoroughly before being prepared for cooking. This is best done at room temperature or by using a dehydrator.

ZESTY PUMPKIN
with cream cheese dip

The plancha is perfect for cooking vegetables such as pumpkin wedges, which you can eat with the skin on. Make sure that all the pumpkin pieces are roughly the same size.

SERVES 4

PUMPKIN

1 small pumpkin or squash (about 800 g/ 1 lb 12 oz)

4 tablespoons brown sugar

juice and zest of 2 unwaxed limes

½ teaspoon sea salt

4–6 tablespoons olive oil

DIP

150 g (5½ oz) cream cheese

4 tablespoons olive oil

sea salt and freshly ground black pepper

EQUIPMENT

1 plancha or cast iron griddle

PREPARATION
20 minutes, plus
10–15 minutes
marinating

COOKING TIME
20–25 minutes

max. max. max.
COOKING METHOD
Direct heat

RESTING TIME
5 minutes

1 Prepare the grill for a medium to high direct heat (180–200°C/ 350–400°F). Put the plancha over a direct heat, close the lid and preheat for 12–15 minutes. Wash the pumpkin, rub dry and cut it in half. Using a tablespoon, remove the seeds and fibres.

2 Cut the pumpkin into even-sized wedges so they will all cook at the same rate.

3 Zest the limes and set aside the zest for the dip. To make a marinade, squeeze the limes and mix the juice with the brown sugar. Season the mixture with sea salt.

4 Rub the pumpkin wedges with the marinade and place on a baking tray. Cover the tray with clingfilm and leave the wedges to marinate for 10–15 minutes at room temperature.

5 In the meantime, make the dip by stirring the lime zest and olive oil into the cream cheese. Season to taste with salt and pepper.

6 Remove the pumpkin wedges from the marinade and pat dry thoroughly. Set aside the marinade. Rub the olive oil into the pumpkin, place the wedges in a single layer on the plancha, close the lid and cook for 20–25 minutes, turning several times. Drizzle over the remaining marinade and serve with the cream cheese dip.

BUNS & ROLLS

If you want your burgers to be really good, it's best to make the buns yourself. These buns are perfect for burgers, but amazing on their own or with a savoury topping, too.

MAKES 8–10

STARTER DOUGH

50 ml (2 fl oz) milk

40 g/1½ oz fresh yeast or 20 g (¾ oz) fast-action dried yeast

20 g (¾ oz) sugar

100 g (3½ oz) plain flour

DOUGH

75 ml (2½ fl oz) milk

350 g (12 oz) plain flour, plus extra for shaping

30 g (1 oz) sugar

10 g (¼ oz) salt

1 egg yolk

1 egg

125 g (4½ oz) butter, softened

GLAZE

1 egg yolk

25 ml (1 fl oz) milk

TOPPING

2–3 tablespoons black and white sesame seeds, *or*

50 g (1¾ oz) grated Cheddar and a pinch of chilli powder, *or*

2–3 tablespoons chopped bacon and ½ finely diced red onion

EQUIPMENT

1 pizza stone, plancha or cast iron griddle

PREPARATION
20 minutes, plus
1 hour 40 minutes rising

COOKING TIME
15–20 minutes

COOKING METHOD
Indirect heat

RESTING TIME
5–8 minutes

1 To make the starter dough, heat the milk until lukewarm (35–40°C/ 95–104°F). Crumble the yeast into the milk, add the sugar and stir until the yeast and sugar have completely dissolved. Sift the flour into a bowl, pour in the yeast mixture and mix thoroughly for several minutes with a whisk. Cover the bowl with clingfilm and leave to rise for about 30 minutes at room temperature.

2 To make the dough, put the flour, milk, sugar, salt, egg yolk and whole egg with the starter dough in a food processor with a dough hook and, on medium speed, knead for 5–8 minutes to form a smooth dough. After half the kneading time, gradually add the butter. Cover the dough with clingfilm and leave to rise for about 45 minutes at room temperature, until it has doubled in size.

3 Place the dough on a floured work surface and knead thoroughly again. Cut the dough into 8–10 pieces, weighing about 75 g (2¾ oz) each and roll into balls. Dust the pizza stone or griddle with flour and arrange the dough balls on it, spaced well apart. For the glaze, whisk the egg yolk with the milk, brush it all over the dough balls and leave to rise for about 25 minutes until twice the size.

4 In the meantime, prepare the grill for a medium to high indirect heat (180–200°C/350–400°F). Brush the dough balls again with the glaze, add the topping of your choice and put the pizza stone or griddle over an indirect heat, close the lid and bake for 15–20 minutes.

SHAPING ROLLS & SPEEDY DOUGH

To make hot dog buns, simply shape the dough pieces into rolls 12–14 cm (4½–5½ inches) long and 2–3 cm (¾–1¼ inches) wide. For best results, all the ingredients should be at room temperature when you start. If you need your rolls to be ready sooner, you can dispense with the starter dough stage and make the main dough directly, kneading all the ingredients together and leaving it to rise for about 45 minutes. However, the downside is that the rolls won't be quite as fluffy.

HERB BUTTER BAGUETTE

The herb butter filling is what makes this baguette irresistible – which is why it's best to make more than one.

MAKES 2

DOUGH

2 tablespoons sugar

20 g/¾ oz fresh yeast or 10 g (¼ oz) fast-action dried yeast

250 ml (9 fl oz) lukewarm water

450 g (1 lb) plain flour, plus extra for shaping

2 tablespoons cider vinegar

1 tablespoon Bread seasoning mix (see page 53)

8 g (¼ oz) fine sea salt

HERB BUTTER

40 g (1½ oz) mixed herbs (such as flat-leaf parsley, chives, chervil, tarragon)

2 garlic cloves

150 g (5½ oz) butter, softened

sea salt and freshly ground black pepper

EQUIPMENT

1 pizza stone

PREPARATION
15 minutes, plus
30 minutes rising

COOKING TIME
20–25 minutes

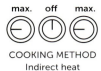
max.　off　max.
COOKING METHOD
Indirect heat

RESTING TIME
5–8 minutes

1 To make the dough, stir the sugar and crumbled yeast into the measured lukewarm water until the sugar and yeast have completely dissolved. Sift the flour into a large bowl, mix roughly with the vinegar, bread seasoning and sea salt, then pour in the yeast water and knead for several minutes with your hands or in a food processor on medium speed until a smooth dough forms.

2 Cover the bowl with clingfilm and leave to rise for about 30 minutes at room temperature, until doubled in size.

3 In the meantime, for the herb butter, sort through the herbs, discarding any wilted leaves, then rinse, shake dry and finely chop. Peel and finely chop the garlic. Thoroughly mix the herbs and garlic with the soft butter. Season the herb butter with salt and pepper to taste.

4 Prepare the grill for a medium to high indirect heat (180–200°C/ 350–400°F). Put the pizza stone on the grate and preheat for 8–10 minutes. Divide the risen dough into 2 and roll out each piece on a floured work surface into a rectangle about 25 × 30 cm (10 x 12 inches), and spread the centre of each piece with herb butter.

5 Loosely roll the rectangles of dough to form 2 baguettes and place them, with the joins underneath, on the preheated pizza stone.

6 Dust the surface of the baguettes with flour and score with a sharp knife at even intervals, only cutting halfway through. Put the baguettes on the pizza stone over an indirect heat and bake for 20–25 minutes, until golden brown. Remove from the grill, leave to cool slightly and serve while still warm.

BAGUETTE

Spring onion baguette

To make a herb purée, blanch 75 g (2¾ oz) flat-leaf parsley leaves and 75 g (2¾ oz) sliced spring onions in boiling water for a few seconds. Plunge into cold water to cool, squeeze out any excess moisture, then purée finely with 125 ml (4 fl oz) water.

To make the dough, thoroughly stir 2 tablespoons sugar and 20 g/¾ oz crumbled fresh yeast or 10 g (¼ oz) fast-action dried yeast into 125 ml (4 fl oz) lukewarm water until the sugar and yeast have completely dissolved. Then mix together 475 g (1 lb 1 oz) sieved plain flour, 2 tablespoons cider vinegar, 1 tablespoon Bread seasoning mix (see page 53), 8 g (¼ oz) fine sea salt and the herb purée in a bowl. Pour in the yeast water and knead the mixture for several minutes with your hands or in a food processor on medium speed to form a smooth dough. Then, as described on page 279, spread the dough sheets with 125 g (4½ oz) soft butter and 50 g (1¾ oz) grated Parmesan cheese before folding and baking.

Beetroot baguette

To make the dough, thoroughly stir 1 tablespoon sugar and 20 g/¾ oz crumbled fresh yeast or 10 g (¼ oz) fast-action dried yeast into 250 ml (9 fl oz) lukewarm beetroot juice until the sugar and yeast have completely dissolved. Then mix 400 g (14 oz) sieved plain flour, 50 g (1¾ oz) sunflower seeds, 2 tablespoons cider vinegar, 1 tablespoon Bread seasoning mix (see page 53) and 8 g (¼ oz) fine sea salt in a bowl, pour in the yeast mixture and knead everything with your hands or in a food processor on medium speed for several minutes to form a smooth dough. Then continue as described on page 279. Brush the dough sheets in the middle with 3–4 tablespoons pumpkin seed oil before folding.

Black baguette

To make the dough, thoroughly stir 1 teaspoon squid ink, 2 tablespoons sugar and 20 g/¾ oz crumbled fresh yeast or 10 g (¼ oz) fast-action dried yeast into 250 ml (9 fl oz) lukewarm water until the sugar and yeast have completely dissolved. Then mix 450 g (1 lb) sieved plain flour, 2 tablespoons cider vinegar, 1 tablespoon Bread seasoning mix (see page 53) and 8 g (¼ oz) fine sea salt in a bowl, pour in the black yeast mixture and knead with your hands or in a food processor on medium speed for several minutes to form a smooth dough. Then continue as described on page 279. Mix 125 g (4½ oz) soft butter with 50 g (1¾ oz) trail mix. Season the fruit and nut butter with sea salt and freshly ground black pepper. Spread the nut butter along the middle of the dough sheets before folding and baking.

BBQ baguette with Cheddar, sun-dried tomatoes & bacon

To make the dough, thoroughly stir 2 tablespoons sugar and 20 g/¾ oz crumbled fresh yeast or 10 g (¼ oz) fast-action dried yeast into 200 ml (7 fl oz) lukewarm water until the sugar and yeast have completely dissolved. Then mix 450 g (1 lb) sieved plain flour, 50 g (1¾ oz) BBQ sauce, 1 tablespoon tomato purée, 25 g (1 oz) diced bacon, 25 g (1 oz) diced sun-dried tomatoes, 2 tablespoons cider vinegar, 1 tablespoon Bread seasoning mix (see page 53) and 4 g (⅛ oz) fine sea salt in a bowl, pour in the yeast water and knead the mixture with your hands or in a food processor on medium speed for several minutes to form a smooth dough. Then continue as described on page 279. Scatter 75 g (2¾ oz) grated Cheddar across the middle of the dough sheets before folding.

BACON FOCACCIA

This Italian classic — hearty and rustic straight from the plancha — is a great accompaniment for meat, vegetables and salads. It also tastes great on its own with a chilled beer. Why not try this recipe with different herbs and cheeses?

PREPARATION
10 minutes, plus
1 hour rising

COOKING TIME
35–40 minutes

COOKING METHOD
Indirect heat

RESTING TIME
5–8 minutes

1 To make the dough, stir the sugar and yeast into the measured lukewarm water until the sugar and yeast have completely dissolved. Sieve the flour into a bowl and mix in the salt, olive oil and lemon pepper. Pour in the yeast water and knead the mixture with your hands or in a food processor with a dough hook at medium speed for several minutes to form a smooth dough. Cover the bowl with clingfilm and leave to rise for about 30 minutes at room temperature until doubled in size.

2 In the meantime, for the bacon mixture, sort through the herbs, discarding any wilted leaves, rinse and shake dry. Strip off the leaves and finely chop them. Mix the chopped herbs with the cheese and bacon.

3 Add two-thirds of the bacon mixture to the dough, with 1–2 tablespoons flour if it seems too wet, and knead the again for several minutes. Cover with clingfilm and leave to rise for 30 minutes.

4 In the meantime, prepare the grill for a medium to high indirect heat (180–200°C/350–400°F).

5 Dust the plancha or pizza stone with a thin layer of flour. Place the dough on the plancha and, using your hands, pull it out into an even layer about 3 cm (1¼ inches) thick. Scatter with the remaining bacon mixture. Put the focaccia on the pizza stone over an indirect heat and bake for 35–40 minutes until golden.

6 Remove from the grill and rest for 5–8 minutes. Drizzle with olive oil before serving.

SERVES 6–8

DOUGH

2 tablespoons sugar

30 g/1 oz fresh yeast or 15 g (½ oz) fact-action dried yeast

300 ml (½ pint) lukewarm water

650 g (1 lb 7 oz) plain flour, plus extra for kneading

10 g (¼ oz) salt

50 ml (2 fl oz) olive oil

1 tablespoon lemon pepper

BACON MIXTURE

40 g (1½ oz) mixed herbs (such as rosemary, thyme, lavender, sage)

150 g (5½ oz) grated cheese (such as Cheddar, Emmental, Gouda)

200 g (7 oz) diced bacon

3–4 tablespoons olive oil

EQUIPMENT

1 plancha, cast iron griddle or pizza stone

TIP: You can shorten the dough's rising time by about 5 minutes if all the ingredients except the fresh yeast are at room temperature.

CHEF'S SPECIALS

SHELBY BURGER SPECIAL

What's the best way to tackle a burger this big? Just take a bite, and you'll figure it out from there.

SERVES 4

4–5 red onions

Basic mayonnaise (see page 58)

50 g (1¾ oz) black truffles

4 coarse veal sausages

8 bacon rashers

4 slices Cheddar cheese

4 eggs

4 burger buns

3–4 tablespoons melted butter, for brushing

PATTIES

400 g (14 oz) minced beef (preferably freshly minced)

400 g (14 oz) minced pork (preferably freshly minced)

1 teaspoon fine sea salt

2 tablespoons Worcestershire sauce

freshly ground black pepper

1–2 tablespoons olive oil

EQUIPMENT

1 hamburger press

1 cast iron GBS pan

PREPARATION
20 minutes

COOKING TIME
25–30 minutes

off   max.   max.

COOKING METHOD
Direct/indirect heat

1 Prepare the grill for a medium to high direct and indirect heat (200–220°C/400–425°F). Place the unpeeled onions over an indirect heat, close the lid and cook for 20 minutes, turning occasionally, until soft. Remove from the grill, leave to rest for 10 minutes, then peel and cut into 5 mm (¼ inch) thick rings. Set aside.

2 For the patties, mix the minced meat with the sea salt and Worcestershire sauce. Season the mixture with pepper to taste. Grease the hamburger press with oil, divide the meat mixture into quarters and form 4 patties. Place the patties between layers of baking parchment.

3 Prepare the Basic mayonnaise. Finely grate two-thirds of the truffles and stir in to the mayonnaise.

4 Put the sausages over a direct heat, close the lid and grill for 3–4 minutes, turning once. Place the patties over a direct heat and grill for 3–4 minutes.

5 Insert the GBS pan over a direct heat and cook the bacon on it until crispy on both sides. Meanwhile, with the sausages still over a direct heat, continue grilling for 3–4 minutes. Turn the patties, cover each with a slice of cheese and continue grilling for 3–4 minutes.

6 When the bacon is crispy, fry the eggs in the pan. Cut open the buns, brush the cut surfaces with butter and grill briefly until golden. Remove all the ingredients from the grill. Cut the sausages diagonally in 1 cm (½ inch) thick slices. Spread some mayonnaise on the bun bases, top with half the onions, a patty and the sausage slices, add another layer of onions and mayonnaise and finish with a fried egg and 2 bacon rashers on each. Grate the remaining truffle over the top, replace the bun lids and serve the burgers warm.

ROYAL LOBSTER

Lobster and chips are a great combination – anyone who has ever enjoyed the lobster version of poutine, Canada's national dish, knows that to be true. Of course, it tastes even better if you make the fries yourself. Brace yourself for a delicious surprise!

SERVES 4

4–5 litres (7–8¾ pints) water

2–3 bay leaves

4 tablespoons coarse sea salt

1 tablespoon black peppercorns

15 g (½ oz) fresh herbs (such as lemon thyme, thyme)

2 live lobsters* (800–900 g/ 1 lb 12 oz–2 lb each)

250 g (9 oz) shallots

2 garlic cloves

75 g (2¾ oz) butter

fine sea salt

freshly ground black pepper

TO SERVE

chips (see page 216)

Cocktail sauce (see page 59)

EQUIPMENT

1 Dutch oven or cast iron casserole

1 cast iron GBS pan

In some countries, live crustaceans such as lobsters must be stunned before being immersed in boiling water.

PREPARATION
15–20 minutes

COOKING TIME
20–25 minutes

max.   max.   max.

COOKING METHOD
Direct heat

RESTING TIME
3–5 minutes

1 Prepare the grill for a high to very high direct heat (240–260°C/ 475–500°F). Place the water, bay leaves, salt, peppercorns and herbs in the casserole over a direct heat, cover with the pot lid, close the grill lid and bring the water to the boil for 6–8 minutes. Put the lobsters head first in the boiling water, replace the pot lid, close the grill lid and cook for 5 minutes.

2 Check the core temperature – it should be 56–58°C/133–136°F). Carefully transfer the lobsters to ice-cold water and leave to cool for 3–5 minutes. Remove the claws and legs from the body, return them to the casserole, cover and cook for a further 2–3 minutes. Then cool the claws in ice-cold water and remove the casserole from the barbecue.

3 Halve the lobster lengthways, remove the stomach sack and rinse out the cavity. Dab the lobster dry.

4 Crack the claws by hitting the widest part with the back of a knife. Then use the blade to carefully cut into the shell on the back of the claw and gently break open with your hands to remove the meat. Insert the GBS pan and preheat for 8–10 minutes. Reduce the grill temperature to a medium to high heat (180–200°C/350–400°F).

5 Bend the leg joints by moving them carefully back and forth, then break them open and remove the meat. Alternatively, cut them open using a pair of strong scissors.

6 Peel and chop the shallots and garlic. Melt the butter in the pan, add the shallots and garlic and cook for a few minutes. Season the lobster halves with salt, place them in the pan with the cut sides down, close the lid and cook for 2–3 minutes. Turn the lobster pieces, season with salt and add the meat from the claws and joints to the pan. Continue cooking for 2–3 minutes then serve the lobster with chips and the cocktail sauce.

SCALLOPS IN THE SHELL

Cooked briefly on the grill then finished in the shell, these scallops are a feast for the eyes – as well as your palate.

PREPARATION
20 minutes, plus 10 minutes marinating

COOKING TIME
about 15 minutes

COOKING METHOD
Direct heat

RESTING TIME
3–5 minutes

1 Prepare the grill for a high direct heat (220–240°C/425–475°F).

2 Remove the scallops from the shells, rub the flesh with oil and season with salt to taste. Cover with baking parchment and put in the refrigerator to marinate for 10 minutes.

3 Clean the fennel bulb, cut it in half and slice it as thinly as possible with a mandolin or knife. Place the melted butter and fennel in the GBS pan over a direct heat, cover with the lid and cook gently for 6–8 minutes. Season with salt and pepper to taste and add the ras el hanout. Add the spinach and tomatoes and allow to wilt. Divide the vegetables evenly between 4 scallop shells.

4 Place the egg yolks with the white wine and vinegar in a small fireproof pan. Season with salt and pepper. Place on the side burner or directly on the grill and beat the mixture for several minutes until

thick and foamy, removing it from the heat now and then so the egg yolk does not curdle. It is ready when the mixture thickens into a creamy sauce. Remove from the heat and stir in the clarified butter, drop by drop at first, then in a steady stream. Set aside.

5 Pat the scallops dry and rub them again with oil. Then put over a direct heat with the grill lid open on just one side and cook for 1–2 minutes.

6 Arrange 2 cooked scallops with the grill markings facing upwards on top of the vegetables in each of the shells. Season with pepper and top with the butter sauce. Put over a direct heat, close the grill lid and cook for 6–8 minutes. Serve the scallop shells on plates, scattered with sea salt.

SERVES 4

8 scallops on the half shell, cleaned

1–2 tablespoons oil

fine sea salt

freshly ground black pepper

coarse sea salt, for sprinkling

VEGETABLES

1 small fennel bulb

3–4 tablespoons melted butter

½ teaspoon ras el hanout

1 handful baby spinach, *washed and spun dry*

100 g (3½ oz) tiny cherry tomatoes, *washed and dried*

BUTTER SAUCE

3 egg yolks

25 ml (1 fl oz) white wine

1 tablespoon tarragon vinegar

150 ml (¼ pint) clarified butter (see below)

EQUIPMENT

1 cast iron GBS pan

1 small fireproof pan

CLARIFIED BUTTER

You can make clarified butter by heating some butter to separate the fat and whey. Melt the butter in a heavy-based saucepan and bring it to a slow simmer, skimming off the froth, until the white whey has settled at the base of the pan. Then carefully pour the clarified butter through a fine sieve into another container to remove any milk solids, leaving the whey in the pan.

SMOKED CHESTNUT SOUP

You might think we're using quite a few accessories here. We are! But this means you get to expand your repertoire of barbecue techniques, and that's always fun.

SERVES 4–6

600 g (1 lb 5 oz) fresh chestnuts

4 red onions

2 garlic cloves

2 bay leaves

50 g (1¾ oz) butter

fine sea salt

freshly ground black pepper

1 litre (1¾ pints) vegetable stock

200 g (7 oz) single cream

TOPPING

1 red apple

zest from 1 unwaxed orange

4 tablespoons pomegranate seeds

EQUIPMENT

1 large aluminium drip tray

1 fine-meshed rotisserie basket

1 vegetable basket

1 smoker box

1–2 handfuls of applewood chips

1 GBS wok or Dutch oven

PREPARATION
10 minutes

COOKING TIME
about 1 hour

off · max. · max.

COOKING METHOD
Direct/indirect heat

RESTING TIME
10–15 minutes

1 Remove the grates from the grill. Place the drip try directly on the flavorizer bars and pour in 500 ml (18 fl oz) water. Prepare the grill to cook using the rotisserie basket over a medium to high direct and indirect heat (180–200°C/ 350–400°F). Cut a cross shape through the shell at the top of each chestnut, then put them in the rotisserie basket and fit it to the rotisserie.

2 Fit the rotisserie in the grill, close the lid and grill for 20 minutes. Remove the roasted chestnuts from the basket, wrap them in a tea towel and leave to rest for 10–15 minutes.

3 Peel the chestnuts and put them in the vegetable basket. Fill the smoker box with the dry chips, place the box on the flavorizer bars over a high heat (220–240°C/425–475°F) and burn for 6–8 minutes.

4 Remove the smoker box, replace the grates and place the box on top. Reduce the temperature to a medium heat (160–180°C/325–350°F). Put the chestnuts in the vegetable basket over an indirect heat, close the lid and roast for about 15 minutes.

5 Remove the chestnuts and smoker box from the barbecue. Insert the wok over a direct heat, close the lid and preheat for 8–10 minutes. Meanwhile, peel the onions and garlic. Cut the onions into thick slices and place in the wok with the garlic, bay leaves, butter and chestnuts. Season with salt and pepper, close the lid and cook for 6–8 minutes.

6 Remove a few whole chestnuts from the wok and divide them among the bowls. Deglaze the wok with the stock, pour in the cream and simmer for 6–8 minutes. Purée the soup using a hand-held blender. Wash, core and dice the apple. Ladle the soup into the bowls, top with the apple, strips of orange zest and the pomegranate seeds. Grind some pepper over the top and serve with toasted baguette, if desired.

CRAZY PIZZA CAKE

This pizza tower is crazy but incredibly delicious. If you're not sure how to serve pizza to 6–8 people all at the same time, let your gas barbecue do the work for you.

PREPARATION
15 minutes, plus
35–40 minutes rising

COOKING TIME
30–35 minutes

COOKING METHOD
Direct/indirect heat

SERVES 6–8

1 x pizza dough (see page 66)

a few basil leaves

3–4 tablespoons olive oil

FILLING

1–2 red onions

3 peppers (one each yellow, red and green)

400 g/14 oz tomato passata

1 tablespoon cornflour

1 teaspoon herbes de Provence

sea salt and freshly ground black pepper

30 thin salami slices

200 g (7 oz) mozzarella cheese, grated

EQUIPMENT

1 pizza stone

1 pizza peel

1 baking tray

1 Prepare the dough as described on page 67.

2 Prepare the grill for a medium to high direct and indirect heat (200–220°C/400–425°F). Place the pizza stone on the grill grate on the left over an indirect heat, close the lid and preheat for 12–15 minutes.

3 In the meantime, peel and finely dice the onions. Core, wash and pat dry the peppers, then dice finely.

4 Shape the dough into 5 equal balls. Then, using your hands or a rolling pin, pull or roll them out on a floured work surface to form 2–3 mm (⅛ inch) thick pizza bases with a diameter of about 25 cm (10 inches).

5 Mix the tomato passata with the cornflour and herbs. Season with salt and pepper to taste. Brush the pizza bases with the tomato mixture and top with the onions, peppers, salami and cheese.

6 Place one pizza on the stone over indirect heat using the pizza peel to move it, close the lid and cook for 4–5 minutes. At the same time, place another pizza on the baking tray on the right side of the grill over a direct heat and cook for 4–5 minutes. Now place the second pizza

on top of the first, place the third pizza on the baking tray, close the lid, cook for 4–5 minutes then place on top of the stack. Bake the remaining 2 pizzas in the same way, one after the other, and place them on top of the stack.

7 Once all the pizzas are stacked up, place the pizza stone in the middle of the grate, reduce the temperature to a low to medium indirect heat (140–160°C/275–325°F), close the lid and cook for 10–15 minutes. To serve, scatter with basil leaves and drizzle with the olive oil.

BACON DREAM

To make sure nothing goes wrong with your bacon pie, cover it with a circle of baking parchment and weigh it down in the middle with a small metal bowl filled with water as it cooks. Just before the end of the cooking time, brush with the BBQ sauce.

SERVES 6–8

600 g (1 lb 5 oz) thin bacon rashers

800 g (1 lb 12 oz) large floury potatoes

fine sea salt

15 g (½ oz) flat-leaf parsley

2 egg yolks

2–3 tablespoons cornflour

freshly ground black pepper

800 g (1 lb 12 oz) minced beef (preferably freshly minced)

500 g (1 lb 2 oz) minced pork (preferably freshly minced)

150 ml (¼ pint) Classic BBQ sauce (see page 57)

EQUIPMENT

1 cast iron GBS pan

PREPARATION
20 minutes

COOKING TIME
35–40 minutes

max. off max.

COOKING METHOD
Indirect heat

RESTING TIME
8–10 minutes

1 Prepare the grill for a medium to high indirect heat (200–220°C/ 400–425°F). Line the GBS pan with baking parchment, then line the inner rim of the pan with bacon. Use the remaining bacon slices to line the base of the pan, starting at the centre, overlapping them slightly and extending them well over the rim.

2 To make the filling, peel and coarsely grate the potatoes and mix with 1 teaspoon sea salt. Leave at room temperature to stand for about 10 minutes. Wash the parsley, shake it dry and finely chop the leaves and stalks. Thoroughly squeeze the moisture out of the grated potatoes, then place in a bowl and mix with the egg yolks, cornflour and half the parsley. Season with pepper.

3 Mix together the minced beef and pork and add the remaining chopped parsley. Season the mixture with a little salt and pepper.

4 Form the minced meat into 3 or 4 sausages of equal length, each one 2 cm (¾ inch) thick.

5 Working from the outside in, cover the bacon base in alternating circles of sausages and potato mixture.

6 Fold the overhanging bacon slices over the filling. Put the bacon pie over an indirect heat, close the lid and cook for 35–40 minutes until the sausages reach a core temperature of 65–68°C (149–154°F). Brush the pie with the BBQ sauce 10 minutes before the end of the cooking time. Remove the pan from the grill and leave the pie to rest for 8–10 minutes before serving.

Tip: As the bacon rashers will shrink as they cook, make sure they overlap in the centre of the pan when you arrange them in place in Step 1.

STEAK TORTILLAS TO GO

This is an unusual but brilliant idea for a relaxed get-together with friends. And the best part is that anything goes!

SERVES 4

STEAK

1 flank steak (600–800 g/ 1 lb 4 oz–1 lb 12 oz and 1–2 cm/½–¾ inch thick)

1–2 tablespoons oil

coarse sea salt

freshly ground black pepper

FOR THE TOPPING

1 red onion

½ each yellow, red and green pepper

1 tomato

a few sprigs of flat-leaf parsley

100 g (3½ oz) drained canned sweetcorn

2–3 tablespoons olive oil

CHEESE SAUCE

100 g (3½ oz) single cream

200 g (7 oz) Cheddar cheese, grated

4 bags tortilla chips (about 125 g/4½ oz each)

EQUIPMENT

1 small fireproof pan

 **PREPARATION**
15 minutes, plus
10 minutes marinating

 COOKING TIME
6–8 minutes

 **COOKING METHOD**
Direct heat

 RESTING TIME
3–5 minutes

1 Prepare the grill for a high to very high direct heat (240–260°C/475–500°F). Pat the steak dry, rub it all over with oil and season with sea salt to taste. Cover with baking parchment and leave to marinate for 10 minutes at room temperature.

2 Peel and finely dice the onion. Wash and core the peppers and tomato and cut into small cubes. Rinse the parsley, shake dry, pluck the leaves and chop roughly. Mix the onion, pepper, tomato, parsley and sweetcorn in a bowl and season with salt, pepper and olive oil.

3 Put the steak over a direct heat, close the lid and grill for 6–8 minutes, turning once, until its core temperature reaches 52–54°C (126–129°F).

4 In the meantime, pour the cream into the fireproof pan over the side burner or directly on the grill rack. Add the cheese and stir until smooth. Remove the steak from the grill, leave it to rest for 3–5 minutes, then season with pepper.

5 Cut the steak into very thin slices across the grain and season the cut surfaces again with salt and pepper.

6 Open the tortilla chip bags and divide the topping between them. Arrange the steak slices on top and finish with the cheese sauce.

TIP: Whether you're going to a match, gig or party, why not meet for a barbecue beforehand, filling up your bag of tortilla chips and enjoying this snack on the way there!

TORTILLAS TO GO

FLAVOUR UPGRADE

Chicken onion rings

For each packet of onion rings (about 125 g/4½ oz), add 3–4 tablespoons chopped iceberg lettuce, 2 tablespoons sliced romano peppers, 2 tablespoons soured cream and ½ grilled and sliced chicken breast. Top with ¼ sliced red onion and 1 tablespoon chopped chives.

Beef-topped crisps
with salt & vinegar

For each packet of salted crisps (about 125 g/4½ oz), add ½ handful of rocket, 1 finely diced tomato, 150 g (5½ oz) grilled rump steak cut into cubes (see page 118) and 2 tablespoons Parmesan cheese shavings. Top with 1 tablespoon olive oil and 1 teaspoon balsamic vinegar. Season with sea salt and freshly ground black pepper to taste.

Grilled sausage & bacon

For each packet of chickpea tortilla chips (about 75 g/2¾ oz),
add ½ handful lamb's lettuce, 3 grilled bacon rashers and
1 sliced grilled sausage (see pages 94–95). Mix 1 tablespoon
crème fraîche with 1 tablespoon olive oil and 1 tablespoon
white balsamic vinegar and spoon on top.

Pork fillet with peppers & spinach

For each packet of paprika or sweet chilli crisps (about 125 g/
4½ oz), add ½ handful baby spinach, 2–3 tablespoons mixed
sliced peppers, 150 g (5½ oz) sliced grilled pork fillet (see page
160 or page 162) and 2 tablespoons Sweet Chilli sauce (see
page 57). Top with 1 teaspoon roasted white and black sesame
seeds and a few fresh coriander leaves.

LEMONADE FROM THE GRILL

As well as the citrus fruits, choose a good-quality, flavoursome honey because it has a big impact on the taste of this lemonade.

SERVES 4–6

8 unwaxed lemons

2 unwaxed limes

6–8 tablespoons white sugar

75 g (2¾ oz) blossom honey

2–3 handfuls crushed ice

4–6 lemon balm sprigs

1–1.2 litres (1¾–2 pints) ice-cold sparkling water

EQUIPMENT

4–6 chilled drinking glasses (about 450 ml/¾ pint each)

PREPARATION
15 minutes, plus
10 minutes marinating

COOKING TIME
6–8 minutes

max.   max.   max.

COOKING METHOD
Direct heat

1 Prepare the grill for a high to very high direct heat (240–260°C/ 475–500°F). Halve the lemons and limes. Scatter the sugar over a large baking tray. Place the citrus fruit on the tray, cut sides down, and leave at room temperature to stand for about 10 minutes.

2 The grill grate should be very clean before you start cooking. Place the citrus fruit on the grate with the sugared sides down over a direct heat, close the lid and grill for 6–8 minutes to caramelize.

3 Remove the cooked citrus fruit from the grill, leave to cool slightly, then squeeze three-quarters of the fruit to remove the juice.

4 Mix the lemon juice with the honey in a small bowl to make a lemon syrup, then place in the refrigerator to chill. Peel the remaining citrus fruit and cut into chunks.

5 To serve, pour the crushed ice into the glasses and top each with 50–60 ml (about 4 tablespoons) of the lemon syrup. Divide the citrus chunks between the glasses and add a lemon balm sprig to each. Top up with ice-cold sparkling water, stir and enjoy.

TIP: You can prepare the lemon syrup well in advance – it will keep for at least 4–5 days in the refrigerator.

SWEET TREATS & DESSERTS

STRAWBERRY TARTE FLAMBÉE
with honey & almonds

SERVES 4

250 g (9 oz) strawberries

4 tablespoons strawberry syrup

4 tablespoons chopped almonds

300 g (10½ oz) soured cream

2 tablespoons clear honey

4 tarte flambée bases* or thin pizza bases (about 30 cm/12 inches in diameter)

a few mint leaves

icing sugar, for dusting

EQUIPMENT

1 pizza stone

*Tart flambée bases are not available to buy in all countries but they don't need yeast so are simple to make. To make your own, mix 250 g (9 oz) plain flour with ½ teaspoon salt, then gradually add 100 ml (3½ fl oz) water mixed with 2 tablespoons oil and knead to form a smooth dough, adding a little more water, a tablespoon at a time, if it seems too dry). Wrap in clingfilm and leave to stand for about 1 hour. Divide into 4 balls and roll out on a floured surface as thinly as possible into circles.

PREPARATION
10 minutes

COOKING TIME
32–40 minutes

COOKING METHOD
Direct heat

RESTING TIME
3–5 minutes

1 Prepare the grill for a high direct heat (220–240°C/425–475°F). Put the pizza stone on the grill rack and preheat for 8–10 minutes. In the meantime, clean and halve the strawberries and mix in a bowl with the syrup and almonds.

2 Stir the honey into the soured cream.

3 Using a spoon, spread the honey and soured cream mixture on the tarte bases, leaving a border of about 1 cm (½ inch).

4 Scatter the marinated strawberries over the tarte flambée bases.

5 Put the topped bases, one at a time, on the pizza stone over direct heat, close the lid and cook for 8–10 minutes until crispy.

6 Remove the finished tarte flambée from the grill and leave to rest for 3–5 minutes. To serve, top the tartes with mint leaves and dust with icing sugar.

TARTE FLAMBÉE

With chocolate, bananas & marshmallows

Top the tarte flambée bases with the honey and soured cream mixture, as described on page 307. Spread 1 tablespoon hazelnut chocolate spread on each base, then top each one with ½ sliced banana and some mini marshmallows (1 handful in total). Put the tartes, one at a time, on the preheated pizza stone as described and cook for 8–10 minutes until crispy, remove from the grill and leave to rest for 3–5 minutes. To serve, scatter 50 g (1¾ oz) roughly chopped chocolate over the top.

With berries & hazelnuts

Top the tarte flambée bases with the honey and soured cream mixture, as described on page 307. Sort through 250 g (9 oz) mixed berries (such as raspberries, blackberries and blueberries, depending on the season), discarding any mushy fruit, and arrange the berries on the prepared bases. Put the tartes, one at a time, on the preheated pizza stone as described and cook for 8–10 minutes until crispy, remove from the grill and leave to rest for 3–5 minutes. To serve, scatter 50 g (1¾ oz) roughly chopped hazelnuts over the top.

With goat cheese, grapes & figs

Top the tarte flambée bases with the honey and soured cream mixture, as described on page 307. Scatter 200 g (7 oz) halved grapes, 2 sliced figs and 200 g (7 oz) sliced goat cheese on the bases. Put the tartes, one at a time, on the preheated pizza stone as described and cook for 8–10 minutes until crispy, remove from the grill and leave to rest for 3–5 minutes. To serve, scatter 50 g (1¾ oz) roughly chopped walnuts over the top, drizzle over a little olive oil and season with salt and freshly ground black pepper.

Tropically topped with coconut

Top the tarte flambée bases with the honey and soured cream mixture, as described on page 307. Scatter 200 g (7 oz) finely diced fruit (pineapple, papaya, mango) and 100 g (3½ oz) redcurrants on the bases. Put the tartes, one at a time, on the preheated pizza stone as described and cook for 8–10 minutes until crispy, remove from the grill and leave to rest for 3–5 minutes. To serve, scatter 50 g (1¾ oz) coconut flakes and a few lemon balm leaves over the top.

STRUDEL PASTRY FANS
with caramelized white chocolate

SERVES 4

150 g (5 oz) white
chocolate

300 g (10½ oz) summer
berries (raspberries,
redcurrants,
blueberries,
blackberries)

150 ml (¼ pint) Berry
compôte (see page 316)

PASTRY FANS

4 sheets of strudel pastry*
or filo pastry
(about 15 × 30 cm/
6 x 12 inches)

4 tablespoons melted
butter

icing sugar, for dusting

EQUIPMENT

1 pizza stone

1 sheet of baking
parchment

*To make strudel pastry,
mix 300 g (10½ oz) strong
bread flour with
½ teaspoon salt. Make a
well in the centre. Mix
175–200 ml (6–7 fl oz)
warm water with
3–4 teaspoons oil.
Slowly add the liquid
ingredients to the well,
mixing well to form a
smooth dough, then
knead for 10 minutes.
Form into a ball, wrap in
clingfilm and leave to
stand for 30 minutes
before rolling out thinly
on a floured surface.*

PREPARATION
10 minutes

COOKING TIME
10–12 minutes

COOKING METHOD
Direct heat

RESTING TIME
3–5 minutes

1 Prepare the grill for a medium to high direct heat (180–200°C/350–400°F). Put the pizza stone over the heat and preheat for 8–10 minutes.

2 Roughly chop the white chocolate. Place the sheet of baking parchment on the preheated pizza stone and spread the chopped chocolate on top. Close the barbecue lid and let the chocolate caramelize for a few minutes until brown. Remove from the pizza stone, allow the chocolate to cool on the baking parchment, roughly chop it into pieces and transfer to kitchen paper to rest.

3 In the meantime, fold each of the 4 sheets of pastry into a fan shape, about 1 cm (½ inch) wide, starting from one narrow edge. Strudel dough works best here, but if you are using filo dough, keep the sheets covered with a damp cloth when not working with them.

4 Crimp the ends together and spread the folded sheets apart to form fans.

5 Place 2 pastry fans on the pizza stone, brush each with 1 tablespoon melted butter and dust with icing sugar. Close the lid and cook for 5–6 minutes until golden brown. Leave to rest for 3–5 minutes before serving.

6 In the meantime, sort through the fresh berries, removing any mushy ones. Sprinkle the warm fans with the chocolate, the fresh berries and Berry compôte, then dust with icing sugar.

TIP: You can place the baking parchment on the pizza stone without soaking it in water beforehand. However, make sure that it does not protrude beyond the edge of the pizza stone, as the overhanging paper could catch fire.

SWEET RIBS

These sweet ribs are quick to prepare and will be a hit with everyone. If you don't like fennel seeds, you can scatter chopped nuts on top instead, or simply serve the ribs with sugar and cinnamon.

SERVES 4

1 puff pastry sheet (about 20 × 20 cm/ 8 x 8 inches)

4 tablespoons melted butter

1–2 tablespoons icing sugar

flour, for dusting

juice and zest of ½ lemon

4 tablespoons clear honey

1–2 tablespoons fennel seeds

EQUIPMENT

1 rectangular pizza stone (44 × 30 cm/17½ x 12 inches) or see tip

1 sheet of baking parchment

PREPARATION
10 minutes

COOKING TIME
12–15 minutes

max. off max.

COOKING METHOD
Indirect heat

RESTING TIME
8–10 minutes

1 Prepare the grill for a medium to high indirect heat (180–200°C/ 350–400°F). Roll out the puff pastry to twice its length on a lightly floured work surface or a large chopping board. Brush it with half the melted butter and dust with half the icing sugar.

2 Fold the pastry sheet in half and roll out again to twice its length, then brush with melted butter and dust with icing sugar. Fold in half again.

3 Place the pastry on the sheet of baking parchment on top of the pizza stone and roll it out to twice its length again. Then carefully slice into 1 cm (½ inch) thick strips, without cutting the baking parchment.

4 Scatter the lemon zest over the pastry sheet. Mix the lemon juice with the honey. Brush the puff pastry with the remaining butter and honey and lemon mixture and scatter over the fennel seeds.

5 Place the pizza stone with the sweet ribs over an indirect heat, close the lid and cook for 12–15 minutes until golden brown. Remove from the grill and leave to rest for 8–10 minutes. Before serving, separate the ribs if necessary.

TIP: If you are cooking the sweet ribs on a round pizza stone, you'll have to halve the dough and bake the ribs in two batches.

CRISPY SWEET BACON

Choose streaky bacon of the best quality and not too highly seasoned. The cocoa content of the chocolate and the choice of crunchy topping are up to you.

PREPARATION
5 minutes

COOKING TIME
8–10 minutes

max.   max.   max.

COOKING METHOD
Direct heat

RESTING TIME
8–10 minutes

SERVES 4

500 g (1 lb 2 oz) thick-cut smoked streaky bacon

1–2 tablespoons oil

100 g (3½ oz) dark chocolate

4 tablespoons caramelized chopped hazelnuts

EQUIPMENT

1 plancha

1 sheet of baking parchment

1 Prepare the grill for a medium to high direct heat (180–200°C/ 350–400°F). Place the plancha on the rack and preheat for 12–15 minutes.

2 Grease the plancha with oil, place the bacon on top, close the lid and cook for 8–10 minutes, turning once. Then drain on kitchen paper and leave to cool completely (preferably on kitchen paper in the refrigerator).

3 Meanwhile, chop the dark chocolate and melt it in a metal bowl over a saucepan of simmering water on the grill rack or side burner.

4 Dip the cold bacon slices into the melted chocolate, scatter over the hazelnuts, place on baking parchment and briefly leave to set. Either enjoy immediately or place the meaty treats back in the refrigerator until the chocolate has completely hardened.

TIP: This sweet and savoury treat is easy to make in advance. You can use any kind of chocolate you like, but the sweeter it is, the greater the contrast with the taste of the salty bacon. In warm weather, sweeter chocolate melts faster than darker chocolate, which has a higher cocoa content.

CRUMBLE with summer berries

For this dessert, the choice of fruit is up to you – and you can also vary the spices, nuts and other ingredients in the crumble. The one rule is that the ramekins will need to be well buttered to prevent sticking.

SERVES 4

CRUMBLE

160 g (5¾ oz) plain flour, plus extra for dusting

½ teaspoon baking powder

100 g (3½ oz) brown sugar

100 g (3½ oz) butter, softened, plus extra for greasing

pinch of cinnamon

BERRY COMPÔTE

250 g (9 oz) frozen mixed berries (such as cherries, cranberries, blueberries, raspberries, strawberries), *defrosted*

100 ml (3½ fl oz) juice from the frozen fruit

1 tablespoon cornflour, *mixed with 2–3 tablespoons water*

6 tablespoons clear honey

EQUIPMENT

4 fireproof ramekins (140–180 ml/5–6¼ fl oz capacity)

PREPARATION
10–15 minutes

COOKING TIME
about 20 minutes

max.   off   max.

COOKING METHOD
Indirect heat

1 Prepare the grill for a medium to high indirect heat (180–200°C/350–400°F). Meanwhile, mix the flour and baking powder in a bowl for the crumble. Add the sugar, butter and cinnamon and rub the mixture into loose crumbs with your finger tips.

2 Generously grease the ramekins up to the rim with butter and dust with a thin layer of flour.

3 For the compôte, bring the defrosted fruit and juice to the boil in a small pan on the side burner, then thicken with the cornflour and sweeten with the honey.

4 Divide half the crumble between the ramekins, then place a quarter of the fruit in each ramekin and top with the remaining crumble.

5 Put the crumbles over an indirect heat, close the lid and cook for about 20 minutes until golden brown. Remove from the grill and serve warm.

CRUMBLE TIMING

You will love this wonderfully quick dessert, which can be cooked while you're cooking the main course – just bake them on the warming rack of your gas barbecue. The crumbles can easily tolerate some temperature fluctuation when the lid is opened and closed, but they might need a bit longer to bake.

CRUMBLE

FLAVOUR UPGRADE

Chocolate crumble
with plums

Prepare the crumble mixture using 120 g (4½ oz) plain flour, 40 g (1½ oz) cocoa powder, ½ teaspoon baking powder, 100 g (3½ oz) softened butter and 100 g (3½ oz) brown sugar as described on page 317. Roughly chop 250 g (9 oz) halved and stoned plums. Bring the fruit to the boil with 100 ml (3½ fl oz) red grape juice on the side burner, thicken with cornflour and sweeten with 4 tablespoons clear honey. Layer the crumbles as described and put over an indirect heat to cook for about 20 minutes. Top with chopped caramelized hazelnuts.

Coconut crumble
with mango & apple

Prepare the crumble mixture using 120 g (4 oz) plain flour, 40 g (1½ oz) desiccated coconut, ½ teaspoon baking powder, 100 g (3½ oz) softened butter and 100 g (3½ oz) brown sugar as described on page 317. Roughly chop 150 g (5½ oz) mango. Cut an apple in half, peel, core and roughly chop. Bring the fruit to the boil with 150 ml (¼ pint) apple juice on the side burner, thicken with cornflour and sweeten with 2–3 tablespoons honey. Layer the crumbles as described and put over an indirect heat to cook for about 20 minutes.

Almond crumble with blueberries

Prepare the crumble mixture using 80 g (2¾ oz) plain flour,
80 g (2¾ oz) ground almonds, ½ teaspoon baking powder,
100 g (3½ oz) softened butter and 100 g (3½ oz) brown sugar
as described on page 317. Sort 250 g (9 oz) blueberries,
discarding any mushy ones, then bring to the boil in 150 ml
(¼ pint) blueberry juice on the side burner, thicken with
cornflour and sweeten with 4 tablespoons clear honey. Layer
the crumbles as described and put over an indirect heat to
cook for about 20 minutes. Dust with icing sugar.

TIP: You could flavour the crumble mixture
with a variety of spices: vanilla seeds, ground
cinnamon, speculoos spice mix and tonka bean
all give crumbles a special flavour.

CLASSIC CHEESECAKE

For a gluten-free version, you could replace the butter biscuits with gluten-free flour, breadcrumbs or gluten-free biscuits.

SERVES 6–8

BASE

50 ml (2 fl oz) melted butter

25 g (1 oz) butter biscuits

FILLING

500 g (1 lb 2 oz) quark (low-fat cream cheese) or cottage cheese

50 ml (2 fl oz) melted butter

6 eggs

zest of 3 unwaxed lemons

juice of ½ unwaxed lemon

150 g (5½ oz) sugar

35g (1¼ oz) cornflour

a few mint leaves

EQUIPMENT

1 cast iron GBS pan or fireproof cake tin (about 30 cm/12 inches in diameter)

TIP: You can use the zested lemons to make a great barbecue lemonade. The recipe is on page 302.

PREPARATION
10 minutes

COOKING TIME
40–45 minutes

COOKING METHOD
Indirect heat

RESTING TIME
15–20 minutes

1 Prepare the grill for a low to medium indirect heat (140–160°C/ 275–325°F). Meanwhile, brush the base and sides of the cast iron pan or cake tin with the melted butter.

2 Put the butter biscuits in a plastic bag and crush into fine crumbs using a rolling pin or blitz them in a food processor. Scatter the biscuit crumbs over the pan to coat, setting aside any remaining biscuit crumbs.

3 Place all the ingredients for the filling in a large bowl and whisk until smooth, or use a food processor.

4 Pour the mixture into the pan, spread it evenly and smooth it down.

5 Put the cheesecake over an indirect heat, close the lid and cook for 40–45 minutes until just set.

6 Remove the pan from the grill and leave the cheesecake to cool for 15–20 minutes. Use a moistened knife to cut into slices and scatter the remaining crumbs and mint leaves on top. Top the cheesecake with the lemon zest.

DELICIOUS LEMON ZEST

For the lemon zest, wash 2 unwaxed lemons under hot running water, then rub dry. Peel off the yellow skin with a peeler and cut into fine strips (or use a zester). Cook the lemon zest with 4 tablespoons clear honey on the side burner or cooker for 1–2 minutes, then leave to infuse for a further 8–10 minutes away from the heat.

CHEESECAKE

RAINBOW CHEESECAKE

If you're expecting a lot of guests, you could make a rainbow cheesecake. It's simple to prepare, but it does take a little time. You will be rewarded with a wonderfully fresh and intense taste. Simply bake two or more variants of the cheesecake on the grill and leave them to cool down. Then layer the cheesecakes on top of each other and top with sauces, fruit or chocolate.

Blueberry cheesecake

For a blueberry cheesecake filling, mix 150 g (5½ oz) blueberry or elderberry jam with 400 g (14 oz) quark or cottage cheese, 50 g (1¾ oz) melted butter, juice of 1 lime, 6 eggs, 50 g (1¾ oz) sugar and 35 g (1¼ oz) cornflour and prepare the cheesecake as described on page 321. To serve, top the cheesecake with 100 g (3½ oz) blueberries or blackberries and dust with icing sugar.

Peanut cheesecake

For a peanut cheesecake filling, mix 100 g (3½ oz) peanut butter (smooth or crunchy) with 100 g (3½ oz) chocolate almond butter, 400 g (14 oz) quark or cottage cheese, 50 g (1½ oz) melted butter, 6 eggs, 100 g (3½ oz) sugar and 35 g (1¼ oz) cornflour and prepare the cheesecake as described on page 321. To serve, top the cheesecake with 3–4 tablespoons peanut butter and 3-4 tablespoons chopped peanuts.

Chocolate cheesecake

For a chocolate cheesecake filling, mix 150 g (5½ oz) chocolate hazelnut spread or Dattella chocolate spread (see page 333) with 100 g (3½ oz) chocolate almond butter, 400 g (14 oz) quark or cottage cheese, 50 g (1¾ oz) melted butter, 6 eggs, 100 g (3½ oz) sugar and 35 g (1¼ oz) cornflour and prepare the cheesecake as described on page 321. To serve, top the cheesecake with 3–4 tablespoons of chopped chocolate.

TARTE TATIN

Serve this French classic with vanilla ice cream, whipped cream or double cream. And if you fancy trying a variation, use apricots, plums or pears instead of apples.

SERVES 6–8

1 kg (2 lb 4 oz) firm apples (such as Gala, Boskoop, Elstar, Jonagold or Braeburn)

juice of 1 lemon

SHORTCRUST PASTRY

300 g (10½ oz) plain flour

150 g (5½ oz) cold butter, cut into cubes

45 g (1½ oz) sugar

1 egg

1 egg yolk

CARAMEL

150 g (5½ oz) sugar

60 g (2¼ oz) cold butter, cut into cubes

butter, for greasing

flour, for dusting

EQUIPMENT

1 cast iron GBS pan or fireproof cake tin (about 30 cm/12 inches in diameter)

1 BBQ ceramic dish (about 30 cm/12 inches in diameter)

2 sheets baking parchment

PREPARATION
15 minutes

COOKING TIME
45–50 minutes

max. max. max.
COOKING METHOD
Direct heat

RESTING TIME
10 minutes

1 Peel and quarter the apples and remove the cores. Pour the lemon juice into a bowl of cold water and add the apple quarters so that they do not turn brown. Set aside.

2 Place the ingredients for the pastry in a bowl and rub in with your fingertips to form a stiff dough, or use a food processor. Cover the pastry with clingfilm and leave to rest for about 20 minutes at room temperature. In the meantime, prepare the grill for a medium to high direct heat (200–240°C/400–475°F). Put the cast iron GBS pan over the heat and preheat for 6–8 minutes.

3 Remove the clingfilm and roll out the pastry between two sheets of baking parchment to a diameter of about 40 cm/ 16 inches. Grease the ceramic dish with butter and coat with a thin layer of flour.

4 Remove the apples from the lemon water and drain. For the caramel, place the sugar and 75 ml (3 fl oz) water in the preheated GBS pan and cook for a few minutes until a light caramel forms. Add the apples with the cold butter cubes and caramelize for 6–8 minutes while stirring. Remove from the grill, leave to cool to room temperature then place the apples and caramel in the ceramic dish.

5 Arrange the apples in a single layer in the ceramic dish, then cover them with the pastry, using the baking parchment to move it without breaking. Tuck the edges of the pastry down inside the edges of the dish.

6 Put the tart over a direct heat, close the lid and cook for 35–40 minutes until golden brown. Remove from the grill and leave to rest for 10 minutes in the dish. Turn the tart out of the dish and serve while it is still warm.

TIP: Don't cut the apples too small, or they will disintegrate when cooked. To make sure they cook evenly, make 2 or 3 lenthways cuts in the apple quarters, without cutting all the way through.

KIDS' CHOICE

CHICKEN TO GO

It's not just the children who will love these little chicken drumsticks with their subtly sweet and crispy skin – food you're allowed to eat with your fingers! Add home-made chips (see page 216) and ketchup, and you'll be the hero of the hour.

SERVES 4

500 g (1 lb 2 oz) chicken drumsticks

1–2 tablespoons olive oil

1 tablespoon sea salt

freshly ground black pepper

GLAZE

4 tablespoons clear honey

juice of ½ lemon

2 tablespoons Spicy tomato glaze (see page 57) or tomato ketchup

PREPARATION
10 minutes

COOKING TIME
25–30 minutes

COOKING METHOD
Indirect heat

RESTING TIME
3–5 minutes

1 Prepare the grill for a medium indirect heat (160–180°C/ 325–350°F). Make a cut around the circumference of each chicken drumstick, all the way to the bone and about one-third of the way from the bone end.

2 Slice through the tendons, then hold each drumstick with the bone end resting on the chopping board and cut the gristle away from the bone.

3 Cut away and pull off all the gristle to leave the ends of the bones clean.

4 Rub the chicken drumsticks all over with oil, then season with sea salt and black pepper to taste. Cover with baking parchment and stand for about 10 minutes to reach room temperature.

5 For the glaze, stir the honey, lemon juice and Spicy tomato glaze or ketchup together until smooth.

6 Put the drumsticks over an indirect heat, close the lid and cook for 25–30 minutes, until the core temperature reaches 76–78°C (169–172°F). About 5 minutes before the end of the cooking time, brush with the glaze until it is all used up. Remove from the grill and leave to rest for 3–5 minutes before serving.

TIP: Take a look at the different chips in the book, in case the kids fancy something different: for example, try the sweet potato fries (see page 265), root vegetable chips or beetroot chips (see page 219).

STICK BREAD
from the barbecue

Bread on a stick – a tasty campfire treat you can also make on a gas barbecue. Why not make double the amount of dough, so you can cook a second batch while the kids are eating the first batch?

SERVES 4

20 g (¾ oz) fresh yeast or 10 g (¼ oz) fast-action dried yeast

275 ml (9¾ fl oz) lukewarm water

1 tablespoon sugar

500 g (1 lb 2 oz) plain flour, plus extra for kneading

4 g (⅛ oz) salt

4 tablespoons rapeseed oil

GLAZE

1 egg yolk

25 ml (1 fl oz) milk

spreads to serve (see pages 332–333)

EQUIPMENT

8–12 ETGS or metal skewers (about 25 cm/10 inches long)

PREPARATION
10–15 minutes, plus
30 minutes rising

COOKING TIME
12–15 minutes

max.   off   max.

COOKING METHOD
Indirect heat

1 For the dough, crumble the yeast into the warm water, add the sugar and stir until the yeast and sugar have dissolved. Sieve the flour into the bowl of a food processor with a dough hook and mix with salt and oil. Pour in the yeast water and, on medium speed, knead for 5–6 minutes to form a smooth dough. Alternatively, this can be done by hand.

2 Cover the dough with clingfilm and leave at room temperature to rise for about 30 minutes until doubled in size.

3 Prepare the grill for a medium indirect heat (160–180°C/ 325–350°F). On a lightly floured work surface, roll out the risen dough into a flat rectangle about 1 cm (½ inch) thick.

4 Cut the dough into 8–12 long strips of equal width.

5 Now wrap the strips of dough around the skewers in a spiral with the edges overlapping slightly, stopping about 5 cm (2 inches) from the tip of the skewer, and press down the end to seal. For the glaze, whisk together the egg yolk and milk.

6 Hang the ETGS skewers on their rack or arrange standard skewers on the grill rack, then brush the bread with the glaze. With the stick breads over a direct heat, close the lid and cook for 12–15 minutes until golden brown. Allow the stick breads to cool slightly, then serve with spreads of your choice.

SPREADS FOR STICK BREAD

FLAVOUR UPGRADE

Pizza spread

Use a vegetable peeler to peel ½ red pepper, then chop into fine dice. Mix with 2 tablespoons drained canned sweetcorn, 100 g (3½ oz) cream cheese, 50 ml (2 fl oz) tomato sauce and 1 crumbled slice of toasted white bread, crusts cut off. Top the spread with fresh basil, if liked.

Apple spread with cream cheese

Wash 1 red apple, pat dry and grate on all sides with a coarse grater then discard the core. Mix the grated apple with 150 g (5½ oz) cream cheese and 2 tablespoons clear honey and refrigerate until ready to serve.

Datella chocolate spread

Bring 80 ml (2¾ fl oz) almond milk to the boil in a small pan and remove from the heat. Add 1 teaspoon cocoa powder and stir until completely dissolved. Leave the cocoa mixture to cool slightly. In a food processor, blend 100 g (3½ oz) pitted dates and 50 g (1¾ oz) almonds with the cocoa mixture to make a creamy spread.

Peanut marshmallow dip

Bring 100 ml (3½ fl oz) milk to the boil in a small pan and remove from the heat. Add 1 handful of white mini marshmallows and stir to combine. Thoroughly mix the marshmallow milk with 2 tablespoons clear honey and 50 g (1¾ oz) peanut butter. Transfer to a small bowl and top the spread with 4 tablespoons peanuts.

COLOURFUL POTATO & SAUSAGE KEBABS

PREPARATION
10 minutes

COOKING TIME
8–10 minutes

COOKING METHOD
Direct heat

1 Prepare the grill for a medium to high direct heat (180–200°C/350–400°F).

2 Cut any large pre-cooked potatoes in half. Cut the sausages into 2 cm (¾ inch) pieces. Clean and core the red pepper, then cut into chunks. Wash and trim the courgettes, pat them dry and cut into 2 cm (¾ inch) thick slices. Put all the ingredients in a bowl, mix with the oil and season to taste with salt and pepper.

3 Now thread the potato, sausage, pepper and courgette pieces on the skewers, alternating the ingredients. Wrap each skewer with 2 bacon rashers, slightly overlapping the edges.

4 Put the skewers over a direct heat, close the lid and grill for 8–10 minutes, turning occasionally, until the bacon is crispy. Remove from the barbecue and serve warm.

SERVES 4

200 g (7 oz) small potatoes, *pre-cooked*

2 sausages, *pre-cooked*

1 red pepper

1 small green courgette (about 200 g/7 oz)

1 small yellow courgette (about 200 g/7 oz)

8 bacon rashers

1–2 tablespoons olive oil

sea salt and freshly ground black pepper

EQUIPMENT

4 wooden or bamboo skewers (about 25 cm/10 inches long), *pre-soaked for at least 30 minutes*

MINCED BEEF KEBABS with crisps

Juicy minced beef coated in crunchy potato crisps – the simplest things can make you smile.

SERVES 4

1 red pepper

1 red onion

2 spring onions

500 g (1 lb 2 oz) minced beef (preferably freshly minced)

1 teaspoon sweet paprika

½ teaspoon fine sea salt

freshly ground black pepper

1–2 tablespoons olive oil

4 tablespoons Classic BBQ sauce (see page 57)

generous handful of roughly crushed paprika-flavoured crisps

EQUIPMENT

8 wooden or bamboo skewers (about 25 cm/ 10 inches long), *pre-soaked for at least 30 minutes*

PREPARATION
10 minutes

COOKING TIME
8–10 minutes

max.   max.   max.

COOKING METHOD
Direct heat

RESTING TIME
5 minutes

1 Prepare the grill for a medium to high direct heat (180–200°C/ 350–400°F). In the meantime, clean, core, pat dry and cut the peppers into small cubes. Peel and finely dice the onion. Trim and wash the spring onions, pat them dry and cut into fine rings. Put the minced beef, finely chopped vegetables and paprika in a bowl and season to taste with sea salt and pepper.

2 Mix the ingredients until well combined. Dampen your hands with water and then press one-eighth of the minced beef around the top of each skewer to form a sausage shape.

3 Brush the minced beef skewers all over with olive oil.

4 Put the skewers over a direct heat, close the lid and grill for 8–10 minutes, turning from time to time. Halfway through the cooking time, brush the meat with the BBQ sauce, close the lid and cook until the core temperature reaches 65–68°C (149–154°F).

5 Dip the cooked skewers into the crumbled crisps in a large bowl until well coated then serve warm.

PARTY BURGERS FOR KIDS

Letting everyone assemble their own burger will be the highlight of any birthday party.

PREPARATION
5 minutes, plus
1 hour rising

COOKING TIME
15–18 minutes

COOKING METHOD
Direct/indirect heat

RESTING TIME
5–8 minutes

1 To make the dough for the buns, heat the beetroot juice until lukewarm (35–40°C/95–104°F). Add the sugar and crumble in the yeast and stir to dissolve. Put the flour, salt, egg and butter in a mixing bowl, pour in the yeast liquid and knead the mixture with your hands for several minutes to form a smooth dough.

2 Cover the bowl with clingfilm and leave at room temperature to rise for about 30 minutes until doubled in size.

3 Knead the dough again on a floured work surface, then shape into 40 g (1½ oz) dough balls. Dust the pizza stone with flour and place the dough balls on it, well spaced apart. To make a glaze, whisk the egg yolk with the milk and brush all over the dough balls. Leave to rise for a further 30 minutes until doubled in size.

4 In the meantime, prepare the grill for a medium to high indirect and direct heat (180–200°C/350–400°F). Brush the dough balls with the glaze again, top with sesame seeds and put the pizza stone over an indirect heat, close the lid and cook for 12–15 minutes.

5 Meanwhile, rub oil all over the chicken breasts and season with salt. Put them over direct heat, close the lid and grill for 6–8 minutes, turning occasionally. Transfer to indirect heat and grill for a further 9–10 minutes until the core temperature reaches 72–74°C (162–165°F). Remove from the grill, season with pepper and leave to rest for 3–5 minutes. Remove the cooked buns from the grill, leave to cool for 5–8 minutes, then slice in half.

6 Place the buns, cut sides down, on the grill grate over direct heat and cook until they are just toasted. Cut the chicken diagonally into 1 cm (½ inch) thick slices. Spread the mayonnaise on the bottom halves of the buns and top with lettuce leaves and chicken slices. Finish with the ketchup and place the top halves of the buns to top.

MAKES 12–14

BURGER BUNS

150 ml (¼ pint) beetroot juice

2 tablespoons sugar

15 g (½ oz) fresh yeast or 7.5 g (¼ oz) fast-action dried yeast

250 g (9 oz) plain flour, plus extra for kneading

5 g (⅛ oz) salt

1 egg

25 g (1 oz) butter, softened

1 egg yolk

25 ml (1 fl oz) milk

1– 2 tablespoons white sesame seeds

FILLING

2 skinless, boneless chicken breasts (about 200 g/7 oz each), *excess fat removed*

1 tablespoon olive oil

sea salt and freshly ground black pepper

lollo rosso lettuce leaves

3–4 tablespoons each of mayonnaise and tomato ketchup

EQUIPMENT

1 pizza stone

PANCAKES with
maple syrup & blueberries

These little pancakes are sweet, fluffy and fruity – and when it comes to the choice of fruit, they're very versatile.

MAKES 12–16

PANCAKES

50 ml (2 fl oz) melted butter

3 eggs

210 ml (7¼ fl oz) milk

50 g (1¾ oz) sugar

½ teaspoon salt

300 g (10½ oz) plain flour

16 g (½ oz) baking powder

4–6 tablespoons oil

TOPPING

8 tablespoons maple syrup

2 tablespoons butter

200 g (7 oz) blueberries

EQUIPMENT

1 cast iron GBS pan or plancha

1 fireproof pan

PREPARATION
10 minutes

COOKING TIME
20–25 minutes

max.   max.   max.

COOKING METHOD
Direct heat

1 Prepare the grill for a low to medium direct heat (150–170°C/300–340°F). Put the cast iron GBS pan over the heat, close the lid and preheat for 8–10 minutes. Meanwhile, for the pancakes, thoroughly mix the melted butter with the eggs, milk, sugar and salt. Sift the flour and baking powder into a bowl and mix with the egg and milk mixture to form a smooth batter.

2 To make the topping, put the maple syrup and butter in the fireproof pan and heat on the grill rack or side burner, stirring, until the butter has melted. Set aside. Generously coat the base of the preheated GBS pan with oil, pour in 1 small ladleful of batter at a time and spread to form a pancake about 8 cm (about 3¼ inches) in diameter. You can cook 3 pancakes at the same time.

3 Scatter the pancakes with a few blueberries, close the lid and cook for 4–5 minutes over direct heat.

4 Turn the pancakes, close the lid and cook for a further 1–2 minutes until ready. Use the remaining batter to make more pancakes in the same way, scattering with blueberries.

5 Stack the finished pancakes on a plate and drizzle with the buttery maple syrup. Serve warm with the remaining blueberries.

PANCAKES

FLAVOUR UPGRADE

Chocolate pancakes
with strawberries

Prepare the pancake batter as described on page 341, adding 1–2 tablespoons cocoa powder to the flour mixture.

Briefly rinse 250 g (9 oz) strawberries in a sieve, then pat dry and hull them. Halve or quarter the strawberries, depending on their size. Gently mix the strawberries with 2 tablespoons maple syrup and arrange on the cooked pancakes then dust with icing sugar to serve.

Vanilla pancakes
with caramel cream

Prepare the pancake batter as described on page 341, adding the seeds of 1 vanilla pod to the milk mixture.

Melt 100 g (3½ oz) creamy toffees in a fireproof pan over a medium to high heat while stirring. Add 50 ml (2 oz) milk, then pour in 150 ml (¼ pint) double cream. Put the caramel cream over a low heat and simmer for 6–8 minutes, stirring occasionally. Add a few sea salt flakes to taste. Beat 150 ml (¼ pint) double cream or whipping cream until it forms stiff peaks. Pour the caramel cream over the cooked pancakes and serve warm with the whipped cream.

Cheese pancakes

Prepare the pancake batter as described on page 341, leaving out the sugar and stirring in 100 g (3½ oz) mixed grated cheese (such as Edam, Cheddar, Gouda) and 1 tablespoon chopped flat-leaf parsley. Season the batter with salt, freshly ground black pepper and freshly grated nutmeg.

Top the finished pancakes with grated Parmesan and basil leaves to garnish.

Herb pancakes

Prepare the pancake batter as described on page 341, leaving out the sugar and stirring in 4 tablespoons finely chopped herbs (such as flat-leaf parsley, chives, chervil).

Top the finished pancakes with sliced tomato and 1–2 finely sliced spring onions. Season to taste with sea salt and freshly ground black pepper. Drizzle with 2 tablespoons olive oil and serve warm.

MARSHMALLOW & FRUIT KEBABS

Grilled marshmallows aren't just a hit with the kids – combine them with fruit to conjure up a quick and delicious dessert.

PREPARATION
10 minutes

COOKING TIME
4–5 minutes

COOKING METHOD
Direct heat

1 Prepare the grill for a high to very high direct heat (280–300°C/535–575°F).

2 Clean and prepare the fruit as appropriate for the variety, then cut into 2 cm (¾ inch) pieces.

3 Thread the pieces of fruit on to the skewers, alternating them with the marshmallows, then brush all over with the oil.

4 Put the kebabs over a direct heat, close the lid and grill for 4–5 minutes, turning once, until golden.

5 Remove from the grill and arrange on plates. Drizzle over the honey, scatter with the grated chocolate and serve.

TIP: The marshmallows will be very hot when you take them off the grill, so don't be in too much of a rush to pop one in your mouth!

SERVES 4

600 g (1 lb 5 oz) mixed fruit (such as pineapple, plums, apricots, peaches, bananas, strawberries)

about 24 marshmallows

1–2 tablespoons oil

4 tablespoons clear honey

1–2 tablespoons finely grated chocolate

EQUIPMENT

8–12 wooden or bamboo skewers (about 25 cm/10 inches long), *pre-soaked for at least 30 minutes*

THE RIGHT WAY TO GRILL MARSHMALLOWS

You need to grill marshmallows over very high heat, as they basically consist of sugar and egg whites held together as a foamy mass with a little bit of starch. If you grilled them at a lower temperature, they would melt and start to run. However, at a high heat, the sugar caramelizes quickly and the marshmallows retain their shape.

CHOCOLATE BANANAS

Use bananas that are ripe but still firm – they should taste sweet without turning too mushy on the barbecue.

SERVES 4

4 bananas

juice of ½ lemon

2 tablespoons brown sugar

4 fun-size chocolate bars with nougat, caramel or nuts, or 4 strips milk chocolate

chocolate biscuit topping, to serve

SAUCE

250 ml (9 fl oz) double cream

4 fun-size chocolate bars with nougat, caramel or nuts, or 4 strips milk chocolate

50 g (1¾ oz) dark chocolate

EQUIPMENT

4 cocktail sticks, *pre-soaked in water*

1 smoking plank, pizza stone or ceramic dish (optional)

1 fireproof pan

PREPARATION
10 minutes

COOKING TIME
8–10 minutes

max.   off   max.

COOKING METHOD
Indirect heat

1 Prepare the grill for a medium to high indirect heat (180–200°C/ 350–400°F). Make 2 cuts in the skin of each banana lengthways from bottom to top, one on each side and about 2 cm (¾ inch) apart.

2 Roll back the skin between the cuts and use a pre-soaked cocktail stick to attach it to the stalk. If necessary, cut a shallow slice off the bases of the bananas so they will stand up and not tip over.

3 Make a lengthways cut down into the flesh of each banana, but do not cut all the way through.

4 Drizzle the lemon juice over the bananas and scatter with the sugar, pushing the ends together lightly to increase the bend in the banana.

5 Push a fun-size chocolate bar or strip of milk chocolate down into the slit in each banana.

6 Put the bananas over an indirect heat, close the lid and cook for 8–10 minutes. To make the bananas easier to handle, you could stand them on a smoking plank, pizza stone or dish.

7 To make the sauce, bring the cream to the boil in a fireproof pan on the side burner or the grill rack over a direct heat. Remove from the heat and stir in the chocolate bars and dark chocolate until melted. Set aside until ready to use.

8 Pour the chocolate sauce over the cooked bananas and scatter over the chocolate topping of your choice.

4-FLAVOUR POPCORN

Barbecued popcorn is always a success – thanks to the constant movement of the rotisserie basket, nothing will burn. Prepare the toppings while the corn is popping: sweet for the kids, savoury for the adults, or the other way round?

SERVES 4

100 g (3½ oz) popping corn

1–2 tablespoons sunflower oil

SALTED CARAMEL

200 g (7 oz) creamy toffees

½ teaspoon sea salt

CHOCOLATE & NUTS

1 chocolate bar with peanuts (50 g/1¾ oz)

200 ml (7 fl oz) double cream

2 tablespoons brown sugar

150 g (5½ oz) trail mix

BUTTER, HONEY & LEMON

50 g (1¾ oz) butter

6 tablespoons clear honey

juice of ½ lemon

sea salt

BACON & CHEESE

8 bacon rashers

40 g (1½ oz) Parmesan cheese, grated

80 g (2¾ oz) Cheddar cheese, grated

sea salt

EQUIPMENT

1 rotisserie and fine-meshed rotisserie basket

PREPARATION
5 minutes

COOKING TIME
6–8 minutes

COOKING METHOD
Indirect heat

RESTING TIME
5 minutes

1 Remove the grates from the grill. Prepare the grill with the rotisserie for a high indirect heat (220–240°C/ 425–475°F). Mix the popping corn in a bowl with the oil.

2 Place the popping corn in the fine-meshed rotisserie basket. Place the basket in the middle of the rotisserie and fix in place with the two screws. Close the rotisserie basket.

3 Wearing BBQ gloves, hook the rotisserie in the prepared grill and close the lid. Leave to cook for 8–10 minutes.

4 Put the BBQ gloves back on and remove the rotisserie, detach the basket and open it. Leave the popcorn to dry for 5 minutes, so it stays crunchy.

ⓐ **With salted caramel**

Blitz the creamy toffees to a powder in a food processor and mix with the sea salt. Sprinkle the salted caramel powder over the popped corn in the rotisserie basket, close the lid and cook for a further 2–3 minutes until the powder has caramelized. Then leave the popcorn to dry as described.

ⓑ **With chocolate & nuts**

Chop the peanut chocolate bar into small pieces and put with the cream, sugar and two-thirds of the trail mix in a fireproof pan over a medium heat and simmer for 6–8 minutes. Drizzle over the popcorn in a bowl and top with the remaining trail mix.

ⓒ **With butter, honey & lemon**

Melt the butter in a fireproof pan over a medium heat, then stir in the honey and lemon juice and season the mixture with sea salt to taste. Drizzle over the popcorn in a bowl while it is still warm.

ⓓ **With bacon & cheese**

Place the bacon in the rotisserie basket with the popping corn and cook the corn as described. Scatter the Parmesan and Cheddar cheeses over the popped corn in the basket, close the lid and cook for a further 1–2 minutes. Leave the popcorn to dry as described then season with sea salt to taste before serving.

INDEX

hamlyn

First published in Great Britain in 2023 by
Hamlyn, an imprint of
Octopus Publishing Group Ltd
Carmelite House
50 Victoria Embankment
London EC4Y 0DZ
www.octopusbooks.co.uk

An Hachette UK Company
www.hachette.co.uk

Originally published under the title
Weber's Gasgrillbibel by Manuel Weyer,
ISBN 978-3-8338-7950-0, by GRÄFE UND
UNZER VERLAG GmbH, Postfach 860366,
81630 München, Germany, www.gu.de

Text copyright © 2021, 2023 GRÄFE UND
UNZER VERLAG GmbH, München
Copyright © 2021, 2023 Weber-Stephen
Products LLC

ISBN 978-0-60063-780-6

A CIP catalogue record for this book is
available from the British Library.

Printed and bound in China

10 9 8 7 6 5 4 3 2 1

Photography: Mathias Neubauer
Recipes & food styling: Manuel Weyer
Illustrations: Fornfest
Design and layout: Arndt Knieper
Layouts adapted by Jeremy Tilston
Cover design: Jaz Bahra

Editorial Director: Eleanor Maxfield
Senior Editor: Alex Stetter
Senior Production Manager: Peter Hunt
Translated by First Edition Translations,
Cambridge

The advice in this book is believed to be
correct at the time of printing, but the authors
and the publishers accept no liability for
actions inspired by this book.

Cookery notes

Both imperial and metric measurements have
been given in all recipes. Use one set of
measurements only and not a mixture of both.

Aluminium foil is used for some recipes in this
book. As acidic ingredients or those
containing salt can corrode aluminium, which
can then leach into food, you should wrap
food in baking parchment first and then in
aluminium foil.